TO VARVARA

We must try

To love so well the world that we may believe,
in the end, in God.

(Robert Penn Warren, 'Masts at Dawn')

ROBERT PENN WARREN
A Vision Earned

ROBERT PENN WARREN
A Vision Earned

Marshall Walker

Paul Harris Publishing

Edinburgh

First published in Great Britain 1979
by Paul Harris Publishing,
25 London Street, Edinburgh.

© Copyright Marshall Walker, 1979

ISBN 0 904505 75 8

6 00 0668881 X

Printed by Robert MacLehose and Company Limited,
Renfrew, nr. Glasgow

Contents

Acknowledgements

I am grateful to Professor Peter H. Butter for practical help with my second visit to the United States and for his advice on preparing these chapters. I have benefited, too, from suggestions kindly made by Dr Andrew Hook, Professor Geoffrey Moore and Mr Hugh C. Rae.

My thanks go to Professor and Mrs Herschel Gower of Vanderbilt University for putting me in touch with Fugitive as well as modern Nashville; to Mrs Harriet Owsley for access to her husband's papers and to the letter from Robert Penn Warren to Andrew Lytle now lodged in the Tennessee State Library and Archives; to the Librarians of the Joint University Libraries in Nashville for their kindness to me and for permission to quote from unpublished material in the Donald Davidson Collection; to the Librarians of Idaho State University at Pocatello for their help with inter-library loans; and to Dr Donald Gallup for admission to the Beinecke Research Library at Yale, where Robert Penn Warren's papers are held.

Mrs Jean Robertson of the University of Glasgow Library has been very helpful as has Mr Ian A. C. Campbell of Marr College. Miss Irene Elsey, Miss Ingrid Swanson and Mrs Wilma Whyte have kindly typed drafts. I am especially grateful to Mrs Valerie Eden for her generous commitment to the final manuscript.

For invaluable help and guidance most generously accorded over many years I thank Dr J. R. F. Buchanan and Mr John A. M. Rillie.

For hospitality given to parts of this book I thank *Scottish International*, *Journal of American Studies*, and *London Magazine*. Grateful acknowledgement is made to Random House, Inc., for permission to quote from the copyrighted works of Robert Penn Warren. Excerpts from *All the King's Men* by Robert Penn Warren are reprinted by permission of Harcourt Brace Jovanovich, Inc., copyright 1946, 1974 by Robert Penn Warren.

My chief debt is to Mr and Mrs Robert Penn Warren for bed, board and bourbon in the summers of 1968 and 1969 and for encouragement and friendship since then. I have tried to return a measure of their kindness in these pages by respecting their privacy:

my few biographical observations are made strictly on the basis of material now in the public domain.

Glasgow, June 1978   M.W.

Chronology

1905   Robert Penn Warren born in Guthrie, Kentucky, 24 April; son of Robert Franklin Warren and Anna Ruth Penn.

1920   Left school in Guthrie and went, for one year, to Clarksville (Tennessee) High School.

1921   Graduated from Clarksville High School and enrolled at Vanderbilt University, Nashville.

1923– Participated in activities of the 'Fugitive Group' in Nashville.
1925

1925   Graduated from Vanderbilt University (B.A., *summa cum laude*).

1925– Graduate student, University of California (M.A., 1927).
1927

1927– Graduate student, Yale University.
1928

1928– Rhodes Scholar, University of Oxford (B.Litt., 1930).
1930

1929   *John Brown: the Making of a Martyr*

1930   Assistant Professor of English, Southwestern College, Memphis; married Emma Brescia.

1931– Assistant Professor of English, Vanderbilt University.
1934

1934– Assistant Professor of English, Louisiana State University,
1942   Baton Rouge (Associate Professor from 1936).

1935   Founded *Southern Review* with Cleanth Brooks and Charles W. Pipkin.

1936   *Thirty-Six Poems.*

1938   *Understanding Poetry: An Anthology for College Students* (with Cleanth Brooks, Albert Erskine and Charles W. Pipkin).

1939   *Night Rider;* Guggenheim Fellow (a second fellowship awarded 1947–48).

1942   *Eleven Poems on the Same Theme;* Professor of English, University of Minnesota, Minneapolis.

1943   *At Heaven's Gate; Understanding Fiction* (with Cleanth Brooks).

1944   *Selected Poems, 1923–1943;* Library of Congress Chair of Poetry (–1945).

1946   *All the King's Men* (Pulitzer Prize).

1947   *The Circus in the Attic, and Other Stories;* New York first production of play (by Warren) based on *All the King's Men,* directed by Erwin Piscator.

1949   *Modern Rhetoric* (with Cleanth Brooks); motion picture of *All the King's Men*—Robert Meltzer Award, Screen Writers Guild.

1950   *World Enough and Time;* Professor of Playwrighting, Yale University (–1956).

1951   Divorce from Emma Brescia Warren.

1952   Married Eleanor Clark (children: Rosanna and Gabriel); elected to American Philosophical Society.

1953   *Brother to Dragons: A Tale in Verse and Voices.*

1955   *Band of Angels.*

1956   Resigned from Yale to give full time to writing.

1957   *Promises: Poems, 1954–1956* (Pulitzer Prize, National Book Award, Edna St Vincent Millay Prize of Poetry Society of America); *Segregation; The Inner Conflict in the South.*

1958   *Selected Essays.*

1959   *The Cave;* elected to American Academy of Arts and Letters. New York production of revised version of *All the King's Men.*

1960   *You, Emperors, and Others: Poems 1957–1960; All the King's Men* (play published).

1961   *Wilderness; The Legacy of the Civil War;* Professor of English Yale University.

1964   *Flood.*

1965   *Who Speaks for the Negro?*

1966   *Selected Poems: New and Old, 1923–1966* (Bollingen Prize in Poetry).

1968   *Incarnations: Poems 1966–1968.*

1969   *Audubon: A Vision* (National Medal for Literature, Van Wyck Brooks Award).

1971   *Meet Me in the Green Glen; Homage to Theodore Dreiser.*

1974   *Or Else—Poem/Poems 1968–1974;* Copernicus Prize for Poetry, Academy of American Poets; National Foundation for the Humanities Lectureship.

1975   *Democracy and Poetry;* elected to American Academy of Arts and Sciences (received the Emerson-Thoreau Award of the Academy).

1976   *Selected Poems, 1923–1975.*

1977   *A Place to Come To;* Harriet Monroe Prize for Poetry.

Abbreviations

Works by Robert Penn Warren:

AHG	*At Heaven's Gate* (New York, 1959)
AKM	*All the King's Men* (New York, 1953)
BOA	*Band of Angels* (New York, 1955)
BTD	*Brother to Dragons* (New York, 1953)
C	*The Cave* (New York, 1959)
CIA	*The Circus in the Attic* (New York, 1947)
F	*Flood* (New York, 1964)
GG	*Meet Me in the Green Glen* (New York, 1971)
JB	*John Brown: The Making of a Martyr* (New York, 1929)
Legacy	*The Legacy of the Civil War: Meditations on the Centennial* (New York, 1964)
NR	*Night Rider* (New York, 1948)
OE	*Or Else—Poem/Poems 1968–1974* (New York, 1974)
PCT	*A Place to Come To* (New York, 1977)
Promises	*Promises: Poems, 1954–1956* (New York, 1957)
SE	*Selected Essays* (New York, 1966)
Segregation	*Segregation: The Inner Conflict in the South* (London, 1957)
SP	*Selected Poems: 1923–1975* (New York, 1976)
SP: 1943	*Selected Poems, 1923–1943* (New York, 1944)
W	*Wilderness* (New York, 1961)
WEAT	*World Enough and Time* (New York, 1950)
WSN	*Who Speaks for the Negro?* (New York, 1965)
YEO	*You, Emperors, and Others: Poems 1957–1960* (New York, 1960)

Others:

Bohner	Charles H. Bohner, *Robert Penn Warren* (New York, 1964)
Casper	Leonard Casper, *Robert Penn Warren: The Dark and Bloody Ground* (Seattle, 1960)

DDC	Donald Davidson Collection; unpublished letters and papers (Nashville, Joint University Libraries)
GWT	John Crowe Ransom, *God Without Thunder* (New York, 1930)
Longley	John L. Longley, Jr, *Robert Penn Warren: A Collection of Critical Essays* (New York, 1965)
Stewart	John L. Stewart, *The Burden of Time: The Fugitives and Agrarians* (Princeton, 1965)
Strandberg	Victor H. Strandberg, *A Colder Fire: The Poetry of Robert Penn Warren* (Lexington, 1965)

Introduction

A full study of a living, active writer faces special difficulties: the evidence is not all in. In the case of Robert Penn Warren, whatever evidence may be yet forthcoming, there should be no doubt about the substantialness of achievement. He is America's most distinguished living man of letters, an *honnête homme* involved with books and humankind and at ease in many *genres*.

Best known in this country as author of *All the King's Men*, Warren has been called 'the pentathlon champion of American literature'.[1] In an age of specialisation he has published in America a biography, ten novels, a volume of short stories, poetry in several kinds, major criticism, socio-historical comment and a play. In the early stages of his career he was overshadowed internationally both by more established and by more obviously experimental American novelists (Fitzgerald, Wolfe, Dos Passos, Faulkner) and in the last ten or fifteen years he has been somewhat eclipsed in the eye of the academic establishment by the Jewish novel (Bellow, Malamud, Roth), the comic-apocalyptic novel (Heller, Barth, Pynchon), the poetry of neurosis (Lowell, Berryman) and what his wife, Eleanor Clark calls 'the Sylvia Plath virus'.[2] Yet Warren began his several treatments of the now fashionable theme of alienation with *Night Rider* as long ago as 1939 and by the forties his poetry had evolved one of the most remarkable and comprehensive styles of the century, able to combine the swift pace of fiction with the intensity of poetry and to compass lyric passion, nervous tension and mythic resonance through a compounding of the formal and the colloquial unmatched in

17

American literature. It seems ironic that if Warren's name is a household word in literate America it is so largely because of his work as a teacher and co-author of the influential textbooks, *Understanding Poetry*, *Understanding Fiction* and *Modern Rhetoric*. This book is primarily concerned with Warren the maker rather than with Warren the critic or teacher.

In addition to an indispensable bibliography compiled in 1968 by Mary Nance Huff,[3] John L. Longley, Jr. has edited a collection of essays on Warren and there is a somewhat elliptical pamphlet by Paul West in the University of Minnesota series on American writers. Klaus Poenicke's *Robert Penn Warren: Kunstwerk Und Kritische Theorie* (1959) gives a compact and accurate account of Southern Agrarianism and an illuminating discussion of Warren's literary theory in the context of the New Criticism. In *Robert Penn Warren: the Dark and Bloody Ground* (1960) Leonard Casper's chapter on Warren's poetry is, possibly for reasons of space, more impressionistic than analytical, but the chapter on Warren the novelist is still useful. Casper's book was a pioneering effort in Warren studies and must still command respect. Charles H. Bohner's *Robert Penn Warren* (1964) is a first-rate introduction. All of these books are now unavoidably out of date to the extent that much of Warren's best work has been done since they were written. The same applies to the accomplished dissertations written by James H. Justus, Mark Linenthal, Jr., and Allen G. Shepherd, details of which are given in the Bibliography. My discussions of Warren's Agrarian affiliations and his earlier fiction owe much to the perceptions of these readers and part of the exhilaration of the early stages of this study came from the discovery that my own readings so often squared with theirs.

Victor H. Strandberg's *A Colder Fire: The Poetry of Robert Penn Warren* (1965) is a scholarly and instructive book which covers the poetry written by 1960 very thoroughly though somewhat undiscriminatingly. Strandberg's concern with the metaphysical quality of Warren's vision tends to instate density of thought as a criterion of excellence; he appreciates the importance of naturalism as a theme in Warren and is always alert to the poetry's imagery but sometimes neglects the dynamics of a poem. A new book on Warren's poetry by

Strandberg, *The Poetic Vision of Robert Penn Warren* (1977),[4] has been announced but, at the time of writing, has not come to hand. As these chapters neared completion Barnett Gutten-berg's *Web of Being: The Novels of Robert Penn Warren* (1975)[5] became available. This book offers a close reading of each of the novels except *A Place to Come To*. Concentrating on the characters, Guttenberg finds that they pursue 'false being', whether through escape into idealism or into world and fact. The thesis is sound and it is earnestly propounded but Gut-tenberg's readings seldom expand beyond the narrow line of his argument, which has the effect of making Warren appear a more abstract writer than he is: the reader feels cheated of flesh and blood.

In his book, *Sur Proust*, Jean-François Revel defines a basic pre-requisite to the kind of study attempted in these pages:

> ... il y a une seule manière de parler d'un auteur, il y a une condition fondamentale qu'il faut remplir: il faut que ce qui lui importait vous importe. Parler d'un auteur, c'est dire en prenant appui sur lui ce qu'on pense soi-même de ce dont il a parlé.[6]

If this expresses what must be one's private justification for the following chapters and for much in their method, it also points a danger, for one must, equally, guard against under-mining critical observation by requiring that what is important to oneself should account for everything of value in the subject. The aim of the present study is to interpret Warren's work, to celebrate it and to 'discriminate values and methods among the individual items of the canon,'[7] with special attention to the interrelations between literary theory and moral vision.

The range of Warren's achievement testifies to the scope and commitment of his human sympathies. Each intellectual act, whether formally poem, novel or one of the interviews with black leaders in *Who Speaks for the Negro?* is of the nature of a poem, according to his own definition of the poem as a way of 'getting your reality shaped a little better'.[8] *Band of Angels* is over-melodramatic and *Wilderness* is flawed by the failure of its hero's consciousness to develop along with the events of the novel; but there is never in Warren's work the meretricious gloss of the merely fashionable, although a popular audience

B

might look to him for a 'good story' complete with fast action, sex, violence and earthy humour. Abstracted from their novels, the mere plots of *World Enough and Time*, *The Cave* or *Meet Me in the Green Glen* would have little to commend themselves to the attention of the serious reader, though, to be sure, the same might be said about the mere plots of many other nineteenth and twentieth-century novelists. Warren is a popular novelist in that his novels have made money and, occasionally, films.[9]

Academic audiences appear to be fearful of such popularity and to suppose that commercial success must inevitably spoil the writer. Indeed, one periodically hears that in Warren's case the worst has long since happened. He is a popular writer in the further sense that in a typical Warren novel there will be something for everybody. What counts, of course, is that underlying the energy, even the violence that is part of his metaphor of the world, as well as of the world itself, is a concern to visualise the meaning of common experience and, without artistic concessions, to make this meaning available in a body of work which, with astonishing success, unites metaphysical and social themes in a single vision. There is a remarkable consistency in his view of the artist's relations to his materials, the nature of the work of art and the ethical life.

Deeply a Southerner, Warren has emerged as the most versatile and vigorous of the Fugitive Group, that astonishing convention of talents who met in Nashville, Tennessee between 1915 and 1928 and included John Crowe Ransom, Allen Tate and Donald Davidson. As Tate predicted soon after Warren's poems began to appear in *The Fugitive*, 'that boy's a wonder—has more sheer genius than any of us; watch him: his work from now on will have what none of us can achieve—power.'[10] The power of Warren's work arises from experience that incorporates the frontier, as well as the town, the plantation, the college and the farm. Though he has long since left the South to live in the North, where he now divides his time between Connecticut and Vermont, he has, nonetheless, remained a Southerner. So he testifies in the opening of *Segregation*:

'I'm glad it's you going,' my friend, a Southerner, long resident in New York, said, 'and not me.' But I went back, for going back this time, like all the other times, was a necessary part of my life. I was going back to look at the landscapes and streets I had known—Kentucky, Tennessee, Arkansas, Mississippi, Louisiana— to look at the faces, to hear the voices, to hear, in fact, the voices in my own blood. A girl from Mississippi had said to me: 'I feel it's all happening inside of me, every bit of it. It's all there.'

I know what she meant.

(Segregation, p. 11)

The eternal return has been as much a part of Warren's own life as it is of the lives of his characters. Contrary to Thomas Wolfe's dictum 'You can't go home again', Warren's work persistently tells us that you *must* go home again—even if, like Jack Burden, Brad Tolliver, Jed Tewskbury or little Billie Potts, it is only:

To ask forgiveness and the patrimony of your crime;
And kneel in the untutored night as to demand
What gift—oh, father, father—from that dissevering hand?

(SP, p. 281)

At home 'the father waits for the son' and only from the father can the son receive forgiveness, the patrimony of his crime and the gift of meaning—as a rule, in Warren, self-knowledge. The Dantesque scheme of *At Heaven's Gate* projects a group of characters who violate nature and Jerry Calhoun, in denying his true father and taking a false father, commits what is for Warren a crucial impiety. In *All the King's Men* Jack Burden adopts a series of false fathers, the most notable being Willie Stark himself. Invariably there is alignment of the true father and the truth of the situation. Warren concedes this himself when he says that the perfect father will act as the great reconciler of the world's chief contraries, resolving the tension between the idea and fact, the Emersonian and the Haw- thornian. The point where fact and idea coincide, the perfect fusion is not, Warren conjectures, in our world: 'But we constantly want to have it in our world, and we only find it by finding a new father, I guess, beyond us, beyond this world'. (Appendix, p. 250). Thus our human case, Southern or other- wise, remains not hopeless but perpetually interesting.

Warren, then, has repeatedly gone home again, imaginatively in his poetry and fiction, and actually in the task of gathering material for *Segregation* and *Who Speaks for the Negro?* (1965). His business is with that region of which Robert Coles speculates in *Farewell to the South*:

> I wonder where else in this country past history and present social conflict conspire to bring forth so much of the evil in people, so much of the dignity possible in people, so much of the 'pity and terror' in the human condition.[11]

Like Hawthorne, Warren has lived 'in the right ratio . . . between an attachment to his region and a detached assessment of it.'[12] His meditations on the Centennial in *The Legacy of the Civil War* are very much concerned with 'past history and present social conflict', with evil and dignity, pity and terror— above all with the effects of simplifying idealisms which would, catastrophically, rob the world of its complexity. He reflects:

> Most Americans are ready to echo the sentiment of Woodrow Wilson that 'America is the only idealist country in the world.' As Reinhold Niebuhr has put it, we live in the illusions of innocence and virtue. We have not grown up enough to appreciate the difficulty of moral definition, the doubleness of experience—what he calls 'the irony of history.'
>
> *(Legacy,* p. 71)

Here Warren defines his own enterprise—the effort 'to appreciate the difficulty of moral definition, the doubleness of experience . . . the irony of history.'

Introduction — Notes

[1] Bohner, p. 17.

[2] Clark, Eleanor, *Eyes, Etc., A Memoir* (London: Collins, 1978), p. 5.

[3] Huff, Mary Nance, *Robert Penn Warren: A Bibliography* (New York: David Lewis, 1968).

[4] Strandberg, Victor H., *The Poetic Vision of Robert Penn Warren* (Lexington: University of Kentucky Press, 1977).

[5] Guttenberg, Barnett, *Web of Being: The Novels of Robert Penn Warren* (Nashville: Vanderbilt University Press, 1975).

[6] Revel, Jean-François, *Sur Proust: Remarques sur A La Recherche Du Temps Perdu* (Paris: René Julliard, 1960), p. 244.

[7] Warren, Robert Penn, (Ed.), *Faulkner: A Collection of Critical Essays* (Englewood Cliffs, N.J.: Prentice-Hall Inc., 1966), p. 21.

[8] Purdy, Rob Roy, (Ed.), *Fugitives' Reunion: Conversations at Vanderbilt, May 3–5, 1956* (Nashville: Vanderbilt University Press, 1959), p. 150.

[9] *All the King's Men*, copyrighted 5 January, 1950, was written and directed by Robert Rossen. Despite an adverse review in *Sight and Sound*, June, 1950, 163–64, 168, the film won Academy Awards for Broderick Crawford as Willie Stark and Mercedes McCambridge as Sadie Burke. Warren was pleased with the film: 'Rossen did a good job with AKM . . . Crawford in the lead is perfect and several minor characters, especially Sadie Burke, are excellent. The handling of atmosphere is fine. The end is different, Willie comes off sort of black-and-white. But that is the price of movies, I guess. You can't do much with ironies and complications in the final effect.' (Letter to Frank Owsley, dated 31 January, 1950. Papers of Frank Owsley, Tennessee State Library and Archives.) By comparison, *Band of Angels*, copyrighted 3 August, 1957, directed in old-school Hollywood style by Raoul Walsh, was a two-dimensional flop, remote from Warren's novel. At the time of writing, Sidney Pollack is directing a film version of *A Place to Come To* with Robert Redford in the leading part.

[10] Letter to Donald Davidson, 17 April, 1924. DDC, File 10.

[11] Coles, Robert, *Farewell to the South* (Boston: Atlantic-Little, Brown, 1972), p. 36.

[12] Warren, Robert Penn, 'Hawthorne Revisited: Some Remarks on Hellfiredness', *Sewanee Review*, **81** (1973), 75.

1

Regionalism, Agrarianism and Literature

Warren's first public image was that of an 'enlightened' conservative Southerner. Like his associates, John Crowe Ransom, Donald Davidson, Allen Tate, Andrew Lytle, he was a 'Fugitive' not only from 'the high-caste Brahmins of the Old South',[1] but from the mainstream of American culture. Like them he deplored the sovereignty of materialism in American life and felt the alienation it imposed on the artist. His contribution to *Who Owns America?* shows his sense of the writer's predicament:

> The contemporary writer . . . must first discover a theme unless he is merely to project in symbol after symbol the frustration he suffers . . . or to project his rebellion and dissatisfaction in a literature of violence and disgust . . . He may be overwhelmed by the sense of his own separateness . . . further, he may feel that something that once bound author and audience together, some common tie of values . . . some sustaining convention, is lost.[2]

So, in an age of dissolving values, Warren sided with those who prized the securities of a tradition. Unlike Allen Tate he was unable to adopt the radical solution of conversion to Roman Catholicism, although many of the intellectual aristocrats who became known as the 'Southern Agrarians' shared an inclination towards orthodox Christianity as well as a general desire, boosted by revulsion from the moral and social character of the

North, for a regeneration of the South's best traditions.

Warren early proclaimed himself a regionalist, but a cautious one. 'Literary regionalism is more than a literary manner,' he wrote in 1936, '. . . only in so far as literature springs from some reality in experience is it valuable to us.'[3] There was no doubt about the 'reality in experience' behind Warren's own writing: 'It never crossed my mind when I began writing fiction that I could write about anything except life in the South. It never crossed my mind that I knew about anything else; knew, that is, well enough to write about. Nothing else ever nagged you enough to stir the imagination.'[4] In his essay on Hemingway (1947), however, the emphasis is less on regionally 'experienced reality' than on the ideas which that reality may embody: 'A writer may write about his special world merely because he happens to know that world, but he may also write about that special world because it best dramatises for him the issues and questions that are his fundamental concerns—because, in other words, that special world has a kind of symbolic significance for him' (SE, p. 85). For a writer who wishes to dramatise his intellectual concepts in terms of this 'special world' of his own experience the chief hazard lies in the possibility that the abstractions, the 'issues and questions', may then run away with him. Striking a proper balance between the autonomy of the 'experienced reality' and its 'symbolic significance' becomes the central problem. If the writer fails to achieve this balance, his symbolic structures may endanger the direct 'regional' inspiration by undermining the concreteness of the 'special world'. Already Warren is alert, like Hawthorne, to the tyrannising effect of an idea on the mind. Even a 'special world' has its birthmarks, and the idea refines them out of existence at peril to itself. There is a clear analogy here between Warren's view of the artist's problem and his view of life. The abstract idea must first of all stand the test of reality before it can lay any claim to validity: 'In literature, ideas leave their cloisters and descend into the dust and heat to prove their virtue anew.'[5] Tragedy in his work most frequently results from a failure to achieve a similar balance between ideals and the dust and heat of the world, 'The malfeasance of nature or the filth of fate.'[6]

Acknowledgement of 'the malfeasance of nature' might appear strange in the context of Agrarianism. Klaus Poenicke notes the apparent similarity between the ideas of John Crowe Ransom in *God Without Thunder* (rustic virtue versus urban depravity) and those of Thomas Jefferson as expressed, for example, in Jefferson's letter of 20 December, 1787 to James Madison:

> This reliance [i.e. on the will of the majority of the people] cannot deceive us, as long as we remain virtuous; and I think we shall be so, as long as agriculture is our principal object, which will be the case, while there remains vacant lands in any part of America. When we get piled upon one another in large cities, as in Europe, we shall become corrupt as in Europe, and go to eating one another as they do there.[7]

Agriculture, Jefferson believed, would enable Americans to avoid the complex fate of Europe. Although the Nashville Agrarians share Jefferson's enthusiasm for the moral value of raising food from the earth, they do not accept his Wordsworthian connection between agrarianism and the life of simple virtue. If the cruel aspects of nature troubled Jefferson, he managed to preserve his faith in its fundamental goodness as the nourishing context for a republic of yeoman farmers. Warren's resurrected Jefferson in *Brother to Dragons*, however, is forbidden any vision of American possibilities not grounded in the realities of human nature, and compelled by the author to acknowledge the permanent existence of sin in the world, even in his own blood. Part of nature is the murder in December 1811 of a Negro slave by his own nephews (the first of the great Mississippi Valley earthquakes assimilates this human convulsion to the natural order in its most violent aspect) and Jefferson comes to see the event as paradigmatic of an ironic world of 'natural' contraries and tangled motives:

> . . . and as History divulged
> Itself, I saw how the episode in the meat-house
> Would bloom in Time, and blooms in all characteristic
> Episodes, and blooms in the lash-bite,
> And blooms in the lost child's cry
> Down in the quarters when the mother is sold.
> Oh, yes, I've heard it, but I know, too,

How vanity and blood-lust may link obscenely
In the excuse of moral ardour, and a cause.

(BTD, pp. 135–36)

At the end of the poem R.P.W. sums up, chanting the lesson in paradox he has provided for Jefferson through this terrible piece of history:

> The recognition of complicity is the beginning of innocence.
> The recognition of necessity is the beginning of freedom.
> The recognition of the direction of fulfilment is the death of the self,
> And the death of the self is the beginning of selfhood.
> All else is surrogate of hope and destitution of spirit.

(BTD, pp. 214–15)

If *Brother to Dragons* disturbs conventional ideas of Jefferson, these lines about complicity, and, in particular, about the death of the self are scarcely Emersonian. Neither was the Agrarianism which influenced Warren. While in Emerson's vision nature achieved increased status as the repository of moral laws to be grasped intuitively, it was, at the same time, diminished from the authoritative art of God to an operation of the human mind. Nature eventually lost its own objective existence and became a human projection in precocious anticipation of the appropriations of modern science. From this it followed, in the inevitable progress of American romanticism, that increasing autonomy and power were attributed to the individual mind: the way was open for the solipsism of an Ahab, the tawdry subjectivity hoisted into godhead of a John Brown, the tragic enterprise of a Jeremiah Beaumont. Emerson himself, on the hunt for something in the world to match his own idea, got short shrift from Warren in 1929:

> Emerson possessed a set of ideas which have been given the interesting name of Transcendentalism; he spent his life trying to find something in man or nature which would correspond to the fine ideas and the big word. In John Brown, Emerson thought he had found his man ... but Emerson was a man who lived in words, big words, and not in facts ... And it is only natural, that Emerson, in his extraordinary innocence, should have understood nothing, nothing in the world, about a man like John Brown ...

matters of fact, the questions of truth or falsehood, were often perfectly inconsequential to the sage of Concord. The sage of Concord so gracefully transcended such things.

(JB, pp. 245–46, 414)

The connection between the sage of Concord and the ideals of industrial progress may not be quite as immediate as F. O. Matthiessen implies when he reminds us that Emerson's *Essays* were declared by Henry Ford to be his favourite reading,[8] but we can take Ford as a ready symbol of everything the Agrarians abhorred. Ford, among others, is the object of Warren's irony in an essay on Ransom: "I have heard, in . . . a church once concerned with the awful mysteries of atonement and election, a sermon on the four modern 'saints', those men who now walk hand in hand with God: i.e. Mr Pupin, Mr Millikan, Mr Ford and Mr, Rockefeller."[9] For Ransom himself in *God Without Thunder*, the myth of scientific perfectibility had replaced the essentially mysterious, inaccessible God of the Old Testament by an amiable, understandable God who, as Ransom puts it, 'developed popularly out of the Christ of the New Testament: the embodiment mostly of the principle of social benevolence and physical welfare' (GWT, p. 5). Modern man's great hope was that he would ultimately enslave nature, but the Agrarians, with Ransom in the lead, sought to re-endow nature with an element of terror and inscrutability. In *A Plea to the Protestant Churches* Cleanth Brooks argues against the reduction of Christian theology to a humanitarian principle, to 'merely a socio-political programme',[10] and Ransom urges the need to bring back to the world a God who is author of evil as well as of good, to give God back his thunder. (John Updike's opposition of the Rev. Eccles and Kruppen-bach, the Lutheran, in *Rabbit, Run* is a contemporary parallel.) The resulting position from the Agrarian point of view is clearly stated in the introduction to *I'll Take My Stand*:

> Religion is our submission to the general intention of a nature that is fairly inscrutable; it is the sense of our rôle as creatures within it. But nature industrialised, transformed into cities and artificial habitations, manufactured into commodities, is no longer nature but a highly simplified picture of nature. We receive the illusion

of having power over nature as something mysterious and contingent. The God of nature under these conditions is merely an amiable expression, a superfluity, and the philosophic understanding ordinarily carried in the religious experience is not there for us to have.[11]

Ransom, again, is thinking in such terms when he writes: 'The moral order is a wished-for order, which does not coincide with the actual order or world order . . . the mind must accept the world order' (GWT, p. 47). We are stuck with the need to recognise and accept an actual world order which includes good and evil, order and chaos, 'the incandescence of the heart's great flare' (BTD, p. 195) as well as 'the stink of the didie' and 'the stench of the shroud' (AKM, p. 54).

II

'The stars', Warren says in a recent poem, 'are only a backdrop for / The human condition', but his stargazing leads to an admission which, a little wryly, reneges against so naturalistic an astronomy:

> The stars
> Love me. I love them. I wish they
> Loved God, too. I truly wish that.

(SP, p. 61)

Although he has never subscribed to a religious orthodoxy, Warren early concerned himself with the conflict between naturalism and what he came to call 'the religious sense'. The Agrarians' attempt to compile a religious, political and aesthetic programme that rejected the modern supremacy of reason was based on the conviction that science and rational philosophy, which flourish by generalisation and abstraction, are not true to the empirical facts of a mixed, mysterious world. For Allen Tate, 'abstraction is the death of religion no less than the death of everything else.'[12] Perhaps the most striking feature of the Agrarian viewpoint is the sophisticated primitivism whereby the appeal to experience is consistently held to be diametrically opposed to the appeal to reason and the scientist held in contempt for assuming that an ordered world compliantly waits to be weighed and measured by his orderly mind. With suave reasonableness Ransom demolishes the poor, complacent scientist: 'The issue is one of fact. Is the actual universe amenable to the laws of science or is it not? Of course the truth is that it partly is, and partly isn't. One of the consequences of too much of the modern scientific training upon us is that we finally come to the point where we mistake the uniformity of nature, which is only the expression of a hope, for the statement of a fact' (GWT, p. 32). In other words, the world is to an indeterminable extent theoretically knowable, but there is an ineffable remainder which is far more important than the data gleaned by reason.

Ransom's view of the poem as a miniature world is clearly analogous, for while the poem does or should, possess a conceptual structure amenable to reason, it is the texture that remains when the structure has been accounted for that finally earns the work the character of a poem by imaging that mysterious irradiation of unparaphrasable meaning that belongs to all the world's phenomena. The imperialist imagination of a humanist like Wallace Stevens, artificer of his own world, who can make a poem take the place of a mountain, is not for Ransom. In *God Without Thunder* the poetic attitude to the natural object is defined as one in which 'we regard the endless mysterious fullness of this object, and respect the dignity of its objective existence after all, in spite of the ambition to mastery that has become more and more habitual with us' (GWT, p. 129). The concreteness of imagery in Warren's poetry and the realism of character and location in his fiction, however philosophical its aim, reflect a similar distaste for abstraction. Stevens himself obviously sensed this reverence for the real in Ransom's poems, writing in *John Crowe Ransom: Tennessean*:

> What John Crowe Ransom does is to make a legend of reality
> ... the reality of which he makes a legend is the reality of
> Tennessee ... He would say that he lives in Tennessee and among

the Tennesseans and it would be the same thing. I don't in the least mean anything romantic. On the contrary, I mean a real land and a real people and I mean Mr Ransom as the instinct and expression of them.[13]

It is one of the aims of this book to show that Warren too is 'the instinct and expression' of Tennessee, Kentucky and other Southern parts and their people.

According to Ransom: 'The religion of a people is that background of metaphysical doctrine which dictates its political economy' (GWT, p. 116). A society's economic structure is, therefore, a reflection of its religious beliefs. Further, we are to see its social structure as determined by its economic practices. Allen Tate clearly proposes such a chain of determinations: 'the social structure depends on the economic structure, and economic conviction is still, in spite of the beliefs of economists from Adam Smith to Marx, the secular image of religion.'[14] The introduction to *I'll Take My Stand* addresses the horrors of the industrial economy in which all human functions subserve the brutalising processes of material production and consumption. Since 'the tempo of our labours communicates itself to our satisfactions . . . these also become brutal and hurried' (p. xxiv). Living in cities in which nature seems readily brought to the heel of technology, joyless economic man is incapable of religious feeling. With the decay of sensibility the amenities suffer and the arts wither from desuetude.

The diagnosis the Twelve Southerners made of the South in 1930 and the remedies they proposed are well summarised in the draft of a letter from Tate to the Editor of *The Macon Telegraph*, a Georgia paper which had printed adverse reviews of *I'll Take My Stand*:

First, we should do well to re-define the South's destiny in the light of a recent display which is simply appalling—the economic ruin of Britain. Like most Southern States, Georgia was settled from the Britain of the Eighteenth Century, which was decidedly agrarian. The agrarian tradition has held out in Georgia, where it only begins today to be shaken. But something like a century ago, without any deliberation but blindly, Britain went industrial, made a vast addition to her population, and built up a trading establishment that was profitable, and very pretty indeed, until just yesterday, when it collapsed. An industrial state is always predatory, in the sense that its population cannot live except by invading and capturing foreign markets. But when these markets are lost, whether through competition, or the development of home industries within the market area, or a general consumers' strike, this population is helpless: it will have to starve, or emigrate, or be supported by doles until it uses up all the capital of that country. Now our own East is taking the same industrial road that Britain took. It is suffering from one of its periodic depressions at this moment, though of course, it does not yet lie permanently broken like Britain. But we should insist that the South does not want to take that road. The South must remain an agrarian bloc, keep down the population of her parasite cities, and seek her old-time happiness under her well-known tradition.

. . . The thing to tell the Southern farmer is, undoubtedly, that he can make much more of a living on the farm than he has lately been led to suppose. His first object should be to make the farm his home, and to provide it by his own labors with the comforts that make country life decent. He must again take to his garden, his orchard, his poultry, his home dairy, he must fix up his fences, his yard, his house. He must think much less about his money crop than he has been doing lately. Often he has come to think only about that, and the result has been that he works in his fields as a hired laborer works in the factory, he defeats his own object by continual overproduction, and he has forgotten the meaning of a home. Will you not urge the Southern farmers to think less about money and more about the dignity that is traditional in the Southern country life?[15]

The Agrarian answer to the disruptions of modern life is that we must re-learn a way of living according to the promptings of sensibility—our combined faculties operating in concert, which will protect us from the ravages of reason and the dehumanising pressures of labour by demanding that our work be pleasurable. Our capitalist, industrial society must be replaced by a distributist, agrarian one, with farming as the model way of living: 'The concrete nature which the farmer knows is at once inscrutable and satisfying to the senses' (GWT, p. 189). By keeping a man in contact with 'concrete nature' while intimating the inscrutability of the world in an enjoyable way, farming becomes itself a kind of poetry, healing the split sensibility of modern industrial man.

What, then, of the suppressed sensibility of the modern black man? Like William Faulkner, Robert Penn Warren demonstrates moral realism, not only in his art but also in the sociopolitical realm. The opinions of both Southerners on the racial question illustrate Ransom's split between wished-for moral order and actual order, the tension between dream and fact. Faulkner says of the Negro's claim to equality: "His equality is inevitable, an irresistible force, but as I see it you've got to take into consideration human nature, which at times has nothing to do with moral truths. Truth says this and the fact says that. A wise person says 'Let's use this fact. Let's obliterate this fact first'. To oppose a material fact with a moral truth is silly."[16] In *Segregation*, Warren describes himself as a gradualist. Like Faulkner he recognises the moral justification of the Negro's claims, but sees the then situation (the mid-fifties) as an interim phase in a long struggle. His final plea is for moderation: 'It's a silly question, anyway, to ask if somebody is a gradualist. Gradualism is all you'll get. History, like nature, knows no jumps.' Warren concludes that by overcoming the present crisis through the operation of its own communal conscience the South could become a source of moral identity and power:

> If the South is really able to face up to itself and its situation, it may achieve identity. Then in a country where moral identity is hard to come by, the South, because it has had to deal concretely with a moral problem, may offer some leadership. And we need any we can get. If we are to break out of the national rhythm the rhythm between complacency and panic.
>
> (*Segregation*, p. 86)

Here we may recall the attitude of Gavin Stevens, the lawyer, in Faulkner's *Intruder in the Dust*:

> . . . the postulate that Sambo is a human being living in a free country and hence must be free. That's what we are really defending: the privilege of setting him free ourselves: which we will have to do for the reason that nobody else can, since going on a century ago now the North tried it and have been admitting for seventy-

five years now that they failed. So it will have to be us . . . But it won't be next Tuesday.[17]

In the boy, Chick Mallison, Faulkner dramatises what he sees as the tenacious autonomy of the Southern conscience:

> . . . that fierce desire that they should be perfect because they were his and he was theirs, that furious intolerance of any one single jot or tittle less than absolute perfection—that furious almost instinctive leap and spring to defend them from anyone anywhere so that he might excoriate them himself without mercy since they were his own and he wanted no more save to stand with them un- alterable and impregnable: one shame if shame must be, one expiation since expiation must surely be but above all one un- alterable durable impregnable one: one people one heart one land.[18]

The final emphasis here, of course, is dangerous in its implica- tion that it might be better to sink together in shame than be forced by someone else to keep afloat, but the moral realism of these passages is based on historical and psychological truth.

Like Faulkner, Warren realises that the ideal moral truth must make its way in the world of fact. Now we can look back to 'The Briar Patch', his pro-segregation essay in *I'll Take My Stand*, and find moral realism there too. On the other hand there is the abstract, ideal, moral proposition that it is desir- able to maintain a humane society in which maximum hap- piness is possible for negroes and whites alike. On the other hand there were the present habits and forms of the traditional organic structure of Southern life, and these were the facts in which any ideal notion had somehow to earn its living. So Warren's essay was a cogent and self-consciously humane defence of segregation, that self-consciousness indicating, Warren later remarked, 'an awareness that in the real world I was trying to write about, there existed a segregation that was not humane.' (WSN, p. 11). The essay conceives of segregation with full legal protection for the Negro, equal educational facilities, equal opportunities, equal pay for equal work. If this sounds today like a hand-out from the South African Information Service, it was, in 1930, for Warren, the most humane possible expression of practical sympathy for the Negro within the structure in which both he and the Negro had been raised. Little Rock was still a long way off and Stokely Carmichael had to wait eleven years to be born. So we should not dismiss the essay as mere compromise, but see it rather as an early example of Warren's moral realism, his design for a moral order within the actual world order, a plan to bring the poetry of idealism into the prose of present fact: 'For we know from history that you do not achieve an ideal spiritual condition and then set up a society to express it. Ideals grow out of the act of living, out of the logic of life; and in a long dialectic, even as they grow, they modify living.' WSN, p. 413).

III

Robert Penn Warren's literary criticism conveys a typically Agrarian evaluation of modern man, but while he criticises the depersonalisations of city life in, for example, *At Heaven's Gate, All the King's Men, A Place to Come To* and the sequence of poems called 'Internal Injuries,' his emphasis falls on the fracture of modern sensibility rather than on the urban dislocations which more particularly troubled some of his associates. In Warren's view, as Frederick McDowell defines it, 'The integrity of poetry and the wholeness of man have both been threatened by our failure to go beyond the scientific to reassert the aesthetic and humanistic.'[19] Ransom, in one of his more querulous moments, declares: 'Science is the order of experience in which we mutilate and prey upon nature; we seek our practical objectives at any cost' (GWT, p. 136). Part of the cost is the loss of individual dignity, for the insistence on industrial progress that results from allegiance to scientific principles denies man personal goals: 'Men are prepared to sacrifice their private dignity and happiness to an abstract social ideal and without asking whether the social ideal produces the welfare of any individual man whatsoever' (*I'll Take My Stand*,

c

p. xxvii). Men, in short, are cheated into co-operating in their own dehumanisation. Submission to an abstract social ideal produces not Whitman's 'average man' but Auden's 'Unknown Citizen', less consumer than consumed, at best a case and at worst a number. While the Agrarians in general seek to bring back a respect for the 'multi-form, recalcitrant, seductive, and violent world', Warren especially stresses the dignity and autonomy of the individual, requiring that the work of a poet be premised on the belief that 'the human creature possesses an inalienable dignity and interest' as in the culture of nineteenth century New England.[20]

The dominion of reason means that 'We freeze from above downwards', Warren says in the poem, 'Toward Rationality' (SP: 1943, p. 41). For Ransom there is only one solution: 'In order to be human we have to have something which will stop action, and this something cannot possibly be reason in its narrow sense. I would call it sensibility' (GWT, p. 190). Warren, committed to breaching the dissociation of intellect from spirit and emotion, defines Ransom's 'sensibility' as the 'harmonious adaptation or rather the functioning together of thinking and feeling.'[21] In his essay on Coleridge (1946) Warren writes: "I cannot admit that our experience . . . is ineluctably divided into the 'magical' and the 'rational' with an abyss between" (SE, p. 272). Hemingway's greatness is attributed to his success in unifying man's twofold endowment by celebrating a code of 'spiritual' values in a style that gives these values life in 'natural' terms. Thoroughly non-theological, Hemingway is thus a 'religious' artist whose work continues to voice Romantic protest against the apotheosis of rationally conceived fact by modern science. This is little short of heroic, for the myth of science may induce faithlessness even in the artist: 'Perhaps we know [our myth of science] and know it too well, knowing that, as Stevenson said, "it provides no habitable city for the soul of man." And in the midst of our competing beliefs, one belief may be lacking: the belief that poetry is worth writing.'[22]

In an earlier essay Warren indicts Sidney Lanier not for faithlessness but for dangerously shallow convictions: here is one poet who might have better served his countrymen and the cause of ideal human value had he, indeed, believed that poetry was not worth writing. Lanier, in Warren's view, typified the dangers of romanticism:

> . . . his theory of personality, his delusion of prophecy, his aesthetic premise, his uninformed admiration of science, his nationalism, his passion for synthesis, his theory of progress . . . He was admired because, as Tennyson in England, he spoke to America, and tardily to the South, in the accent of its dearest anticipations . . . Perhaps we should know Lanier. He may help us to assess our heritage.[23]

Nearly twenty years later Warren's essay on Faulkner (1951) diagnoses the ills of the modern world in clearly related terms, though any one of the Agrarians might have written such a passage as this:

> The modern world is in moral confusion. It does suffer from a lack of discipline, of sanction, of community of values, of a sense of mission . . . it is a world in which self-interest, workableness, success provide the standards of conduct . . . in which the individual has lost his relation to society, the world of the power state in which man is a cipher . . . in which man is the victim of abstraction and mechanism, or, at least, at moments feels himself to be.
>
> (SE, pp. 65–66)

Faulkner's Yoknapatawpha is hung up on the guilt of slavery, the agony of the Civil War, the ignominy of Reconstruction and the soulless tawdriness of modernism. Representative moderns are such perverted figures as Popeye, the gangster of *Sanctuary*, 'a kind of dehumanised robot, a mere mechanism, an abstraction' (SE, p. 65), and Flem Snopes whose sexual impotence signifies his exclusion from the realm of human involvement. Snopesism (i.e. all that Faulkner thinks of as modernism in a capitalistic society) has 'abolished the concept, the very possibility of entertaining the idea of virtue. It is not a question of one idea and interpretation. It is simply that no idea of virtue is conceivable in the world in which practical success is the criterion' (SE, p. 67). Snopesism's chief blasphemy is against Faulkner's—and Warren's—profound respect for 'the common human bond' (SE, p. 78). Popeye and the Snopeses are the mechanistic anti-community forces that lead to all modern alienations; in a world which sees material progress as its ideal the responsible artist declares, '*Non serviam*' and makes alienation his theme. Both the regional and the proletarian movements in literature strove for an organic society which would respect the creative impulse and restore to the estranged artist his function as 'a man speaking to men'.[24]

If Warren, like his fellow Agrarians, consistently urges the need for an organic society, his theory of art has long been recognised as organicist in principle. In Warren's opinion and that of his co-author, Cleanth Brooks, a successful work of art will be, 'a unified construct, a psychological whole . . . an organism not only greater than but different from the sum of its parts . . . the poetic quality resides in a functional combination of factors rather than in the intrinsic nature of any single factor.'[25] Brooks and Warren display their critical resilience in defence of modern poetry, insisting that organic unity can subsist even in aggressively difficult and distorted expression:

> The unity which the poet has attempted to attain is not an easily won unity, but one wrested from recalcitrant and discordant materials. Consequently, such poetry has been characterized by ironical devices, wrenched rhythms, abrupt transitions, apparent discords, non-decorative metaphors, deficiency of statement, and when successful, has attained its unity only in terms of a total intention.[26]

It is significant that 'ironical devices' head the listed characteristics of 'difficult poetry'. Irony has for long enough been at a premium among practitioners and followers of what we tend, slackly, to call the New Criticism, as a guarantee of that complexity which we associate with the kind of writing on which this criticism has conferred most honour. The poem is seen as an organism, a space-wandering monad held together by its internal inter-inanimation of parts. While Warren insists on close attention to the functional relationship between the internal parts of any work of art, his organicism has never been of that ivory tower variety which would banish both author and world, leaving merely the words throbbing away on the page rejoicing in their own inter-inanimations. From the earliest

Fugitive days the words on the page had a larger context. Warren clarifies this point in his interview with the writer:

> MW: There is a notion that the Fugitives were a group of people who went in for *close reading* of one another's poems and whose critical standards were what we would call objectivist. This I take to be a fallacy.

> RPW: There was no theorising that I can think of around that point, If you are going to criticise individual poems you have to talk about the actual words on the page, this line or that line, this word or that word, but as I remember the discussions, they were very far ranging and all sorts of implications might come in. It was hit or miss. There were many temperaments here, and certainly some of the people were very much concerned with history in the relation of literature to the historical materials, or how one stage of history emphasises one kind of poetry. For instance, some of the people in the group were very deep in balladry which would be anything *but* biased toward formalism . . . The next phase of the group's interest—several years later— moved over to the matter of society and history. So this would, in a way, refute the notion of this being a little group of formal- ists working out a theory of pure, limited, objectivist poetry . . .
>
> (*Appendix*, pp. 242)

Indeed, the relationship between art and life is constantly stressed in Warren's writing as, for example, in the conclusion of his essay on Coleridge, where he suggests a definition of the function of poetry explicitly in terms of the inevitable dis- cordancies of life: 'If poetry does anything for us, it reconciles, by its symbolic reading of experience (for by its very nature it is in itself a myth of the unity of being), the self-devisive internecine malices which arise at the superficial level on which we conduct most of our living' (SE, p. 272).

The aesthetic theory of Ransom varies the basic idea of organic unity by splitting the work of art into the two com- ponents of structure and texture, the former being translatable into logical terms for the welfare of the *ego*, while the latter caters to the needs of the *id*.[27] If this is a surprisingly scientific scheme to come from an arch-Agrarian, the important point here is that for Ransom, 'the poem is a loose logical structure with an irrelevant local texture.'[28] The 'not quite resolvable dualism' of his definition, the idea that art is a 'strain of contraries'[29] and that its special cognitive value resides in this 'strain' is echoed in different ways by other Fugitive and Agrarian writers. Allen Tate's key term is 'tension';[30] Cleanth Brooks is a connoisseur of 'paradox,'[31] Warren's term—with, perhaps an unconscious debt to Louis MacNeice—is 'impurity'.[32]

The rôle of irony as Warren prescribes it in 'Pure and Impure Poetry' (1943) is to ensure an inter-inanimation between the pure idea and the world which we know to be rich in impurities:

> Poetry wants to be pure, but poems do not. At least, most of them do not want to be too pure. The poems want to give us poetry, which is pure, and the elements of a poem, in so far as it is a good poem, will work together toward that end, but many of the elements, taken in themselves, may actually seem to contradict that end, or be neutral toward the achieving of that end . . . [Poems] mar themselves with cacophonies, jagged rhythms, ugly words and ugly thoughts, colloquialisms, clichés, sterile technical terms, headwork and argument, self-contradictions, clevernesses, irony, realism—all things which call us back to the world of prose and imperfection.
>
> (SE, p. 4)

Warren tackles the problem by comparing three love poems: Tennyson's 'Now sleeps the crimson petal, now the white', Shelley's 'Indian Serenade' and *Romeo and Juliet*. The first two, he says, aspire to purity of effect and exclude the sordid and the realistic. *Romeo and Juliet*, on the other hand, includes the Nurse's vulgarity and the bawdy scepticism of Mercutio. In suggesting that all poets should make their peace with Mercutio, Warren implies that Mercutio is really lurking in Shelley's would-be 'pure' poem all the time simply because Mercutio lurks in the world itself. Better to invite Mercutio into the poem than have him lurk. So, when Warren himself writes a love poem, as, for example, the early 'Bearded Oaks' (SP, pp. 308–9) his intention is to assert the permanence of love precisely in the face of the most inward kinds of opposition, the decay of passion and the erosions of time:

> I do not love you less that now
> The caged heart makes iron stroke
> Or less that all that light once gave
> The graduate dark should now revoke.

As an *invited* guest Mercutio is enlisted on the poem's side and with him supplying criticism from the inside, the romantic dream is proof against external attack. The poet's dream of ideals is itself a 'destructive element': Stein, in *Lord Jim*, might be addressing the poet in his workshop as well as Everyman in his life in the speech Warren finds so important for understanding Conrad:

> A man that is born falls into a dream like a man who falls into the sea. If he tries to climb out into the air as inexperienced people endeavour to do, he drowns—*nicht wahr?*—No! I tell you! The way is to the destructive element submit yourself, and with the exertions of your hands and feet in the water make the deep, deep sea keep you up.
>
> (SE, p. 44)[33]

The dream will destroy a man who attempts to deny it by living 'naturally' on the dry land of the naturalistic world, in recoil from the risk of full humanity. Man, as a natural creature, "is not born to swim in the dream, with gills and fins, but if he submits in his own imperfect, 'natural' way he can learn to swim and keep himself up, however painfully, in the destructive element" (SE, p. 45). Shakespeare's Mercutio, Warren's 'caged' heart and 'iron' stroke are the necessary recognitions that man's way of submission to the destructive element of the dream is always 'natural', imperfect. At the end of the essay on *Pure and Impure Poetry* we move from aesthetics to morals, from literature to life:

> This method, however, will scarcely satisfy the mind which is hot for certainties; . . . The new theory of pure purity would purge out all complexities and all ironies and all self-criticism. And this theory will forget that the hand-me-down faith, the hand-me-down ideals, no matter what the professed content, is in the end not only meaningless but vicious. It is vicious because, as parody, it is the enemy of all faith.
>
> (SE, p. 31)

In the essay, 'Knowledge and the Image of Man' (1955), Warren relates aesthetics to living by endowing literature with cognitive value. Poetry, that is 'literature as a dimension of the creative imagination' provides a kind of knowledge, an image of man. This knowledge is knowledge of 'form', and 'form' which springs 'from the deep engagement of spirit with the world' is the discovery of the 'rhythm' of that engagement. 'Form', which is known 'only by experiencing it . . . gives man an image of himself, for it gives him his mode of experiencing, a paradigm of his inner life, his rhythm of destiny, his tonality of fate'. By defining 'our deepest life', it gives us, 'in new self-awareness, a yet deeper life to live.'[34] This 'deeper life' is not merely contemplative, for the deepened awareness of self which literature provides must find expression in action. Poetry itself is action, like that of the saint who 'proves his vision by stepping cheerfully into the fires' (SE, p. 29).

Chapter One—Notes

[1] Foreword to *The Fugitive*, **1** (April, 1922), 1.

[2] Warren, Robert Penn, 'Literature as a Symptom', in *Who Owns America? A New Declaration of Independence*, ed. Herbert Agar and Allen Tate (Boston and New York: Houghton Mifflin Company, 1936), pp. 266 ff. and 270.

[3] Warren, Robert Penn, 'Some Don'ts for Literary Regionalists', *American Review*, **7** (Dec, 1936), 142.

[4] Cowley, Malcolm, (Ed.), *Writers at Work: The Paris Review Interviews* (London: Secker and Warburg, 1958), pp. 171–72.

[5] Brooks, Cleanth and Warren, Robert Penn, *Understanding Fiction*, 2nd ed. (New York: Appleton-Century-Crofts, 1959), p. xvii.

[6] 'The Child Next Door', in *Promises*, SP, p. 221.

[7] Koch, Adrienne and Peden, William, (Eds.), *The Life and Selected Writings of Thomas Jefferson* (New York: Random House), p. 441. Klaus Poenicke also quotes this passage from the famous letter to Madison in his *Robert Penn Warren: Kunstwerk Und Kritische Theorie*, p. 14. I am much indebted in this chapter to Poenicke's discussions of agrarianism and the New Criticism as well as to Mark Linenthal Jr's 'Robert Penn Warren and the Southern Agrarians'.

[8] Matthiessen, F. O., *American Renaissance* (New York: O.U.P., 1941), p. 368.

[9] Warren, Robert Penn, 'John Crowe Ransom: A Study in Irony', *Virginia Quarterly Review*, **11** (Jan, 1935), 97.

[10] *Who Owns America?* p. 325.

[11] Twelve Southerners, *I'll Take My Stand: The South and the Agrarian Tradition* (New York: Harper Brothers, 1930. References are to the reprint by Harper Torchbooks, New York, 1962), p. xxiv.

[12] Tate, Allen, *Reactionary Essays on Poetry and Ideas* (New York: Charles Scribner's Sons, 1936), p. 168.

[13] Stevens, Wallace, *Opus Posthumous* (New York: Alfred A. Knopf, 1957), p. 260.

[14] Tate, *Reactionary Essays*, p. 182.

[15] 29 Nov, 1930. DDC, File 43.

[16] Interview with Russell Howe published in *The Reporter*, March 22, 1956, reprinted in James B. Meriwether and Michael Millagte, eds., *Lion in the Garden: Interviews with William Faulkner, 1926–1956* (New York: Random House, 1968), p. 260.

[17] Faulkner, William, *Intruder in the Dust* (Harmondsworth: Penguin Books Ltd, 1960), p. 149.

[18] *Ibid.*, p. 202.

[19] McDowell, Frederick P. W., 'Robert Penn Warren's Criticism', *Accent*, **15** (Summer, 1955), 173–96.

[20] *Who Owns America?* pp. 265–67.

[21] 'John Crowe Ransom: A Study in Irony', *Virginia Quarterly Review*, **11** (Jan, 1935), 112.

[22] Warren, Robert Penn, 'The Present State of Poetry: III. In the United States', *Kenyon Review*, **1** (Autumn, 1939), 389.

[23] 'The Blind Poet: Sidney Lanier', *American Review*, **2** (Nov, 1933), 45.

[24] *Who Owns America?* p. 276.

[25] Warren, Robert Penn, and Brooks, Cleanth, 'The Reading of Modern Poetry', *American Review*, **8** (Feb, 1937), 439.

[26] *Ibid.*, 448.

[27] See Ransom's two articles, 'Poetry: I. The Formal Analysis,' and 'Poetry: II. The Final Cause', in *Kenyon Review*, **9** (Spring, Summer, 1947), 436–56, 640–58.

[28] Ransom, John Crowe, *The New Criticism* (Norfolk, Conn.: New Directions, 1941), p. 280.

[29] Ransom, John Crowe, *The World's Body* (New York: Charles Scribner's Sons, 1938), p. 4.

[30] Tate, Allen, *Reason In Madness, Critical Essays* (New York: G. P. Putnam's Sons, 1941), p. 72.

[31] Brooks, Cleanth, *The Well Wrought Urn: Studies in the Structure of Poetry* (New York: Harcourt Brace, 1947), p. 3.

[32] In his Preface to *Modern Poetry, A Personal Essay* (London: O.U.P., 1938) MacNeice writes: 'This book is a plea for *impure* poetry, that is for poetry conditioned by the poet's life and the world around him.' MacNeice is especially concerned to distinguish between the poet's proper business and the 'purity 'of *fin de siècle* aestheticism.

[33] Conrad, Joseph, *Lord Jim* (London: Dent, 1946), p. 214.

[34] Longley, pp. 244–46.

2

Early Poetry

Throughout Robert Penn Warren's work there is an effort to balance the data available to reason with the insights of intuition. Despite his association with men like Tate and Ransom and their call to re-endow the world with mystery, the young Warren's temperament drove him hard towards a morbidly naturalistic view of things. In a post-Darwinian world the young poet inclined to believe that being 'rolled round in earth's diurnal curse, / With rocks, and stones, and trees' was in the end all man could reasonably hope for. The sequence of poems called 'Kentucky Mountain Farm'[1] which Warren expanded from one poem to seven between 1926 and 1935, shows the poet attempting to make stoical virtue out of such necessity. The first poem in the sequence, 'Rebuke of the Rocks' (SP, p. 319), defines the moon as 'obscene' and 'mad' for dictating the natural cycle of birth, generation and death. The 'little stubborn people of the hill' are enjoined to abandon their attempts to breed any 'tender thing among the rocks' and instead to 'keep the sweet sterility of stone.' One is reminded of Yeats's escape from 'those dying generations at their song' only to realise how at once imaginatively evasive and romantically appealing was his other country of Byzantium by comparison with Warren's stern, all too imaginable, *ultima Thule*.

If the rebuke of Warren's rocks is stern, however, it is also compassionate. If the poet is bitter about the moon's heartless dominion, there are pity and admiration in his apostrophe, 'O little stubborn people of the hill', and in the magisterial cadences of the rhymes a tone of lament prompted, no doubt, by Warren's personal knowledge of the meagre rewards that often attended the efforts of mountain farmers in his home state of Kentucky. This softens the austerity of the poem's injunction to naturalism and prepares us for a further softening in the second poem, 'At the Hour of the Breaking of the Rocks' (SP, p. 319), in which the rocks themselves are borne

> Down shifting waters to the tall, profound
> Shadow of the absolute deeps,
> Wherein the spirit moves and never sleeps
> That held the foot among the rocks, that bound
> The tired hand upon the stubborn plough,
> Knotted the flesh unto the hungry bone,
> The redbird to the charred and broken bough,
> And strung the bitter tendons of the stone.

Like Yeats in 'Sailing to Byzantium' Warren is pulled away, in the course of his meditation, from the strict position in which he begins. Yeats's emigration from mortality to the Byzantium of eternal art is suddenly qualified by the concluding lines of his poem which foresee his singing to 'lords and ladies of Byzantium / Of what is past, or passing, or to come.' Keeping a drowsy Emperor awake is all very well, but addressing lords and ladies even of Byzantium on the subject of passing time strongly suggests a backward glance to those dying generations supposedly left behind. Warren's creation of a spirit of the deeps reminiscent of Wordsworth's impelling and pervading spirit in 'Tintern Abbey', is, similarly, an important subversion of the naturalistic point of view of the first poem. This is not to suggest that the informing spirit of Warren's poem implies the profound faith in the unity of human life, nature and the infinite that Wordsworth affirms. There might seem to be oneness in Warren's absolute deeps only in the sense that through death the individual joins in the annihilation common to all; yet the conception of a spirit that bestows characteristic life on each thing in the world and the attribution, however ironic, of 'bitter tendons' to stone indicate unease in the strict naturalistic stance.

In Part III, 'History among the Rocks' (SP, p. 320), the poet tries to console us, and perhaps himself, by imaging death as a body, pared to its minimum, carried into the peace of watery oblivion:

> Think how a body, naked and lean
> And white as the splintered sycamore, would go
> Tumbling and turning, hushed in the end,
> With hair afloat in waters that gently bend
> To ocean where the blind tides flow.[2]

But the soldiers of the Civil War died less antiseptically: the rocks have a reductive way with the great ideals and issues of history:

> In these autumn orchards once young men lay dead—
> Gray coats, blue coats. Young men on the mountainside
> Clambered, fought. Heels muddied the rocky spring.
> Their reason is hard to guess, remembering
> Blood on their black mustaches in moonlight.

The repetition of 'Their reason is hard to guess' in the next line makes us wonder if intellectual weariness has tossed the poet to the stony breast of naturalism: however perplexed he may be about the motivations that prompted young men to action in the Civil War, he cannot summarily dismiss the enigma of their fate by proving it empty of moral content like the fall of the apple 'in the quiet night', although he might wish to, to be rid of the problem.

The birds in Sections IV–VI[3] are all images of life, counteracting the emphasis on mutability in Parts I–III. The cardinal, jay and hawk of these poems amount to another kind of rebuke to the mordant poet, balancing the rebuke of the rocks. To be sure, the poet punningly reveals that the lizard, 'devout as an ikon', not the bird, is his spiritual 'cardinal' (SP: 1943, p. 81), but in Part V, 'The Jay' (SP: 1943, pp. 81–82), another bird humbles the human observer. As it chases the autumn leaves, the jay's participation in the seasonal process underlines the poet's failure of nerve, his capitulation to time and death. The hawk in Part VI, 'The Watershed' (SP: 1943, p. 82), provides a further lesson in humility. Like Ted Hughes's 'Hawk Roosting', this bird, from its great height, sees everything:

> His gold eyes scan
> The crumpled shade on gorge and crest
> And streams that creep and disappear, appear,
> Past fingered ridges and their shrivelling span.
> Under the broken eaves men take their rest.

To see all is to know all—though perhaps the tenuous logic of this proposition was partly responsible for Warren's omitting the section from later printings of the sequence. The comprehensive vision of the hawk has both instructed the poet in his own myopia and increased his yearning for certitude. Thus the three birds have exposed him as deficient in joy, in the capacity to live in time, and in the faculty of vision. Yet these creatures' victories over 'the sweet sterility of stone' do tentatively suggest possibilities.

In the final section, 'The Return' (SP, p. 321), however, Warren denies these hopeful implications, ending the sequence in what appears to be a completely negative attitude, though now replacing the first section's bitterness with resignation. The central image is of a falling leaf joining its own reflection:

> Again the timeless gold
> Broad leaf released the tendoned bough, and slow,
> Uncertain as a casual memory,
> Wavered aslant the ripe unmoving air.
> Up from the whiter bough, the bluer sky,
> That glimmered in the water's depth below,
> A richer leaf rose to the other there.
> They touched; with the gentle clarity of dream,
> Bosom to bosom, burned on the quiet stream.

Victor H. Strandberg interprets this imagery as an account of 'the dying leaf thus returning to its deeper self in time . . . time being represented here as *still* waters', and notes that, 'By contrast with the ultimate return of self to deeper self, the return of self to a different self on a temporal level, such as the return of a son to his mother, is marked by disappointment and superficiality.'[4] The second half of the poem seems to support this reading:

. . . And he, who had loved as well as most,
Might have foretold it thus, for well he knew
How, glimmering, a buried world is lost
In the water's riffle or the wind's flaw;
How his own image, perfect and deep
And small within loved eyes, had been forgot,
Her face being turned, or when those eyes were shut
Past light in that fond accident of sleep.

Strandberg's perception of the contrast between two kinds of return of self as the particular focus of this poem in the sequence would seem to be endorsed by a letter from Warren to Donald Davidson:

I feel that within the limits of its intention the 'Letter of a Mother' is easily my most finished poem. 'Kentucky Mountain Farm' is second because it presents a more specialized and perhaps more subtle if weaker treatment of the same attitude as that of the first poem named.[5]

The 'attitude' of 'Letter of a Mother' (SP: 1943, pp. 87–88) is, certainly, like the attitude towards 'the return of self to a different self on a temporal level' in Strandberg's reading of 'The Return'. In 'Letter of a Mother' it is part of the son's 'illegal prodigality of dream' to suppose that there can be a meaningful return to the mother, for although his body is 'held mortmain' of the mother's womb, he has also been 'merchandised / Unto the dark' and the mother flesh cannot summon back

The tired child it would again possess
As shall a womb more tender than her own
That builds not tissue or the little bone,
But dissolves them to itself in weariness.

Both poems deal with the failure to get back to some perfect, original conception of oneself and, implicitly, with the resulting diminution of selfhood. But in 1926, when Warren wrote his letter to Davidson, 'Kentucky Mountain Farm' comprised only one poem, 'At the Hour of the Breaking of the Rocks', which is much more concerned with the problem of holding a naturalistic view of things than with the important but narrower subject of the self. 'Letter of a Mother' is about the displacement of a sentimental view by a naturalistic one.

In the first part of 'At the Hour of the Breaking of the Rocks' Warren salutes the resolute men of the Kentucky hills:

> . . . the taciturn
> Lean men that of all things alone
> Were, not as water or the febrile grass,
> Figured in kinship to the savage stone.

This hard kinship, however, cannot protect man from the process of time whereby, in Warren's elemental and apocalyptic imagery, 'the lean men have passed', 'the rocks are stricken' and borne down to the 'absolute deeps' which so clearly echo the dissolving 'womb more tender' than the mother's in 'Letter of a Mother'. As this was the section of 'Kentucky Mountain Farm' which Warren wrote first, it is reasonable to expect that the sequence of poems growing out of it should share its purpose, i.e. to contemplate man's fate in naturalistic terms in order to find out how well these terms work. This is still the purpose in Section IV. 'The Return', first published in 1930, which is incidentally about the problem of the self but centrally about the adequacy of the kind of vision with which the poet has been experimenting throughout the sequence. Repeatedly, as we have seen, the naturalistic position is assumed only to be questioned or qualified. The son in 'Letter of a Mother' is in no doubt that the separation of himself from his mother that began at birth has been a continuing, irreversible process and that there can be no reunion for him except with death, fancifully conceived as the ultimate mother. Yet the very lament of the poem is so strong that it creates its own opposition to such naturalistic certainty. There is more to this than biology!

In 'The Return' the depletion of self caused by the discovery that one's image has not been preserved is the note on which the poem ends. Yet, counterbalancing this naturalistic insistence on the power of time ('the water's riffle') and chance ('the wind's flaw'; 'that fond accident of sleep'), we have had the beautiful intimation of a completed, enriched self in the imagery of the falling leaf and its reflection in the still water of the stream. The 'backward heart' may lack a voice with which to recall the 'vagrant image' of its former self but the speaker has seen an example of perfect self-fulfilment enacted in the natural world. By intensifying the poet's sense of loss, this suggests the possibility of a tragic view of life—and tragedy does not sit well with naturalism—even that things might be otherwise in human experience. Again, naturalism is questioned by nature.

The poems in 'Kentucky Mountain Farm' foreshadow the R.P.W. of *Brother to Dragons* who 'proves that only a synthesis of perspectives can teach us to live responsibly.'[6] In imagery scrupulously drawn from the locale Warren knows so well, the poems deal with the themes of a selfhood, time, history and idealism all within the frame of an unremitting testing of the poet's terms and positions. This testing is itself the most important activity in the sequence—an act of becoming by the poet who, in 1939, felt that the question, 'Can man live on the purely naturalistic level?' was the central issue for modern literature.[7]

II

It is remarkable that Warren should have achieved so early in his career the sophistication and polish evident in 'At the Hour of the Breaking of the Rocks'. Three years earlier, in 1923, his first published poem, 'The Golden Hills of Hell', appeared in *Driftwood Flames*, a booklet produced by the Poetry Guild, an undergraduate literary club at Vanderbilt University. Nearly twenty years later Allen Tate still remembered being surprised by the shy young poet and his poem:

> I became aware of a presence at my back and turning round I saw the most remarkable looking boy I had ever laid eyes on. He was tall and thin, and when he walked across the room he made a sliding shuffle, as if his bones didn't belong to one another. He had a long quivering nose, large brown eyes, and a long chin—all topped by curly red hair. He spoke in a soft whisper, asking to see my poem; then he showed me one of his own—it was about Hell, and I remember this line:
> Where lightly bloom the purple lilies . . .

He said that he was sixteen years old and a sophomore. This remarkable young man was 'Red', Robert Penn Warren, the most gifted person I have ever known.[8]

The poem recalled by Tate merits some attention not only because it gives an indication of Warren's writing before he had come under the influence of the Fugitives, but also because it shows an early attempt to present an earned vision through the use of paradox and by way of symbolic landscape:

> O, fair the Golden Hills of Hell,
>   Where lightly rest the purple lilies;
> There, as all the saints tell
>   Lightly nod the lilies.
>
> Dim beyond the scarlet river,
>   Slenderly and slow they nod,
> Glimpsed from where the splendours quiver
>   On the minarets of God.
>
> False tales the saints tell
>   Of the slender lilies;
> For I have knelt on the Hills of Hell
>   Among the withered lilies.[9]

The poem, somewhat precociously, tries to convey the desolation of sin: saints aver the appeal of sin, but the sinner is miserable. Already there is a characteristic element of paradox —the beauty of the lilies and the pain they signify—but the affected, Decadent manner offers the reader a pose instead of an experience that can be felt as genuine. Perhaps the best effect is the implication that the saints are false because they lack experience, a hint of the mature Warren's conviction that a vision must be earned in living.

The meeting described by Allen Tate was Warren's introduction to the Fugitives. Early in 1924 he joined the staff of the journal to which by this time he had contributed three dramatic monologues. The first of these, 'Crusade',[10] won a place in the competition for the Nashville, Poetry Prize and is superior in some respects to the two succeeding poems, although there is too much alliteration after the style of Old English—Warren wrote Anglo-Saxon imitations for Donald Davidson—and the

D

cataloguing of melodramatic particulars soon becomes monotonous:

> We have not forgot the clanking of grey armours
> Along frosty ridges against the moon,
> The agony of gasping endless columns,
> Skulls glaring white on red deserts at noon;
> Nor death in dank marshes by fever,
> Flies on bloated bodies rotting by the way,
> Naked corpses on the sluggish river,
> Sucked from the trampled rushes where they lay.

Characteristically, the poem is about a quest, being the recollections of a soldier in the service of Count Raymond of Provence
on the night after the capture of Jerusalem, and Warren does
succeed in presenting narrative content in verse form. The
concluding lines anticipate the tension between naturalism
and idealism which, as we have seen, would soon become a
typical source of energy in his work. Here, as one might expect,
a Romantic attitude is struck:

> We have now won through these to the Tomb of God;
> Here is a hole where once lay sacred bones.
> Red crosses have greyed on our hauberks.
> Souls may be whiter for gazing on white stones.
> Here is the Tomb as when our Lord had risen,
> Here is the Tomb, but yonder promised peace.
> Can rock and dust presage a fabled heaven?
> This low malignant moon gives no surcease
> Nor any opiate of forgetfulness
> For the sob and choke of remembered sorrow . . .
> We have no solace in this bitter stillness.
> We shall be still enough tomorrow.

If T. S. Eliot is an influence in this poem[11] 'After Teacups',[12]
the second monologue, begins as an imitation of 'Gerontion':

> I was not on the parapets at Cretae
> Dreading sails black against the red low moon,
> When my ruin overthrew me.
> Nor did it claim me with the plunge of Grecian spears
> Surging up in dark ships from the sea
> That ancient night. There rode no portent of my fears

On the long breeze sweeping in from Cyprus;
Nor later with the rank mists when I fought
Bogged in the marshes, clubbing my arquebus.

The effect here is sarcastic, the speaker evoking grand possibilities only as a preface to the mock-heroic revelation that
his ruin has overthrown him in 'Mme Atelie's salon' where his
gestures and poses remind us all too clearly of J. Alfred
Prufrock.[13] The last lines of the third monologue, 'Midnight',[14]
are unmistakably Eliotesque:

Your gaunt uncomprehending eyes
Clutch at me as I start to rise
Rattling my newspaper, saying, 'It is late'.
You draw the pins, release your flood of hair.
Am I doomed to stand thus ever,
Hesitating on the stair?

In spite of its over-straining the poem does convey the man's
nightmarish sense of exclusion from the turbulent inner world
of his mate and his awareness of his own ineffectuality. Another
poem, related to 'Midnight' in theme was published the following year as one of three sonnets under the title 'Portraits of
Three Ladies':

Strangely her heart yet clutched a strange twilight,
One that had lured with dreams down a cypressed way
To glens where hairy-haunched and savage lay
The night. Could ever she forget that night
And one black pool, her image in the water,
Or how fat lily stalks were stirred and shifted
By terrible things beneath, and how there drifted
Through slimy trunks and fern a goatish laughter?
Sometimes at dusk before her looking glass
She thought how in that pool her limbs gleamed whitely:
She heard her husband watering the grass
Or his neat voice inquiring, 'Supper dear?'
Across the table then she faced him nightly
With harried eyes in which he read no fear.[15]

This is a long way from the parapets of Cretae: imagery is
striking, precisely expressive and skilfully deployed to characterise levels of experience achingly out of phase with each
other. The juxtaposition of the wife's repressed sexuality and

the husband's banality is smoothly accomplished in the sestet; desolation and hopelessness are compacted into the last line where the phrase 'in which he read no fear' concludes the poem with a true, if limited, irony.

The poems Warren submitted to *The Fugitive* in 1924 strongly reflect the depression which overcame him in that year, and apparently led to attempted suicide in May. An impassioned letter from Tate to Davidson sheds some light:

> Well, it has happened . . . I am MAD—mad as hell . . . God! I wish I were there. I am sure that I am the only person who doesn't look on Red as a merely interesting monstrosity mostly to be avoided. I don't accuse you of this; I only mean that it is the temper of the environment, and this temper has probably had much to do with his breakdown . . . Don't deceive yourself that he did it because he was 'convinced he would never be a poet.' It shows, finally,—that statement—his fundamental courage. He rejected the meaner way, that of telling the truth about his anguish. Red is no simpleton; it isn't a mere despair of youth, a maudlin self-pity working itself into the hysteria of suicide. It is simply that he has been beaten down so consistently and brutally, that his emotional needs have met frustration so completely, that he was driven into a blind alley. . . . There's one thing you might do, however: keep Mims away from him in any form. Mims and what he represents is a very significant factor of disturbance in Red's mind. There is no reason why Red shouldn't survive in an intelligent environment, and if he doesn't survive there it will be a tremendous indictment of our whole system of ideas; here, let me say that he isn't persecuted by persons, but by hostile ideas, and the persecution is of course a mere figment in the popular mind but very real to an intellectual mind like Red's.[16]

Youthfully self-conscious about his physical appearance, Warren was further oppressed by the traditionalism of Dr Edwin Mims, then head of the Vanderbilt English Department. A letter from Tate to Davidson, dated 17 April, 1924, includes the following expression of concern for Warren: 'Incidentally, I hope Dr Mims won't keep nagging at him (I doubt if you know whereof I speak), for he's very sensitive, and while the Doctor's solicitude is well-meant it is wholly irrelevant; he no more understands Red than he does the fourth dimension.'[17] The young Warren must have felt intolerably frustrated both personally and intellectually, despite his sustaining associations with the Fugitives. Intellectually he held back from religious orthodoxy ('False tales the saints tell') while his physical unhappiness led him to expect only further misery in a life lived on the naturalistic level. He had reached an *impasse*: both the world of nature and the world of ideas were against him.

The poems of this period are much possessed by death. 'Three Poems'[18] offer, rather obscurely, three different perspectives on death and 'Death Mask of a Young Man'[19] reads like self-dramatisation. In July Tate visited Warren at his family home in Guthrie, Kentucky, and wrote to Davidson: 'Red is in better condition than I've seen him in over a year, strong, healthy looking, heavy with good appetite; he sleeps ten hours a night.'[20] The improvement in Warren is reflected in the new objectivity with which he treats the theme of death, as in the tribute to 'Alf Burt, Tenant Farmer'.[21] Mortality is also the subject of 'Easter Morning: Crosby Junction'[22] in which the clichés of the preacher are tartly answered by the thoughts of one of his listeners:

'Rejoice, ye Righteous, Christ from the tomb is come!'
(The crocus, a christ, breaks its black bulb, the tomb.)

'Now ye that believe on Him are not to die—'
(Through the window the voice importunate and high
Rejects the confutation of the stone
That in the churchyard marks the mortal bone)—

'But inherit life eternal—have ye no fear!'
(Indeed there are no murderers buried here
But godly flesh is rumoured to decay
And if here flourish not the rank green bay

The cedar hath an hungry root and long.
How may we sing who have no golden song,
How may we speak who have no word to say,
Or pray, or pray,—who would so gently pray?)

If this is a crisper effort than 'Alf Burt' it is also more blatantly contrived and despite the intensifying of feeling in the last stanza, technical proficiency does not quite rescue the poem from the cheapening effect of its sarcasms.

The same issue of the magazine printed 'To a Face in the Crowd'[23] (SP, p. 324–25). Tate wrote to Davidson on 20 January 1927 referring to a visit from Mark Van Doren to whom he had read material by the Fugitives. Van Doren 'was astonished at the quality of the group as a whole. He was knocked cold by Red ... You know Red is pretty close to being the greatest Fugitive poet. There are certain obstructions to this realisation, of course. He is the only one of us who has *power*. "Letter of a Mother" and "To a Face in the Crowd" are the only poems in the collection to which the description great can be applied—in spite of a few technical imperfections in both of them.'[24]

The face of the brother seen in the crowd is presumably that aspect of the speaker's own character which drives him to action:

> My brother, brother, whither do you pass,
> Unto what hill at dawn, unto what glen
> Where among the rocks the faint lascivious grass
> Fingers in lust the arrogant bones of men?

The quest for fulfilment in action must be futile in the context of the nature which lubriciously savours its reductive power over human life. The stanza thus recognises both the obligation to act and the tendency to surrender despairingly to the rule of nature whereby all human effort is beset by frustration and ends in death.

> Beside what bitter waters will you go
> Where the lean gulls of your heart along the shore
> Rehearse to the cliffs the rhetoric of their woe?
> In dreams, perhaps, I have seen your face before.

The speaker has difficulty in convincing even himself that his effort amounts to more than rhetoric. The intention of the last line of this stanza is apparently to keep the accusation of ineffectuality aimed at the speaker himself, linking his other, dream self with the forbears mentioned in the following stanzas. As a result the implications of 'rhetoric' are carried forward as a possible judgement of the 'fathers' actions too.

A certain night has borne both you and me;
We are the children of an ancient band
Broken between the mountains and the sea.
A cromlech marks for you that ultimate strand

And dolorous you must find the place they stood.
Of old I know that shore, that dim terrain,
And know how black and turbulent the blood
Will beat through iron chambers of the brain

When at your back the taciturn tall stone,
Which is your father's monument and mark,
Repeats the waves' implacable monotone,
Ascends the night and propagates the dark.

Will the potential self of the speaker respond to the challenge
of a tragic past, or will he lapse into dispirited ineffectuality?
It is, after all, reasonable to be afraid: 'Men there have lived
who wrestled with the ocean', the speaker knows, but 'the
polyp was their shroud', echoing the lustful grass of the first
stanza. We are left wondering, but even heroic renunciation
of the night leads, in the poem's final stanza, only to weariness
as the speaker and his other self are 'Borne in the lost proces-
sion of these feet', like Eliot's Dantesque crowd flowing over
London Bridge in 'The Waste Land'.

The poem's admission that the 'woe' it discusses may be
'rhetoric' acts as a cover for some strained poeticisms, but the
force of the poem carries the reader over these defects and it is
a new force in Warren's work, marking a crucial stage in the
maturing of his art. This force derives not merely from his
ideas or from his skill with image and phrase, but from his
discovery of irony as principle and method. It is not the kind of
irony which puts bite into the ending of the sonnet from
'Portraits of Three Ladies', but a double perspective which is
maintained throughout the poem from first to last as the life
of heroic action is simultaneously extolled and undercut by
naturalistic scepticism. The ending does not finally destroy the
vision of possible heroic action; the sense of likely failure rather
emphasises the majesty of the forefathers. The inclusiveness
which energises Warren's poem closely answers the description
of irony given by John Crowe Ransom in the same issue of
The Fugitive:

Irony may be regarded as the ultimate mode of the great minds—it presupposes the others. It implies first of all an honourable and strenuous period of romantic creation; it implies then a rejection of the romantic forms and formulas; but this rejection is so unwilling, and in its statements there lingers so much of the music and colour and romantic mystery which is perhaps the absolute poetry, and this statement is attended by such a disarming rueful comic sense of the poet's own betrayal, that the fruit of it is wisdom and not bitterness, poetry and not prose, health and not suicide. Irony is the rarest of the states of mind, because it is the most inclusive; the whole mind has been active in arriving at it, both creation and criticism, both poetry and science.[25]

The qualities of Warren's mature writing could hardly be better defined. For the first time in 'To a Face in the Crowd' he achieved a poem which is 'inclusive' in the sense defined here and within the following year he embarked on the 'Kentucky Mountain Farm' sequence with 'At the Hour of the Breaking of the Rocks'. In the late summer of 1925, after graduating from Vanderbilt, Warren went to the University of California as a graduate student. On the train for Los Angeles on 8 August, 1925 he wrote to Andrew Lytle, revealing his capacity for severe self-criticism and the extent to which he was now in possession of his own poetic, with irony replacing sarcasm as the key:

I think that my philosophy of poetry is right, at least for me, who am a relativist and who consequently would not erect it into a criterion. I feel that it is right, but I also know that my method demands discipline; it is far too romantic in essence with too much sarcasm. I have never achieved a real irony which is the true alloy. If I may pursue a metallurgical metaphor, sarcasm is a sort of plating that flakes off and is not integral, while a true irony alloys the softer ore of romanticism and makes it usable.[26]

III

From the University of California Warren went to Yale for
further graduate study. In 1928 he won a Rhodes Scholarship
to Oxford and in the following year published his major
contribution to the Agrarian cause, the critical biography,
John Brown, the Making of a Martyr. While working on his
Bachelor of Literature dissertation for the University of Oxford
he also wrote the essay, 'The Briar Patch', for the symposium,
'I'll Take My Stand'. On his return to America he taught at
Southwestern College in Memphis, then at Vanderbilt University. In 1934 he took up an appointment at Louisiana State
University where with Cleanth Brooks and Charles W. Pipkin
he founded *The Southern Review*. In 1936 he produced his first
collection of verse, *Thirty-Six Poems*.

One anonymous, unsympathetic reviewer, betraying his
misunderstanding of Warren's intentions, nevertheless defined
the strategy not only of several of these early poems but of
many that were yet to come:

> Mr Warren shares in the difficulties of his generation; he has been
> forced to be both critic and poet, to the detriment of his poetry.
> While grateful for the light cast by his criticism, one nevertheless
> cannot but be sorry that the critical spirit has entered into the
> poet. In these poems ratiocination often hampers the free expres-
> sion of poetic sensibility, and emotion is stifled by thought.[27]

In Warren's view, of course, the overflow of powerful feeling
which might have gratified the reviewer would have been too
'pure'. The Wordsworthian poem, 'Man Coming of Age'
(SP: 1943, p. 69), about the death of the speaker's childhood
self, fails just because it is too smooth. It is not just lack of
'ratiocination' which is to blame—there is plenty of 'thought' in
the poem. It is simply that the poem does not cover the case
comprehensively enough. 'The Return: An Elegy' (SP:
pp. 315–16), on the other hand, succeeds magnificently in
covering the case by counterpointing in appropriate tones
'poetic', rationalistic and primitive responses to the death of

the speaker's mother. A discordantly irreverent fancy vivifies his painful incapacity for the luxury of simple cathartic grief:

> give me the nickels off your eyes
> from your hands the violets
> let me bless your obsequies
> if you possessed conveniently enough three eyes
> then I could buy a pack of cigarettes.

If Warren's method saves him from the sentimentality which he chiefly distrusts, Morton D. Zabel was quick to spot its dangers:

> The method is a valuable one; dryness of irony and omniscience is combined with humour or compassion in an extremely effective way, but it is a way that easily falls into its own kind of banality. The feeling of the poem is enervated to the point of exhaustion; a serious method has declined into personal convention and victimised its author.[28]

While the method may keep 'purity' at bay, it sometimes results in a contrived tortuousness, essentially as self-indulgent as the inverted sentimentality of some of Hemingway's writing. Sarcasm can return to cheapen the effect as in 'Letter from a Coward to a Hero' (SP, pp. 291–93):

> Though young, I do not like loud noise:
> The sudden backfire,
> The catcall of boys,
> Drums beating for
> The big war,
> Or clocks that tick at night, and will not stop.
> If you should lose your compass and map
> Or a mouse get in the wall,
> For sleep try love or veronal,
> Though some prefer, I know, philology.
> Does the airman scream in the flaming trajectory?

The coward, unlike some, is not fooled by big words: philological grandeur (like 'flaming trajectory') will not soften the fact of death; but the intellectual smartness of the third and second last lines mars this otherwise fine poem in which the writer's praise for the valiant is set against his worldly suspicion that disaster will result from the hero's simple devotion to an abstract virtue. Disaster itself is characterised in lines which beautifully illustrate Warren's flair for substantialising the abstract:

> Disaster owns less speed than you have got
> But he will cut across the back lot
> To lurk and lie in wait.
> Admired of children, gathered for their games,
> Disaster, like the dandelion, blooms,
> And the delicate film is fanned
> To seed the shaven lawn.

Some of *Thirty-Six Poems* are mannered, some are impenetrable. 'Eidolon' (SP, pp. 229–300) is commended by John L. Stewart[29] for its sensitive evocation of night in the country. For example:

> All night, in May, dogs barked in the hollow woods;
> Hoarse, from secret huddles of no light,
> By moonlit bole, hoarse, the dogs gave tongue.

and more particularly:

> The boy, all night, lay in the black room,
> Tick-straw, all night, harsh to the bare side.
> Staring, he heard; the clotted dark swam slow.

This unfortunately gives way to the flatulence of 'unappeasable riot / Provoked, resurgent, the bosom's nocturnal disquiet', 'belled their unhouselled angers' and 'fanged commotion rude'. Strandberg is probably right in his guess that "the 'eidolon' of the title refers to the phantom-self which escapes from the hounds" and 'returns to eternity',[30] but the reader is likely to find the 'nocturnal disquiet' as perplexingly unaccounted for as the 'curse of hell-black hate' for the father of the speaker in 'Genealogy' (*Thirty-Six Poems*, p. 28). 'Toward Rationality' (SP: 1943, p. 41) is singled out by Zabel as an extreme example of brainy and overplotted ingenuity.[31]

There is always an appeal open to taste in such matters, but among the best poems in *Thirty-Six Poems* are the brilliantly multitoned 'Pondy Woods', 'History', 'Letter from a Coward to a Hero', 'The Last Metaphor', 'Problem of Knowledge', 'For a Friend who thinks himself Urbane', 'The Garden' (after Marvell), and 'Garden Waters'. 'History' (SP, pp. 294–96) considers the significance of human effort in the context of the decline in values prophesied by the speaker. It is as though Warren were pondering a world in which the naturalistic view urged in 'Rebuke of the Rocks' had prevailed, robbing man of moral sense and human feeling. Before descending to their promised land the pioneers pause, anticipating the future and considering their own motive in bringing it into being. The future holds material prosperity but moral decay:

> In the new land
> Our seed shall prosper, and
> In those unsifted times
> Our sons shall cultivate
> Peculiar crimes,
> Having not love, nor hate,
> Nor memory.

Some, conscious of their deficiencies, will seek meaning in the actions of their ancestors, but without success because, as Cleanth Brooks puts it: 'The absolutes are gone—are dissolved, indeed, by our consciousness of the past—by our consciousness of a plurality of histories and meanings.'[32] Human experience is defined as a continuous, futile effort to grasp 'certainty' which, in any case, is 'blank' and 'fanged'. Their morale gone, why do the pioneers descend?

> The act
> Alone is pure.
> What appetency knows the flood,
> What thirst, the sword?
> What name
> Sustains the core of flame?
> We are the blade,
> But not the hand
> By which the blade is swayed.
> Time falls, but has no end.
> Descend!

The significance of 'flood', 'sword' and 'flame' depends on their active fulfilment of their own natures. Thus the poem answers the naturalistic view of 'Rebuke of the Rocks' in which the 'lean men' were commanded to renounce their humanity. If 'sweet sterility' is appropriate to stone, action is appropriate to man: it is man's nature to seek a vision of himself, but he can find it only by creating it. The pioneers must push beyond self-doubt, descend into further action and somehow keep themselves afloat in the 'destructive element' of their dream. Such 'alloy of fact' as the intellectual formulation of experience is insufficient: the vision must be lived to be earned.

IV

In 1942 Warren joined the staff of the University of Minnesota. By now he was known as co-editor with Cleanth Brooks of *Understanding Poetry* (1938) and as author of *Night Rider* (1939), his first novel. Also in 1942 New Directions published *Eleven Poems on the Same Theme* in their 'Poet of the Month' series. It was, the booklet's blurb maintained, high time Warren the poet were better known:

> The poems of Robert Penn Warren are among the finest being written in America in these times. But because he has devoted himself to academic and editorial duties and to the writing of fiction, the number of his poems has been small, and he is not nearly so well-known as a poet as he deserves to be. The best critics have singled him out again and again for conspicuous praise, but their enthusiasm has not yet been transmitted to a large public—a state of affairs which is in itself an indictment of American publishing.

Blurbs are by nature inflationary, but *Eleven Poems on the Same Theme* justified its publisher's encomiums, making a contribution to modern literature worthy of the year in which Eliot completed *Four Quartets* with the publication of 'Little Gidding'.

'Monologue at Midnight' (SP, pp. 307–8), a finely controlled metaphysical treatment of love's mortality, introduces the themes of innocence, guilt, time and separateness which will be developed through the sequence. 'Philosophers / Loll in their disputatious ease', says the poet whose uneasy, passionate business is to make the philosophers' abstract terms live for the reader in imagery that will animate his sensibility as in the Donne-like lines which define the true magnitude of lover for lover:

> The match flame sudden in the gloom
> Is lensed within each watching eye
> Less intricate, less small than in
> One heart the other's image is.

In 'Revelation' (SP, 300–1) the boy's sense of guilt locks him in a world remade by the violence within himself:

> Because he had spoken harshly to his mother,
> The day became astonishingly bright,
> The enormity of distance crept to him like a dog now,
> And earth's own luminescence seemed to repel the night.

The boy is passing through a necessary stage of the maturing process, for, the poet asserts, 'In separateness only does love learn definition.' Such definition achieved, the individual must become reconnected to the human community. The boy of this poem is a recognisable precursor of Jack Burden, Jeremiah Beaumont, Jed Tewksbury and other leading figures in Warren's writing, all of whom illustrate the process described in 'Knowledge and the Image of Man':

> . . . man's process of self-definition means that he distinguishes himself from the world and from other men. He disintegrates his primal instinctive sense of unity, he discovers separateness. In this process he discovers the pain of self-criticism and the pain of isolation. But the pain may, if he is fortunate, develop its own homeopathic cure. In the pain of self-criticism he may develop an ideal of excellence, and an ideal of excellence, once established, implies a depersonalized communion in that ideal. In the pain of isolation he may achieve the courage and clarity of mind to envisage the tragic pathos of life, and once he realizes that the tragic experience is universal and a corollary of man's place in nature, he may return to a communion with man and nature.[33]

Eleven Poems on the Same Theme takes us into the 'pain of self-criticism and the pain of isolation' within which we are disconnected from our essential selves and from the 'general human communion' (SE, p. 54). Dogged by our repressions, we are too stained by living to regress into remembered innocence. Instead, we must accept our propensity for evil, and, matured by our visit to inner space, return to the world of time, error and responsibility.

The eleven poems in the sequence take Warren a stage further from the tempered naturalism of 'Kentucky Mountain Farm'. 'History' recognised the categorical imperative of action; now action is set in a scheme of values derived from the 'ideal of excellence' learned in 'the pain of self-criticism'. Self-criticism prompted Warren to put naturalism to the test again in the sequence 'Mexico is a Foreign Country: Five Studies in Naturalism' (SP: 1943, pp. 51–57).[34] In 'The World Comes Galloping: A True Story' the poet appears to subscribe to the dry stoicism of the old man who, regarding the 'street's astonishing vacancy' after a horseman has racketed through it, refers not to the horseman but to the vacancy when he says, '*Veni galopando el mundo*' (SP, p. 303). A more cheerful naturalism is tried in 'Small Soldiers with Drum in Large Landscape' (SP, pp. 304–5), in which 'all Nature's jocund atoms bounce / In tune to keep the world intact.' The soldiers are part of this activity:

> And shrouded in the coats and buttons,
> The atoms bounce, and under the sky,
> Under the mountain's gaze, maintain
> The gallant little formulae.

Naturalism defines the soldiers inhumanly as atoms contained in uniforms, but the last line shows that the poet's attention has been caught not merely by 'the composition's majesty', the diminutive figures against the wide landscape, but by the feeling that the atoms maintain a configuration of order and purpose among the little marching community. If Warren's naturalism was subtly qualified in 'Kentucky Mountain Farm', the 'impurity' of it here reflects the distance he had come in his thinking by way of *Eleven Poems on the Same Theme*: a truly atomic view of life perceives no gallantry.

In 'Bearded Oaks' (SP, pp. 308–9) the lovers lie, practising 'for eternity', in shared separateness from the world, like 'twin atolls on a shelf of shade'. 'Crime', 'Original Sin: a Short Story', 'Pursuit', and 'Terror', deal with the problem from which the lovers have temporarily escaped: how to live with the inevitable derelictions of life in time. The poems imply certain prerequisites for meaningful life by dramatising the problem in striking, often surrealistic images. Warren explains[35] that the 'you' of 'Terror' (SP, pp. 284–86) is modern man and what he lacks is 'that proper sense of the human lot, the sense of limitation and the sense of the necessity for responsible action within that limitation. I should call that sense, when it is applied inclusively, the religious sense—though I don't insist on this.' The poem discusses ways in which man seeks escape from his limitations. He may prefer suicide to 'the damp worm-tooth of compromise', or try to deny his mortality scientifically, by prolonging physical life, hence the allusion to Alexis Carrel in stanza six. He may seek to lose himself in the kind of violent action described in the fourth stanza:

> So some, whose passionate emptiness and tidal
> Lust swayed toward the debris of Madrid,
> And left New York to loll in their fierce idyll
> Among the olives, where the snipers hid;
> And now the North, to see that visioned face
> And polarize their ion of despair,
> Who praise no beauty like the grace
> Which greens the dead eye under the rocket's flare,
> They fight old friends, for their obsession knows
> Only the immaculate itch, not human friends or foes.

Those who fought in Spain on the side of Russia, then in Finland 'over bitter Helsingfors' against the Russians, were evading their own natures, like Brad Tolliver in *Flood*, preferring to fight grand abstractions than struggle with the disgrace of the void within themselves. An example of 'adequate definition'—that is, of the self—is offered in the image of 'the criminal king', presumably Macbeth, who 'kisses the terror', embracing the defining fact of his degradation. The picture is

like that of Conrad's Mr Kurtz in *Heart of Darkness* acknow-
ledging, at last, 'The horror! The horror!' in terms of which he
must be defined. Seeing only 'an empty chair', the 'you,'
though, doubtless, less steeped in evil, achieves no comparable
redemption.

'Pursuit', 'Original Sin: A Short Story', and 'Crime' are all
addressed to the 'you' of 'Terror' as well as to the reader. In
'Crime' (SP, pp. 290–91) we are advised to 'Envy the mad
killer'. His motive was the basic desire for happiness or peace,
and, unlike us, he has been neither deflected by guilt nor
thwarted by repression. Acting decisively and without guile,
he has won in his weariness a firmness of identity which we fail
to achieve. The mad killer 'cannot seem / To remember what it
was he buried under the leaves', but our memory perpetually
'drips, a pipe in the cellar-dark', reminding us of our repressed
selves and the object we shall never grasp 'bright on the bottom
of the murky pond'. The doctor in 'Pursuit' (SP, pp. 286–88)
finds no symptoms of physical disorder to explain the vague
malaise that afflicts the 'you', and accordingly prescribes 'a
change of scene'; but Florida offers neither an escape from the
problem—even the flamingo's neck is 'a question'—nor the
relief of meaning. The 'you', Warren explains, "doesn't know
how to look for the answer or quite what he is looking for. If
he did know, he might get an answer, or a hint of it, even from
the little old widow, the past of the sufferers who seem to have
some truth which the you has missed."[36]

If self-definition eludes the 'you' in 'Pursuit', the tables are
turned in 'Original Sin: a Short Story' (SP, pp. 288–89) where
it is 'more dogged than Pinkerton'. (BTD, p. 28). Warren
suggests that we all try to dodge the categorical imperative of
identity just as the ambitious provincial will suppress his lowly
background. Warren's audacity with language here is entirely
successful: the poem does not suffer from the opacities that
diminish 'Terror', for the powerful imagery defines itself as the
poem unfolds:

Nodding, its great head rattling like a gourd,
And locks like seaweed strung on the stinking stone,
The nightmare stumbles past, and you have heard

E

It fumble your door before it whimpers and is gone:
It acts like the old hound that used to snuffle your door and
    moan.

You thought you had lost it when you left Omaha,
For it seemed connected then with your grandpa, who
Had a wen on his forehead and sat on the veranda
To finger the precious protuberance, as was his habit to do,
Which glinted in sun like rough garnet or the rich old brain
    bulging through.

But you met it in Harvard Yard as the historic steeple
Was confirming the midnight with its hideous racket,
And you wondered how it had come, for it stood so imbecile,
With empty hands, humble, and surely nothing in pocket:
Riding the rods, perhaps—or Grandpa's will paid the ticket.

Here the poem defines a crucial motif in Warren's work. Our
original sin is not the fact of our identity, but our recoil from it.
At the end of the poem the denied self 'stands like an old horse
cold in the pasture', waiting for the 'you' to wake up and
acknowledge it as his own; in 'The Ballad of Billie Potts' it
proves lethal.

'The Ballad of Billie Potts'[37] is Warren's first extended use of
a particular historical incident in verse. Warren explains in an
introductory note that he first heard the story from an old
lady who was 'a relative' of his (SP, p. 271). She assumed that
the events occurred in a region of Western Kentucky between
the Cumberland and Tennessee Rivers. This section of the state
is known as 'Between the Rivers', hence the repetition of the
phrase like a refrain throughout the ballad, connecting its
locale with Mesopotamia, that other 'land between the rivers',
birthplace of man and scene of his original sin. Warren thus
'subtly hints as early as line 2 of this poem the origin (and
outcome) of the myth he is recreating in terms of New World
innocence and its Fall.'[38]

The point of the interpolated argument is that Little Billie
cannot continue to live with the denial of himself implicit in
his false innocence and must cleanse himself by accepting his
identity. The reader may feel a disproportion between the
simple ballad story and the richly imagistic commentary.
John Crowe Ransom is really complaining about this when he

criticises Warren's use of characters who cannot speak for themselves.[39] Warren's point, however, is that *we* must discern the burden of meaning, make a beginning of Little Billie's end. We must work at this, like the poet himself, and with his help. Little Billie's vacuity is an accusing image of our false, evading selves: we must fill in the blank by recognising the logic of his life and the justice of his death. Our criminal innocence must be actively destroyed by our engagement with the poem: we must bend to the parental spring *aware* of the hatchet raised in benison.

In the final ballad sequence Little Billie's parents are forced to accept the verdict of the birthmark, which is 'shaped for luck'. In the misfortune which so justly overtakes them Warren again exposes the limitations of naturalism. Billie's parents had lived naturalistically, observing only jungle law, the survival of the fittest, as they cold-bloodedly prepared death for each rich victim. The killing of their son forces them out of purely animal existence and into experience, albeit primitive, of the human realities of grief, tenderness and kinship. Discovering their true identities as murderers, they are converted from cunning brutes to vulnerable humans. They are rudimentary figures, of course, but we can see their final state as an image of basic human experience which further devalues the naturalistic view with which Warren has been recurrently concerned. Echoes of the 'Rebuke of the Rocks' will continue to be heard in Warren's writing, but poems like 'History', 'Crime', 'Pursuit', 'Original Sin: a Short Story', and 'The Ballad of Billie Potts' surely vindicate the 'little stubborn men' of his earlier imagination in their 'breeding' of human life despite the discouragements of nature.

Chapter Two — Notes

[1] ' Kentucky Mountain Farm' includes a number of poems, one or more of which comprises the sequence at each printing. 'At the Hour of the Breaking of the Rocks' appeared first in *American Caravan*, edited by Van Wyck Brooks *et al.* (New York: The Macaulay Company, 1927) p. 803. The last part to appear was 'The Jay', printed as Part V of the

sequence in *Thirty-Six Poems*. Of the seven parts printed in SP: 1943, four appear in SP. References are to SP where possible, otherwise to SP: 1943.

[2] *Cf.* Jeremiah Beaumont's vision of the naturalistic peace for which he longs in the image of 'his own body, naked and faintly gleaming in the depth, flowing on with the inner current, on and on' (WEAT, p. 452).

[3] Omitted from SP.

[4] Strandberg, p. 21.

[5] 19 Sept, 1926. DDC, File 2.

[6] West, Paul, *Robert Penn Warren*, Univ. of Minnesota Pamphlets on American Writers, No. 44 (Minneapolis: Univ. of Minnesota Press, 1964), p. 20.

[7] Warren, Robert Penn, 'The Present State of Poetry: III. In the United States', (*Kenyon Review*, **1** (Autumn, 1939), 391.

[8] Tate, Allen, '*The Fugitive* 1922–1925: A Personal Recollection Twenty Years After,' *Princeton University Library Chronicle*, **3** (April, 1942), 81–82. According to Louise Cowan this meeting took place in the Spring of 1923. If so, Warren was probably seventeen. See Louise Cowan, *The Fugitive Group, a Literary History* (Baton Rouge: Louisiana State University Press, 1959), pp. 106–8.

[9] *Driftwood Flames* (Nashville: The Poetry Guild, 1923), p. 41.

[10] *The Fugitive*, **2** (June–July, 1923), 90–91.

[11] The second stanza's opening lines are clearly modelled on the beginning of 'The Waste Land', Part V:

After shouting and trumpets and the crash of splintering lances,
After these and weeping . . .

[12] *The Fugitive*, **2** (Aug–Sept, 1923), 106.

[13] In his letter to Davidson of 19 Sept. 1926 Warren referred to the 'obvious and wavering experimental quality' of 'After Teacups' and 'Midnight'.

[14] *The Fugitive*, **2** (Oct, 1923), 142.

[15] *Double Dealer*, **6** (Aug–Sept, 1924), 192.

[16] 24 May, 1924. DDC, File 11.

[17] DDC, File 10.

[18] *The Fugitive*, **3** (April, 1924), 54–55.

[19] *The Fugitive*, **3** (June, 1924), 69.

[20] 11 July, 1924. DDC, File 12.

[21] *The Fugitive*, **3** (Dec, 1924), 154.

[22] *The Fugitive*, **4** (June, 1925), 33.

[23] *The Fugitive*, **4** (June, 1925), 36; SP, p. 324.

[24] DDC, File 26.

[25] *The Fugitive*, **4** (June, 1925), 64.

[26] *Andrew Lytle Papers*, Tennessee State Library and Archives, Nashville.

[27] " 'Thirty-Six Poems' by Robert Penn Warren," *Nation*, **142** (25 March, 1936), 391.

[28] Zabel, M. D., 'Problems of Knowledge', *Poetry*, **48** (April, 1936), 39.

[29] Stewart, p. 458.

[30] Strandberg, pp. 25–26.

[31] Zabel, p. 39.

[32] Brooks, Cleanth, *Modern Poetry and the Tradition* (Chapel Hill: Univ. of North Carolina Press, 1939), p. 86.

[33] Longley, p. 241.

[34] Reprinted as 'Mexico is a Foreign Country: Four Studies in Naturalism' in SP, pp. 302–07, omitting 'Siesta Time in Village Plaza by Ruined Bandstand and Banana Tree', Part II in SP: 1943.

[35] Warren, Robert Penn, 'Notes', in *Modern Poetry, American and British*, ed. Kimon Friar and John Malcolm Brinnin (New York: Appleton-Century-Crofts, 1951), pp. 541–43.

[36] Warren, 'Notes', p. 542.

[37] 'The Ballad of Billie Potts' appeared first in *Partisan Review*, **11** (Winter, 1944), 56–70, then as the opening poem in SP: 1943. It is reprinted in SP, pp. 271–84.

[38] Strandberg, p. 115.

[39] Ransom, John Crowe, "The Inklings of 'Original Sin'," *Saturday Review of Literature*, **27** (20 May, 1944), 10–11.

3

Short Stories

Leonard Casper criticises the title story of Warren's collection,
The Circus in the Attic, for 'sprawling' and finds it 'hobbled'
by its method.[1] Charles H. Bohner says it is 'rambling and
diffuse'.[2] Certainly, the story is ambitious: Warren not only
outlines the tragedy of one man's wasted life, but comments on
the meaning of history and chronicles a hundred and fifty
years of a Southern town's existence, thereby implying an
assessment of his region. Critics have judged the story a
failure because it reads like an underdeveloped novel. The
reader is, indeed, likely to consider Warren's stories in relation
to his novels if only because many of the novels contain short
stories, readily separable from the novels in which they appear.[3] Bohner reminds us of Warren's farewell to the *genre* of the
short story in the autobiographical note on 'Blackberry
Winter'[4] supplied for *Understanding Fiction,* concluding that
" 'The Circus in the Attic' . . . points to a weakness in many of
the stories included in this collection. The prodigality of
Warren's talent, his gift for sustained narrative and invention
seems cramped within the confines of the short story."[5]

Possessed of Warren's extended fictions, we can see the
grounds for this response to his stories. Undoubtedly, 'The
Circus in the Attic' (1947) contains in abundance the stuff of a
novel. Equally, we might complain that the author of *Eleven
Poems on the Same Theme* and 'The Ballad of Billie Potts'

could have produced a sheaf of characteristic poems from the
material expended in the tale. Warren's valediction to the
short story indeed suggests that poetry must take the responsibility for his giving us no further short fictions: 'poems
are great devourers of stories'.[6] The dog that follows Bolton
Lovehart along the creek bank on the Sunday afternoon of his
baptism 'like an image of medieval hunger and scabrous,
slack-dugged humility and mournful, infinite forgiveness'
(CIA, p. 20) clearly belongs to the same iconography as the
'old hound' and 'old horse' of 'Original Sin: A Short Story'.
We might have had yet another poem on the same theme
instead of this arresting prose representation of Bolton's guilt.
The story of Cassius Perkins and Seth Sykes might have made
a Civil War ballad complete with commentary on the ironies of
history. But it is a perverse and niggardly criticism which
neglects the particular merits of a work simply because the
work might have taken another form.

The opening of 'The Circus in the Attic' places the reader in
the modern age of the highway which is 'like a ribbon of
celluloid film carelessly unspooled across green baize' (CIA,
p. 3). The highway in Warren's work is often a symbol of
modern man's confident and careless superficiality, his substitution of motion for meaning and his preference for illusion.
Thus *All the King's Men* opens with Jack Burden travelling
along Highway 58: 'Way off ahead of you, at the horizon where
the cotton fields are blurred into the light, the slab will glitter
and gleam like water, as though the road were flooded. You'll
go whipping toward it, but it will always be ahead of you,
that bright, flooded place, like a mirage' (AKM, pp. 3–4). The
narrator of 'The Circus in the Attic' realises that 'you' will not
penetrate beneath the surface of what Bardsville has become in
the age of the highway—merely a place to stop for gas, oil
and lunch before 'you .. whirl southward through the afternoon into the heart of Dixie' (CIA, p. 13). The ironic use of the
cliché, 'heart of Dixie', implies the inability of the highway
traveller to see into the heart of anything and the buttonholing,
accusatory 'you' draws the reader from *his* headlong pursuit of
the glittering 'mirage', inviting him to deny his own superficiality by pausing long enough to notice the details which are

only a blur for the unthinking traveller. As in the story of Billie Potts, there is more to Bardsville than immediately meets the eye.

The first page of the story describes the approach to Bardsville in realistic details which typify the wasting of the rural South by the modern age considered from an Agrarian point of view, but the picture goes beyond regional concern and Agrarian bias. The disfigurements of the landscape brought about by wartime industrialisation reflect the peculiar derelictions and distresses of the mid-twentieth century. The image of the Negroes' washing 'hanging abjectly on crazy lines like improvised flags of surrender among ruins' (CIA, p. 3) is at once a reminder of the South's defeat in the Civil War and a symbol of its further decline under the impact of the modern world. If Bardsville itself seems aloof from the valley of chaos, the truth about its monument reveals the extent to which its citizens are out of touch with reality.

The impurities of history are suppressed by man's need for illusions to live by. History's data are accidents: one of Bardsville's Civil War heroes was carried, drunk, on a bolting horse, into the ranks of the enemy, and the other was shot down by the Union Cavalry to whom he offered assistance. Jake Velie knows enough of the truth about Cassius Perkin's heroism to remark sardonically, 'Mought as well put up that moniment with a jug of cawn whisky carved on top lak hit wuz a angel on a tombstone' (CIA, p. 8); but nobody hears him. Even if the people of Bardsville had heard him, 'They would not have believed him or his truth, for people always believe what truth they have to believe to go on being the way they are' (CIA, p. 8). In *The Legacy of the Civil War* Warren reviews the American national identity in terms of the same human failing. Money for Bardsville's monument is raised by 'The United Daughters of the Confederacy, the defenders of ancient pieties and the repositories of ignorance of history' (CIA, p. 5), and it is Bolton Lovehart, specialist in unreality, who undertakes a history of the town.

Simon Lovehart, Bolton's father, is a representative Southerner in that he perverts his private history into an alibi for inertia. His satisfyingly physical one-answer system is provided by the minnie ball which knocked him off his horse at the Battle of Franklin: with a little help from the prayer book he can explain everything in terms of that fortuitous piece of metal. He thus exemplifies the Southern talent for explaining and excusing everything by reference to the War: 'By the Great Alibi the Southerner makes his Big Medicine. He turns defeat into victory, defects into virtues' (*Legacy*, p. 55).

The rhythm of Bolton Lovehart's life is a series of abortive bids for freedom, each followed by a return to captivity and retreat into fantasy. His alien baptism fails to release him from his claustrophobic Episcopalian background; he is snatched back from the circus and neither his academic ambition nor his liaison with Sara Darter nor his predictable pleasure in selling tickets for the illusions screened at the local theatre is any match for his mother's emotional blackmail. After his father's death, Bolton's life becomes another model of Southern fatalism, with Mrs Lovehart as his 'Great Alibi' for failure. When she is finally betrayed by her seemingly relentless heart and can no longer determine his life, history takes over. His rôle as the town's authority on the wider world ends with the War. His wife is killed in circumstances that proclaim the falsity of the respectable image she had been at such pains to build and the death of her son in Italy further demonstrates the caprice of history. Inevitably he returns to the attic, although we are not told whether he finds the strength to carve and paint another surrogate world for his frustrated sensibility to hide in.

By its unifying focus on the story's central symbol, the epilogue effectively summarises the points Warren has made about the meaning of history. His selection of personal histories has reduced history itself to a common denominator of unreality. Only the sketchily portrayed Janie Murphy Parton has a healthy attitude towards the past. Warren's treatment of illusion in this story may seem unduly critical in the context of his Conradian belief in 'the dream', but the dream must be made to work in the world and that is what the illusions of Bardsville fail to do. The Civil War monument is almost forgotten, 'concealed in a riot of purple-tufted ironweed, flame-tufted milkweed, and sassafras growth' (CIA, p. 4). Simon Lovehart's 'truth' detaches him from his family; his wife's idea of motherhood isolates herself and her son from the human bond; Bolton's fantasy of the circus seals him off from the real world. Only Janie, abandoning her illusions, will 'return to a communion with man and nature', thus giving a hint of the method for living Warren suggests in 'Knowledge and the Image of Man'.

The time known as blackberry winter is a spell of unseasonable weather which interrupts summer when blackberries are ripe. It is a climatic incongruity, like T. S. Eliot's 'Midwinter spring' in 'Little Gidding'. Warren's most famous short story began as 'a way of indulging nostalgia' for the childhood freedom of being allowed to go barefoot in summer and for the strange 'feeling of betrayal when early summer gets turned upside-down and all its promises are revoked by the cold-spell, the gully-washer.'[7] 'Blackberry Winter' (1946), therefore, developed out of familiar rural materials which could smoothly extend into a representation of Paradise and Fall without any forcing of basic realism. The story perfectly succeeds in fusing 'experienced reality' and 'symbolic significance'. The basic strategy is to create and maintain a tension between the point of view of the nine-year-old boy and that of the man he has become thirty-five years later, while suggesting, through symbolic representation and occasional observations of the middle-aged man, the differences which the years have made in his evaluation of this spot of time. The signatures of things are there for the young Seth to feel and wonder at—the flood, the trash washed out from beneath Dellie's cabin, the tramp—and the mature Seth is able to read them.

Much of the story's excellence consists in the mature Seth's ability to articulate meanings without falsifying the feelings he experienced when a boy. It is June, time for going barefoot, but Seth's mother has told him to put on his shoes because it is blackberry winter. The boy's response is precisely given although the language belongs to the man: 'You do not understand that voice from back in the kitchen which says that you cannot go barefoot outdoors and run to see what has happened and rub your feet over the shivery wet grass and make the perfect mark of your foot in the smooth, creamy red mud and then muse upon it as though you had suddenly come upon that single mark on the glistening auroral beach of the world' (CIA, p. 64). Seth is both Crusoe and Adam in a closed familiar world of initial perfection where time is the space in which something that has happened 'stands solid'. He might muse safely over that perfect footprint, for it would betoken no sinister intruder. But a mysterious stranger enters on this day of disruptions, natural and human, leaving an imprint on the boy's sensibility that alters him irrevocably, marking his Fall from childhood innocence and his introduction to a mortal, complex world of ambiguity, insecurity and change.

Seth is still secure in the intimate safety of his father's saddle when he looks upon the natural disorder imaged by the cow, 'dead as a chunk', in the swollen creek, but his composure is shaken when he finds Dellie's model yard fouled by rubbish : 'It was not anything against Dellie that the stuff had been under the cabin. Trash will get under any house. But I did not think of that when I saw the foulness which had washed out on the ground which Dellie sometimes used to sweep with a twig broom to make nice and clean' (CIA, p. 79). The mature Seth does not blame Dellie, but the boy knows only that something ordered and clean is now inexplicably confused and besmirched. Dellie herself had been changed by the mystery of the 'woman-mizry' which Old Jebb will not explain but which somehow causes the disproportionate 'awful slap' that reduces Little Jebb to tears and sends Seth running from such sudden ugliness and misunderstanding.

It is the tramp, the mysterious stranger with his shabby city clothes, sinister knife and vicious language, who finally deprives the boy of his childhood certainties. The tramp does not merely symbolise evil : Seth's 'Where did you come from?' and 'Where are you going?' (CIA, pp. 85–86) are questions that spring from an instinctive recognition of 'this lost, mean, defeated, cowardly, worthless, bitter being as somehow a man'.[8] The tramp has no personal identity : his face is 'perfectly unmemorable' (CIA, p. 69) and he enters the story simply as 'the man' (CIA, p. 64). Like a creature of unknown origin he comes 'up from the river and had come up through the woods' (CIA, p. 65). He moves 'like a man who has come a long way and has a long way to go' (CIA, p. 66). He is an Ancient Mariner, fixing the young Seth with his intimation of human possibilities beyond anything the boy has known, or a Leech Gatherer from a far region, come to astonish the boy for his simple view of the world. Old Jebb confirms the admonition when Seth asks him to explain Dellie's 'woman-mizry':

> "Hit is the change," he said, "Hit is the change of life and time."
> "What changes?"
> "You too young to know."
> "Tell me."
> "Time come and you find out everything."
>
> (CIA, p. 82)

The mature Seth of the epilogue has learned that time is not space after all, but movement through change. He realises now that his own 'change of life and time' began on that day thirty-five years ago, when he followed the mysterious stranger out of Eden and into the greater, doubtful world.

In 'Original Sin: A Short Story' the identity from which the 'you' of the poem has fled includes guilty feelings towards 'your grandpa, who / Had a wen on his forehead and sat on the veranda / To finger the precious protuberance, as was his habit to do' (SP, p. 288). 'When the Light Gets Green' (1936) foreshadows this poem as well as the later 'Court-Martial' (SP, pp. 228–32), though on the surface it is little more than a portrait of the narrator's grandfather based apparently, on Warren's own (Appendix, p. 243). The story's concern, however, is with the conflict in the boy's feelings towards Grandfather Barden, which recalls the painful incapacity for 'pure' emotion in the narrator of 'The Return: An Elegy'. Warren begins the story with an engaging childhood example of purity and impurity, the split between real and ideal:

> My grandfather had a long white beard and sat under the cedar tree. The beard, as a matter of fact, was not very long and not white, only gray, but when I was a child and was away from him at school during the winter, I would think of him in my mind's eye, and say: He has a long white beard.
>
> (CIA, p. 88)

There is no easy warmth in the narrator's recollection, but its precision of detail conveys the importance of his grandfather to him, hence the delicate pain of his oscillation between respect for the old man's Civil War past and still straight carriage, and revulsion from his shrunken body and nicotine-stained moustache. The use of green—'the wavy green mirror' (CIA, p. 88), the 'dark green' cedars (CIA, p. 90), the light that 'gets green' before the storm (CIA, p. 94)—to represent the ominous ambiguity of experience is a forced device; but the image of the hen 'trying to peck up a piece of hail' (CIA, p. 95) echoes exactly the boy's feeling of bafflement by his initiation in the doubleness of the heart. The story is slight, but effective within its limits.

'Christmas Gift' (1937) demonstrates that 'our human communion'[9] may assert itself in the most unpropitious circumstances. The grayness of the raw winter weather matches the quality of Seth Alley's life, while, despite Bill Stover's crudities, the warmth of the store and the doctor's office corresponds to a limited but genuine human kindliness missing from the boy's experience. It is after the boy's exposure to human warmth that he and the doctor, drawn together by the desolation of the landscape, exchange their Christmas gifts. Perhaps this could not have happened if Bill Stover's mean remarks had not prompted the store-keeper to give the boy candy. Warren's view of cause and effect in human relations developed from instances like this—and like the lives of the Partons in 'The Circus in the Attic—into Jack Burden's theory of the spider web in *All The King's Men*: 'I eat a persimmon and the teeth of a tinker in Tibet are put on edge' (AKM, p. 234).

The next four stories in the collection illustrate 'the mal-feasance of nature or the filth of fate' in the defeat of personal ideals of living. The rather too obvious point of 'The Love of Elsie Barton: A Chronicle' (1946) is that Elsie's ideal of order, unaccompanied by any real knowledge of herself, cannot withstand life's elemental pull towards chaos, although she does apparently profit enough from experience to send her daughter away from home and the possibility of a fate like her own. 'Goodwood Comes Back' (1941) ends in obvious irony: the country boy comes home, but his ambition to own a piece of ground in the country is realised by the corrupt method of marrying a girl with a half-interest in land. He has prostituted himself in the city and brought the habit back with him. The city made a drunkard of him but the country kills him through the agency of his brother-in-law. Neither of these stories represents Warren at his best. 'The Love of Elsie Barton' is too long for its content and 'Goodwood Comes Back' seems little more than an indistinctly enunciated Agrarian protest against the urban waste land and the poisoning ideal of material success.

In John M. Bradbury's opinion 'The Patented Gate and the Mean Hamburger' (1947) is a case of narrow understanding in the narrator and 'extruded' Agrarian message.[10] But the narrator is clearly qualified both to report and interpret. A local man—'I had seen Jeff York a thousand times' (CIA, p. 121)—he observes convincingly from the beginning: the whole story evolves between the early, repeated image of Jeff York's 'cast-iron brogans' and his inexorable wife's new-found expertise in high heels (CIA, pp. 120, 121 and 133). Authenticity of response inheres in the language. There is the folk precision of 'the corn was good and the tobacco unfurled a leaf like a yard of green velvet' or 'a pinch of salt to brighten it on the tongue' (CIA, pp. 123, 126), and the cadence of formal Southern speech in 'he stands there in that silence which is his gift' (CIA, p. 121). Warren establishes the patented gate and the hamburger stall as credible symbols of the ambitions of the two main characters, so that the ending, though shocking in the manner of Faulkner or Flannery O'Connor, is tragic rather than melodramatic. Jeff York is ancestrally equipped for a life of rural striving but not for the insight that could have forestalled his sacrificing the dream he had made real to the obsession of a wife who parodies the clichéd Southern female. Ironically, a contrivance of the modern age represents escape from the tradition of toil and loss: 'The gate was the seal Jeff York had put on all the years of sweat and rejection. He could sit on his porch on a Sunday afternoon in summer, before milking time, and look down the rise, down the winding dirt track, to the white gate beyond the clover, and know what he needed to know about all the years passed' (CIA, p. 124). The wonder of modernism in the mechanical patented gate is a step towards the denial of those years in the sleazy modernism of the hamburger stand.

'A Christian Education' (1945) is superficially about the failure of Mr Nabb's ideal to work in the world, but this time the story's focus is blurred by an unsatisfactory narrator. The ages given for Alec Nabb in the last paragraph establish that the narrator is recalling events of at least nineteen years earlier, but the tone and language employed are more appropriate to the boy he was at the time of Silas Nabb's death and invest the story with an archness which undermines credibility. A sense of guilt may be responsible for his clipped, ironic presentation of the Nabbs, but it is the moment of his own detachment that he remembers with revealing, if elementary lyricism:

> The bottom of a pond is the softest place in the world and dark deep down, not water and not mud, just like velvet in the dark, only softer, and when my hand touched bottom that time, just for a split second I thought how nice it would be to lie there, it was so soft, and look up trying to see where the light made the water green.

> (CIA, p. 141)

This echoes the lover's retreat from the world to rest 'Upon the floor of light, and time' in 'Bearded Oaks' (SP, p. 308) and anticipates Jasper Harrick's underground pleasures in *The Cave* (C, pp. 240–41) as well as the attraction the earth holds for Angelo Passetto in *Meet Me in the Green Glen* (GG, p. 116).

'Testament of Flood' (1935), another variation on the theme of initiation, re-introduces us to Mrs Beaumont, the Elsie Barton of 'The Love of Elsie Barton: A Chronicle', and her daughter, Helen. This brief story is a finely controlled development of the opening image in which the boy's imagination catches the meaning of Elsie Beaumont's life: 'So dry, she was like those bits of straw and trash lodged innocently in the branches of creek-bottom sycamores as testament of long-subsided spring flood—a sort of high water mark of passion in the community' (CIA, p. 163). It is Steve's growing perception of the flood's rising again in Helen that so discomfits and compels him in his adolescent movement out of innocence to a sense of 'the strict and inaccessible province' which the girl precociously seems to have entered. Helen's detachment from the 'straight lines and cold angles' of geometry suggests her intimacy with 'another world whose lines all curved voluptuously toward some fulfillment he could not possibly understand' (CIA, p. 165). Prompted by the girl's 'mild and satirical gaze', the boy does understand enough to know that when she cannot answer the teacher's question he must not supply the answer: to associate himself with the teacher's world would be to proclaim himself a dullard in the richer lore possessed by the girl. The story is a testament of the flood of feeling in Steve too, and it succeeds because the boy's point of view, clear and sustained, is so sensitively rendered in the language of the author and thereby interpreted.

Sarcasm, which Warren had come to abjure in his poetry, is cleverly employed in the Hawthornian black humour of 'The Confession of Brother Grimes' (1947). The narrator's flippancy is itself a judgement of Brother Grimes's real crime which, of course, is the egoism of believing that his use of hair dye for twenty years is fittingly punished by the deaths of five people. This is not a parody of Warren's 'cosmic web philosophy' as Casper suggests[11] but rather of the fundamentalist's paranoid association of ideas. Paranoia induced by unhappy early lives, guilt-inspiring wives and fading dreams of academic success also afflicts the two Professors exposed in 'The Life and Work of Professor Roy Millen' (1943) and 'The Unvexed Isles' (1947). The stories balance each other: Professor Millen is diminished by his use of a student as emotional scapegoat while Professor Dalrymple, though humbled, grows in moral stature. Both stories are psychologically astute, but technically, somewhat clumsy and predictable.

'Her Own People' (1935) is a deft, small-scale study in race relations, a subject with which Warren became more explicitly concerned in the fifties and sixties with *Segregation* and *Who Speaks for the Negro?* The black girl, Viola, virtually admits her lie, but resists passively, taking to her bed in the home of the Negro family with whom she is an unwelcome lodger. Ironically, she brings blacks and whites into exceptional contact with each other, but as a 'white-folks' nigger', she is herself culturally dispossessed, belonging to neither race. Thus, in a story which deserves to be better known, Warren represents an aspect of the alienation wrought by the Southern caste system.

'Prime Leaf' (1931) is printed last in *The Circus in the Attic*, but was Warren's first published story and is an obvious precursor of *Night Rider*, his first novel. Both works have the same historical source in the Kentucky tobacco wars, both present the same sort of characters and problems,* Mr Sullivan, the young farmer-attorney in 'Prime Leaf', is apparently under the influence of Mr Hopkins and is active in the Association. To this extent he foreshadows Mr Munn in *Night Rider*. Mr Hopkins is an extraverted, practical man like *Night Rider's* Bill Christian, and old Mr Hardin is a prototype of Captain Todd. Big Thomas Hardin does not anticipate the fate which he, as a man of fact rather than of idea, should expect and Percy Munn's efforts to realise himself in action bring only increased isolation and emptiness. Both men die. Between fathers and sons (old Mr Hardin and Big Thomas, Captain and Benton Todd) the same kind of opposition, that between idea and fact, holds the relationships in vivid tension. Neither father is able to save his son and each is made guilty by his son's death. As a result, Little Thomas is prematurely initiated in his tragic realities of the world beyond the farm, so concluding Warren's book of innocence and experience.

The list of writers whom Warren is thought to resemble in these stories is flatteringly comprehensive, if nothing else, including Chekhov, Sherwood Anderson, Lardner, Joyce, Faulkner and Caldwell.[12] The moral is that while influences may be detected, definition of them is variable, subjective and critically not very useful. Warren is certainly a better novelist and poet than he is a writer of short stories: his stories are very uneven in quality and 'Blackberry Winter' is justly known as the best of them. Some are weak, some slight; several—they include 'The Circus in the Attic', 'Christmas Gift', 'The Patented Gate and the Mean Hamburger', 'Testament of Flood', 'Her Own People' as well as 'Prime Leaf'—have much to say and, saying it effectively, are valuable contributions to an art in which rules are only made to be broken.

---

* Although much of the story's interest—lacking from *Night Rider*—is in its subdued portrayal of family tensions.

F

Chapter Three — Notes

[1] Casper, pp. 98–99.

[2] Bohner, p. 105.

[3] These stories, or versions of them, have often been published separately in advance of the complete novels. See Mary Nance Huff, *Robert Penn Warren: A Bibliography* (New York: David Lewis, 1968), pp. 54–56.

[4] Brooks, Cleanth and Warren, Robert Penn, *Understanding Fiction*, 2nd ed. (New York: Appleton-Century-Crofts, 1959), p. 643.

[5] Bohner, p. 105.

[6] *Understanding Fiction*, p. 643.

[7] *Understanding Fiction*, p. 640.

[8] *Understanding Fiction*, p. 642.

[9] *Understanding Fiction*, p. 642.

[10] Bradbury, John M., *The Fugitives: A Critical Account* (Chapel Hill: University of North Carolina Press, 1958), pp. 197–8.

[11] Casper, p. 95.

[12] See Bradbury, John M., in *The Fugitives: A Critical Account*, p. 197; Farelly, John, in a review of 'The Circus in the Attic' in *New Republic*, **118** (26 Jan, 1948); O'Connor, William Van, in another review in *Western Review*, **12** (Summer, 1948); Prescott, Orville, in *Yale Review*, **37** (Spring, 1948), 575–76.

4

Dreams and Identities

Warren's first full length prose work, *John Brown, the Making of a Martyr*, is a carefully researched study of an exploiter of hand-me-down ideals whose impurities had been purged away by a nation hot for certainties. 'I never did intend murder, or treason, or the destruction of property, or to excite or incite slaves to rebellion, or to make insurrection' (JB, p. 40). Thus John Brown at his trial. He only intended to liberate slaves without bloodshed, as he falsely declared he had done in Missouri the year before. C. Vann Woodward, following Warren, comments: 'How these statements can be reconciled with the hundreds of pikes, revolvers, and rifles, the capture of an armoury, the taking of hostages, the killing of unarmed civilians, the destruction of government property, and the arming of slaves is difficult to see. Nor is it possible to believe that Brown thought he could seize a Federal arsenal, shoot down United States Marines, and overthrow a government without committing treason.'[1] Warren observes of the trial speech: 'It was all so thin, that it should not have deceived a child, but it deceived a generation' (JB, p. 40). The Transcendentalists rushed to canonise Brown; the North had its martyr and an idea. Warren's biography examines that idea in the context of the prosaic facts and the ironies implicit in the characters of John Brown and those who helped and applauded him. The book is a study of one of the dreams by which America maintained her identity for much longer than a generation. At times, no doubt, it pulls too far towards the condition of the novel to satisfy the scholarly historian and sometimes its revelation of ironies is sarcastically toned as in this account of a night during Brown's spell in Hudson, Ohio:

> One night the quiet routine of the cabin occupied by the two young men was broken into by a run-away slave, who appealed to them for aid in his flight toward the 'North Star'. They took him in, as almost any Northern citizen would have done if the pursuit were not too hot or no scrupulous sheriff near. Levi Blakesly went into the settlement for provisions, leaving the renegade in the keeping of his friend. Suddenly, the pair in the cabin heard the noise of horses' hoofs; John Brown helped the negro through a window and told him to hide in the underbrush near the house, while he himself prepared to defend his charge. But the noise was only caused by some neighbours riding past on their way home, and John Brown went outside to find the frightened black fellow. He found him lying behind a log. 'I heard his heart thumping before I reached him', said John Brown. Incidentally, he seized on the opportunity to again swear eternal enmity against slavery.
>
> Later John Brown had a son named John Brown Jr. Strangely enough, this son once related this same story with a few circumstantial embellishments, making himself an eye witness as well. Again John Brown concealed the fugitives in the dark woods at the noise of approaching horses; and again he was able to find and fetch them in by the guiding sound of startled heartbeats. Again John Brown swore eternal enmity to slavery. Some people have professed surprise at the coincidence; others have professed surprise only at the acoustics of Hudson township, Ohio.
>
> (JB, pp. 21–22)

Warren might have repudiated the use of sarcasm in his verse, but he is not above using it to point an implausibility in the John Brown story. The sarcasm here may remind us that this is an Agrarian's attempt to demythologise a Northern martyr, but the idea of the martyr is fairly melted back into the impure elements of history and of Brown's own nature. 'After all,' Warren writes, "one cannot afford to read the motives that took John Brown to Kansas as being pure and simple. He merely went there with his eyes open. One of his daughters once made a candid remark on the subject: 'Father said his object in going to Kansas was to see if something would not turn up to his advantage' " (JB, p. 106). The irony, of course, is that the only pure thing about Brown was precisely his faith that something would eventually turn up to his advantage, as, in the event, it did. This was the abstraction he pursued with such fanaticism and energy to the end when he realised that death on the scaffold would provide him with the inestimable advantage of becoming a myth.

A substantial contribution to the interpretation of American history, *John Brown, the Making of a Martyr* is engaged with questions to which Warren returns in his fiction and poetry: the discrepancies between myth and reality, idea and fact; the problem of identity; the interaction between society and the individual. An essay in philosophical biography, the book was a prelude to his becoming what he calls in his discussion of Conrad's *Nostromo* a 'philosophical novelist':

> The philosophical novelist, or poet, is one for whom the documentation of the world is constantly striving to rise to the level of generalisation about values, for whom the image strives to rise to symbol, for whom images always fall into a dialectical configuration, for whom the urgency of experience, no matter how vividly and strongly experience may enchant, is the urgency to know the meaning of experience. This is not to say that the philosophical novelist is schematic and deductive. It is to say quite the contrary, that he is willing to go naked into the pit, again and again, to make the same old struggle for his truth.
>
> (SE, p. 58)

This expands Warren's earlier idea that the poet earns his vision by subjecting it to hostile elements: it is the point at which Warren's aesthetics and his ethics elide. The novelist fails either if his treatment is too abstract—'schematic and deductive'—or if his 'generalisation about values' is swamped by unordered detail. The excessively abstract writer is typified by T. S. Stribling, whose values are inadequately embedded in the texture of his novels.[2] Thomas Wolfe is the exemplar of uncontrolled abundance. Warren concedes 'an enormous talent' and great subjective intensity in Wolfe's fiction, but it is an intensity naively generated because it is unrelated to a coherent philosophical point of view (SE, pp. 170–83). Joseph Conrad is the supreme philosophical novelist, not just because of the distinction, and amenability to Warren, of his philosophy, but because his ideas are incarnate in the concrete terms of his stories. Of Conrad's famous assertion in the Preface to *The Nigger of the Narcissus* that he wanted above all to make the reader 'see' Warren says: 'All of this seems to me, however, to mean nothing more than that Conrad was an artist, that he wanted, in other words, to arrive at his meanings immediately, through the sensuous renderings of passionate experience, and not merely to define meanings in abstraction, as didacticism or moralising' (SE, p. 57). This is precisely the kind of artist Warren seeks to be.

John Brown, the Making of a Martyr is a philosophical enquiry which is rooted in the rich circumstantiality of history. Warren's first two philosophical novels, *Night Rider* and *At Heaven's Gate*, are both remarkable performances which fail to achieve the best of which he is capable chiefly because they are too schematic. It is in *All the King's Men* that, with the creation of Jack Burden as narrator, Warren first finds a wholly satisfactory method for expressing in fiction his philosophical concerns through 'the sensuous renderings of passionate experience.' Indeed, the powerful coincidence of thought and feeling in Jack Burden—reflected in the often coarse energy of his language with its profusion of concretising images— makes him more Metaphysical than Romantic if we invoke Eliot's criterion of unified sensibility. The immediacy of meanings in *All the King's Men* is never quite equalled until *A Place to Come To*, in which first person narrative is also employed, with Jed Tewksbury a clear descendant of Jack Burden.

Warren's conception of life is based on a view of man's rôle as 'religious' in the sense in which he finds Hemingway a religious writer whose special quality resides in 'the quest for meaning and certitude in a world which seems to offer nothing of the sort' (SE, p. 107). *A Farewell to Arms* is, he says, 'a religious book; if it does not offer a religious solution it is nevertheless conditioned by the religious problem.' Warren shares Hemingway's tragic sense of *nada*, of 'the world with nothing at its centre.' Hemingway's heroes counteract the meaninglessness of the natural realm by fidelity to a code (SE, p. 87). For Conrad, and for Warren himself, there is the 'idea': the 'Platonic vision is what makes life possible in its ruck and confusion' (SE, p. 54). We must all serve the idea: 'The lowest and the most vile creature must, in some way idealize his existence in order to exist, and must find sanctions outside himself,' (SE, p. 43). *Nostromo*, illustrates the inevitable defeat of the idea, the 'contamination of the vision in the very effort to realise the vision' (SE, p. 53), but foreknowledge of defeat does not free man from the obligation to give the 'idea' life in the real world. 'Wisdom' is the recognition of this condition and redemption' is earned by acting in terms of it.   (SE, p. 54).

II

Guthrie, Kentucky is a small defunctive town near the Tennessee border, left high, dry and depressed by the tide of progress. When Warren was born there on 24th April, 1905 it thrived as a tobacco market town, a railway junction serving the Black Patch region whose era of economic and political turmoil provided him with some of his earliest impressions and the material for 'Prime Leaf' and *Night Rider*. Warren's first novel is more coherent but much less interesting than his second. *Night Rider* is an oppressively monolithic story of one man's failure to live simultaneously in the real and the ideal world; in Jamesian fashion the reader's attention is continually focused on a single central figure and, except for the Proudfits, the other characters are more or less clearly defined by their relation to him. *At Heaven's Gate* is more panoramic, livelier in characterisation and philosophically richer than *Night Rider*. *All the King's Men* combines the thematic clarity of *Night Rider* with the fullness and variety of *At Heaven's Gate*.

Percy Munn's integrity of being is only an appearance, but some early readers of *Night Rider* were taken in by it. Mina Curtiss, reviewing for *The Nation*, saw Munn's story as 'the inevitable tragedy of the liberal'.[3] Christopher Isherswood agreed: 'Percy Munn is conceived as a figure of tremendous significance: he is the noble liberal gone astray in a world of power politics.'[4] But there is nothing particularly noble or liberal about Mr Munn. As the story develops he is educated into a capacity for some of the other-directed feelings we would associate with a liberal disposition, but he is not much ennobled by his own suffering. Initially he has little interest in the Association of Growers of Dark Fired Tobacco and his goal in life has no reference beyond himself: 'if he desired anything of life, that thing was to be free, and himself' (NR, p. 13). Drawn into the Association against his will and in his essentially vague search for self-definition through action, Munn dies as he has lived, 'without concern for direction' (NR, p. 460). The 'natural attitude' of Lawyer Munn's mind, we are told early in the first chapter, is one of 'logical, sceptical scrutiny' (NR, p. 13), useful attributes in a liberal, but his scepticism soon wilts. The principle that meaning must be found in action is commendable in itself, but Munn is neither free nor sceptical enough to see that the particular action proposed fundamentally corrupts the principle. Angus Wilson sees Munn much more clearly than Curtiss or Isherwood when he discovers in him an 'essentially contemporary horror: the little, empty, unfulfilled person who finds in the Party not so much an ideal, or a means to material ambition, but a realisation of himself in action and violence.'[5]

Munn is incapable of bringing the world and the idea into phase with each other. Once he has been drawn into social involvement by the speech he finds himself making to the crowd gathered to hear of the Association and its aims, he believes that the idea must save the world. 'There is nothing here', he tells the people, 'but an idea', (NR, p. 26). When he discovers that neither idealism nor enlightened self-interest is sufficient to ensure the success of the Association, he is ready to join the Brotherhood. The idea will not redeem the world, so the world must redeem the idea. Munn longs to simplify his life (NR, p. 131), but although the march on the warehouses is relatively successful, it serves only to complicate matters further and Munn, less and less equal to events, enters the final stage of his decline in which the world displaces the idea and he descends into nature.

As his life holds increasingly little hope for the future, Munn attempts, like his remote and faded cousin, Ianthe Sprague, to live exclusively in the present, a blasphemously naturalistic condition in the framework of Warren's moral economy. Blankly absorbed in the present, he denies memory and closes his mind 'like a valve against all thoughts of the future' (NR, pp. 218–19). Shortly before he dies he hears that he is the father of a son whom he will never see. This epitomises the rupturing of time which Warren often suggests through the relationship of father to son. Captain Todd's son is killed, Bill Christian's son is long dead, Senator Tolliver is childless as is Willie Proudfit, and Bunk Trevelyan's children have died. The continuity of history, the flow of related facts out of which meanings are generated, is lost in this disjunction.

Warren's development of the two women in Munn's life, May, his ideal but ineffectual blonde wife and Lucille, his worldly, energetic dark mistress, objectifies the self-division which is further clarified by the contrasts made between Munn and other characters, prototypes of the *dramatis personae* found in later fictions. Captain Todd lives by the ideal and resigns from the Association as soon as its contamination by the Brotherhood becomes clear: he is honourable but, ultimately, ineffectual. Benton, his son, an immature projection of the old man's heroic idealism without his pragmatism, joins the night riders and is killed. The gap which widens between father and son to the point of death reflects the split in Munn himself. The idealistic Captain Todd is offset by two characters of naturalistic bias: Mr Christian, who is sustained by his animal energy, and Mr Sills, who lives, just as inadequately, by facts.

Despite the book's obvious symbolic pattern of darkness and light, its over-all quality is grimly monochrome. It is a novel of considerable invention and power which, nevertheless, has a depressing instead of a tragic effect. There is, in Percy Munn's destruction, an inevitability reminiscent of the tightly wound spring of tragedy which, as Jean Anouilh says, will always uncoil of itself. From the opening scene, where the press of the crowd on the train foreshadows the pressures that lie ahead for Munn, fate controls him as it had controlled the life of Mordecai Munn, his uncle, who came home from the

Civil War and one peaceful morning, while lighting his pipe, fell off the steps of his porch and broke his neck. But tragedy requires a greater potentiality for self-realisation and a more strenuous effort of will than Munn displays. Angus Wilson says of him: 'Though he seems content at the beginning his life is really a husk in which rattles something bigger, which he does not understand.'[6] It is his craving for self-definition which rattles, but it is a sign of his incapacity for such self-definition that he feels himself 'in the grip of an impersonal fatalism' (NR, p. 113) and his actions are 'as unaimed and meaningless as the blows of a blind man' (NR, p. 114). Essentially a static character, Munn encloses the reader in a hopeless case.

Some relief is provided by Willie Proudfit's story. Proudfit does not judge Munn but we are presumably meant to believe that Munn is affected by the story of violence, alienation and final redemption. Like the Indians, Proudfit had discovered the inadequacy of living in naturalistic terms and come to believe in the authority of intuition and spirit. Munn's failure, his inability to kill Senator Tolliver and thus realise himself at last in terms of the idea, is underlined by Proudfit's tale which includes many of Warren's motifs: the son's rejection of the father; westward flight and decline to bestial innocence; regeneration begun in isolation; the mandatory return home signifying self-realisation. The story operates in *Night Rider* as the myth that could save Percy Munn, but he is too fatalistic, too inert morally, to follow its lines in his own life.

III

Excellent in itself, Willie Proudfit's mythic story is obtrusive as a model, a set piece containing an over-explicit metaphor of the alternative to Percy Munn's empty life and meaningless death. In Warren's second novel the model is more effective because it is much better integrated. *At Heaven's Gate* counterpoints the main action with a contrasting mythic sub-plot in the testimony of the Cain-like Ashby Wyndham. As in *Night Rider*, the image of personal reclamation is found in humble and rustic life. The chapters of Wyndham's statement alternate with the main action from the beginning and the converging of the two plots in chapter 23 is, therefore, unforced and convincing.

While the Ashby Wyndham story is an impressively original *tour de force*, there is in the novel, Warren says, 'a good deal of the shadow not only of the events of that period but of the fiction of that period.[7] Slim Sarrett's bohemianism recalls Faulkner's satire on the artists in New Orleans of the twenties in *Mosquitoes* (1927) and the critique of big business implicit in Bogan Murdock's corrupt practices may owe something to the value Faulkner puts on money in *Sartoris* (1929) by appointing Flem and Byron Snopes to positions in the Sartoris bank. Sue Murdock carries obvious echoes of Hemingway's Brett Ashley in *The Sun Also Rises* (1926) and Jerry Calhoun is plainly kin to Fitzgerald's Nick Carraway in *The Great Gatsby* (1925).

Identifying Warren's 'unreal city' as a combination of Nashville and Memphis, Malcolm Cowley intereprets *At Heaven's Gate* as almost a *roman à clef* with the university as Vanderbilt and Bogan Murdock as Senator (Colonel) Luke Lea of Tennessee who was jailed for his part in the seventeen-million-dollar failure of the Asheville Bank and Trust Company.[8] The combination of military rank and civic disgrace in Senator Lea's career makes him, in fact, a more likely model for Bogan Murdock's father, ex-Confederate Major Lem Murdock. Bogan Murdock would then be the fictional counterpart of the Senator's son, Luke Lea Jr. But this narrow-eyed deciphering is beside the point. Warren himself indicates the intended scope of his book when he remembers how deep he was in Dante at the time of composition. The Seventh Circle of Hell 'provided with some liberties of interpretation and extension, the basic scheme and metaphor for the whole novel. All of the main characters are violators of nature.'[9] The principal violations are by Bogan Murdock as usurer, Slim Sarrett as abuser of sex, Ashby Wyndham, before his conversion, as violent against God. Although Jerry Calhoun does not fit into any of Dante's categories, his impiety in taking Murdock as his false father is another crime against nature (Appendix, pp. 249–50).

The novel's thematic richness is analysed by James H.

Justus in one of the best pieces of critical writing on Warren's fiction.[10] Justus sees that the novel concerns a world in which Agrarian values—the integration of personality, a sense of mutual responsibility, and a harmony between man and nature—are conspicuously absent. As a result, the world of *At Heaven's Gate* is one in which the self has to attempt its own recreation. Warren's juxtaposition of the two narratives points clearly to the central idea: the separation in modern life between an amoral, anti-Agrarian pragmatism and a traditional acceptance of ideal supernatural standards. Warren does not mean that man's full humanity can be achieved by either disposition alone: as a natural creature, man must learn how to earn and cherish the ideal while still belonging to the world.

The people surrounding Bogan Murdock are defined by their relation to his self-justifying desires, like the characters in Willie Stark's retinue in *All the King's Men*. Dorothy Murdock has come to recognise her husband's essential coldness but she is too weak and demoralised to escape. Murdock's son, Ham, is a vacuous tool of his father's will while his daughter Sue's struggle to escape is complicated by the fact that she is also drawn to him like any self-respecting modern Electra. Jerry Calhoun wants to be a replica of his boss and seeks authentication by marriage to Sue. Private Porsum, whose image as an honest man of action is falsified by Murdock's use of him, doggedly evades the implications of his master's methods. Duckfoot Blake, the Wemmick to Jerry's Pip, is the exception and the only character in the Murdock world who achieves freedom and identity. He foreshadows Jack Burden not only in his intelligence, the vitality of his language and his breezy cynicism, but also in his self-redeeming conversion from detachment to a belief that 'everything matters' (AHG, p. 372), which finally aligns him—a man of intellect—with Ashby Wyndham—the man of faith.

Most of the characters in *At Heaven's Gate* commit variations on the theme of 'Original Sin: A Short Story' by repudiating the definition of themselves implied in their origins. Jerry, Sue and Jason Sweetwater recoil from their family backgrounds, foreshadowing the identity crises of Isaac Sumpter in *The Cave*, Brad Tolliver in *Flood*, Cy Grinder in *Meet Me in the*

Green Glen and Jed Tewskbury in *A Place to Come To*. Bogan
Murdock amends his own past by recasting his father's as a
model of Southern honour while Slim Sarrett, finding his middle-
class parentage and early history inappropriate to the artist
he is determined to be, invents a family background to go with
his bohemian style of life. Denials of the past are balanced by
equally distorting denials of the present in Jerry's Uncle Lew
who lives in terms of the hatred he constantly refuels in himself
by recalling injustices of the past, and in old Major Murdock
whose sense of time froze with his killing of Goodpasture. In
'Rattlesnake Country' Warren asks: 'Is *was* but a word for
wisdom, its price?' (SP, p. 49). By this token, most of the
characters in *At Heaven's Gate* are fools.

Just before her death Sue Murdock discovers that the two
dominant men in her life, apparently so different, are really the
same type. Both are cold manipulators of other people and
Sarrett's art is as abstract, sterile and ruthless as her father's
finance. Despite his professed artistic creed—"the artist . . .
doesn't have to 'make up' himself or his own life" (AHG,
p. 150)—Sarrett's life is a lie, an attempt to manipulate reality
into the terms of his idea, as remorseless as Murdock's sacrifice
of the idea to money and power. Both Sarrett and Murdock
exercise great destructive force on others but as men both
are, like Isaac Sumpter in *The Cave*, essentially nothing, mere
figments of their own corrupt imaginations. This is what
Duckfoot Blake realises of Murdock when he tells Jerry:
'Bogan Murdock aint' real . . . Bogan Murdock is just a dream
Bogan Murdock had' (AHG, p. 373).

Literally and figuratively a self-made man, Bogan Murdock
is perhaps too much the Agrarian's stereotype of abstract
capitalist manipulation to be fully credible. He is viewed from
several perspectives by different characters and we are left
to speculate about him as did Warren's friend, Frank Owsley,
the Vanderbilt historian who shares the novel's dedication
with his wife and whose comments on the early novels Warren
especially appreciated:

Bogan Murdock leaves the reader in some doubt until his final
statement at the end of the book clinches the conclusion that he

was just what his daughter thought him to be—no different fundamentally from Slim. Still, one has a persistent feeling that Bogan, despite his dominating passion for power, had a real love for his children. Sue never could get away from the feeling and neither can the reader.[11]

If Bogan Murdock is the most ambiguous character in the novel and Duckfoot Blake the most appealing,[12] Jason Sweetwater and Ashby Wyndham are, intellectually, the most challenging. Together they carry Warren's discussion of the fact-idea dilemma into its subtlest reaches. Both men make their bid for identity in terms of an idea of social justice,[13] one political, the other religious, which they attempt to make work in the world and both are well delineated, substantial characters in whom we can believe. The reason for Sweetwater's failing Sue is consistent with Warren's belief in the inadequacy of Marxism—or of any 'one-answer system'[14] (Appendix, pp. 261–62). As limited in its way as his father's cloying blend of Southern chauvinism and Episcopalianism, the insufficiency of Sweetwater's belief in social justice is exemplified by his moral rigidity: he cannot marry Sue because he has decided that marriage is exploitation, the equivalent of legalised prostitution (AHG, p. 312). For Sue, Sweetwater's firm sense of himself is therapeutic after her disappointments in her father, Calhoun and Sarrett; but he fails her because his rigid idea of himself 'in terms of a single principle' (AHG, p. 293) will not yield to meet the instance of need in another person.

'The Statement of Ashby Wyndham' makes a brilliant contribution to both the narrative excitements and the philosophical action of the novel. Ashby's progress from man of nature to man of God indirectly brings about Murdock's exposure, but at the end of the novel Ashby is still in jail, unable even to pray, woefully perplexed by the idea that his conversion of Pearl has led to murder. In James H. Justus's terms, his attempt to recreate himself seems to have resulted in tragedy. God appears to have abandoned him; his might as well be the last *cri de coeur* of Jeremiah Beaumont in *World Enough and Time*: 'Oh, was I worth nothing, and my agony? Was all for naught?' (WEAT, p. 512). In contrast, Bogan Murdock rides his disgrace to become a Nixon-like object of the town's pity.[15] Warren must intend the irony to focus our attention on the inward state of each man. Murdock is an inhuman void. Ashby's final state anticipates the necessary interim condition Warren describes in 'Knowledge and the Image of Man': his feeling of emptiness and the terms of his confusion 'in the pain of isolation' are themselves proof of his human worth and the best hope for his redemption.

IV

Shortly after the publication of *All the King's Men* Frank Owsley wrote to Warren: "Your mastery of the use of prose seems about complete; the manner and ease with which you change your levels of writing always puts me in mind of an automobile term or terms, 'free wheeling' and 'liquid drive.' "[16] The key to the novel's fluency is Jack Burden whose language, tough yet intellectual, casual yet precise, swings from minutely observed detail to philosophical abstraction without breaking its stride. More than any other character in Warren's novels (Jed Tewksbury runs second in *A Place to Come To*) Jack Burden exemplifies what Eric Bentley sees as Warren's double endowment: 'There is Warren the critic, the cosmopolitan, the scholar, the philosopher, and there is Warren the *raconteur*, the Kentuckyan, the humourist, the ballad maker.'[17] Warren is forceful and fluent both as philosopher and story-teller, but he does not always succeed in marrying philosophy and story. In the doubly endowed character of Jack Burden, Warren found a method of unifying the elements of his most famous book. It is part of the purpose of this study to show that in Warren's work the best is not an enemy of the good, but the creation of Jack Burden is largely responsible for making *All the King's Men* not only Warren's best work of fiction but also one of the great and enduring American novels.

Jack Burden's linguistic 'liquid drive' takes him from Sadie Burke's face, 'a plaster-of-Paris mask of Medusa which some kid had been using as a target for a BB gun' (AKM, p. 50), to the dignified prose of the Cass Mastern story (AKM, pp. 170–

200); or from Willie Stark pacing machine-like in his two-dollar hotel room, his legs 'plungers in a big vat and you were the thing in the vat, the thing that just happened to be there' (AKM, pp. 75–76), to the lyricism of the novel's last paragraph. Reflecting Jack's belief that 'Life is Motion' (AKM, p. 160), his language is itself constantly in motion as he experiments with ways of saying what he feels or has seen. The effect is often deliberately comic, as when he reflects on Tiny Duffy's misjudgement of Willie Stark:

> Not that I much blame Duffy. Duffy was face to face with the margin of the mystery where all our calculations collapse, where the stream of time dwindles into the sands of eternity, where the formula fails in the test tube, where chaos and old night hold sway and we hear the laughter in the ether dream. But he didn't know he was, and so he said, "Yeah."
>
> (AKM, p. 22)

The mock-heroic inflation is pointed by Duffy's openly cynical, demotic 'Yeah', but the quick-fire exaggerations of the passage are felt as attempts to catch the truth of the moment as Jack retrospectively assesses it: history, he has come to realise, is shaped by such moments. Years after failing to read the future in the unimpressive figure of 'Cousin Willie from the country' (AKM, p. 21) Duffy tries to offer the Boss an unacceptable opinion:

> The Boss whipped his head around to look at Mr Duffy so fast all of a sudden there wasn't anything but a blur. It was as though his big brown pop eyes were looking out the back of his head through the hair, everything blurred up together. That is slightly hyperbolic, but you get what I mean.
>
> (AKM, p. 24)

While shaping his image Jack concedes the experimental element in the description, involving us in the fundamental process of the book which is the record of his experiment in becoming.

Both character and chorus, Jack is involved in yet detached from the life of the book, participating in the event and then glossing its meaning. This squares with Warren's formulation of the philosophical novelist, 'for whom the documentation of the world is constantly striving to rise to the level of generalisation about values' (SE, p. 58). Jack's progress in *All the King's Men* is through the 'sensuous renderings of passionate experience' (SE, p. 57) towards the 'generalisation about values' of the novel's closing pages in which he reaches an understanding of the fact-idea dilemma and a sense of his own identity defined in terms of relationships.

As a novel of ideas *All the King's Men* possesses a complexity lacking in *Night Rider* and *At Heaven's Gate*, without being philosophically over-insistent. Philosophical control is maintained throughout and images 'fall into a dialectical configuration' (SE, p. 58), but the novel is not felt to be as schematic as some of Warren's other books, partly because the scheme itself is so richly populated both by ideas and by characters. Artistically *All the King's Men* succeeds on Warren's own critical terms. The characters are all embodiments of ideas: Willie Stark, the man of fact—with Lucy his wife-mother, Sadie Burke and Anne Stanton his carnal and ideal mistresses— is contrasted to Adam Stanton, the man of idea, and the conflict is finally resolved by Jack, the narrator, whose burden is to learn the meaning of Willie Stark, his rise and fall. These are not simply cardboard figures with allegorical labels because Warren, chiefly through the agency of Jack Burden's language, gives them such life that they are both credible in themselves and as the expression of moral states.

In Joyce Cary's *To Be a Pilgrim* Edward Wilcher tells his brother:

> No-one has written a real political novel—giving the real feel of politics . . . of people feeling the way: of moles digging frantically about to dodge some unknown noise of walking on a slack wire over an unseen gulf by a succession of lightning flashes.[18]

By this definition *All the King's Men* is a political novel, whatever else it may be. It is, indeed, a veritable handbook of politics: we are given 'the real feel' of building a corrupt political machine which invites its own destruction and in addition to the study of political psychology we are shown techniques for coercing legislators and quashing impeachment proceedings. *All the King's Men* is a political novel in that it

G

deals continually with political processes and actions along the
lines suggested to Warren by the career of Huey P. Long,
Governor of the State of Louisiana from 1928 until his assassina-
tion in 1935. The novel began as a play called *Proud Flesh*[19]
(Appendix, pp. 246–47) and the name of the Huey Long figure
in the play was Talos, "the name of the brutal, blank-eyed
'iron groom' of Spenser's *Faerie Queene*, the pitiless servant of
the knight of justice." This element, Warren tells us, remained
in the change from play to novel, and Willie Stark remained in
one way, Willie Talos: 'Talos is the kind of doom that democracy may invite upon itself' (AKM, p. x). This is a political
subject; but Warren cautions us about limiting his book by a
narrowly political interpretation: 'The book, however, was not
intended to be a book about politics. Politics merely provided
the framework story in which the deeper concerns, whatever
their final significance, might work themselves out' (AKM,
p. x). The fact that some critics have focused on the framework
attests to Warren's mastery of the material he was able to
gather between 1934 and 1942 while teaching at Louisiana
State University in Baton Rouge. By Edward Wilcher's
definition Warren's book is a much better political novel than
either John Dos Passos's lusty *Number One* (1943) or Adria
Locke Langley's sentimental *A Lion is in the Streets* (1945).[20]

The resemblance of Willie Stark to Huey Long had a good
deal to do with the immediate success of Warren's book, but
Warren is at pains to forestall thoughts of a *roman à clef*: 'I
do not mean to imply that there was no connection between
Governor Stark and Senator Long. Certainly, it was the career
of Long and the atmosphere of Louisiana that suggested the
play that was to become the novel. But suggestion does not
mean identity, and even if I had wanted to make Stark a
projection of Long, I should not have known how to go about
it' (AKM, p. ix). The danger of identifying Willie Stark with
Huey Long is illustrated by a comment made by Long's
biographer, T. Harry Williams, on what he takes to be the
thesis of Warren's novel:

> . . . that the politician who wishes to do good may have to do
> some evil to achieve his goal. This was the course that was forced
> on the hero of Warren's novel Willie Stark, who was a politician

much like Long. It is also the course that Long, faced with a relentless opposition, felt he had to follow. Stark was in the end possessed by the evil or the method and was destroyed.[21]

Williams is clearly right that Stark is possessed by the evil or the method and that he is destroyed, but the causes of his destruction include something else: a craving for virtue.

John Brown, the Making of a Martyr is a study of a man much like Stark. During the interview appended to this study Warren says of Brown:

> . . . the man had some kind of constant obsessive interest for me. On the one hand he's so heroic, on the other he's so vile, pathologically vile. Some fifteen years ago, when Edmund Wilson was working on *Patriotic Gore,* we'd meet at parties and he would say, 'Red, let's go and sit in the corner and talk about the Civil War', and we always did. And the subject of Brown once or twice came up, and he once said, 'But he's trivial, he's merely a homicidal maniac—forget him!' Now this is *half* of Brown. In a strange way the homicidal maniac lives in terms of grand gestures and heroic stances, and is a carrier of high values, but *is* a homicidal maniac! This is a strange situation; and the split of feeling around Brown makes the split of feeling in a thing like my character Stark almost trivial.
>
> (Appendix, pp. 248–49)

We would have to agree that John Brown's impact on history has been much greater than that of Huey Long, Kingfish of Louisiana, but there is nothing trivial about the split in Willie Stark or in the nature of his fate. Willie is doubly split. His apparently benevolent despotism brings material improvement to the state but is conducted in the interest of Willie's vengeful lust for power and in a spirit of contempt for the people: 'Man is conceived in sin and born in corruption and he passeth from the stink of the didie to the stench of the shroud' (AKM, p. 54). This is the only fact for Willie, and his dynamic celebration of it brings him a perversely heroic dimension. But he remains, in Warren's sense, 'pure', monovalent, and so is further split because his one naturalistic fact becomes itself an inflexible abstraction that fails to account for the 'dream', the element of virtue which is also a metaphysical object of fact in a complex world.

Willie's career is concisely imaged in Jack Burden's description of the highway to Mason City:

> You look up the highway and it is straight for miles, coming at you, with the black line down the centre coming at you and at you, black and slick and tarry-shining against the white of the slab, and the heat dazzles up from the white slab so that only the black line is clear, coming at you with the whine of the tires, and if you don't quit staring at that line and don't take a few deep breaths and slap yourself hard on the back of the neck you'll hypnotise yourself and you'll come to just at the moment when the right front wheel hooks over into the black dirt shoulder off the slab, and you'll try to jerk her back on but you can't because the slab is high like a curb, and maybe you'll try to reach to turn off the ignition just as she starts the dive. But you won't make it, of course.
>
> (AKM, p. 3)

Willie is a follower of the black line, acting according to his interpretation of life in terms of corruption. He cannot see the white ground on which the black line is imposed, symbolic here of other human categories, other possibilities. Mesmerised by his own black abstraction, Willie finally loses control. He tries, we may say, to 'turn off the ignition' but he has already started his dive to destruction. There is, of course, a meretricious motive behind the free hospital and health centre in that the building and its facilities will commemorate the greatness of Willie Stark and buy him votes. He is, nevertheless, making his bid for virtue, refusing to allow the hospital to be engulfed in the graft typical of his administration and assuring Adam Stanton that 'I'll keep you clean all over' (AKM, p. 275). Willie discovers that man cannot successfully navigate his way through life if he takes his bearings from the black line alone, for man cannot escape virtue. So virtue lies in wait for Willi because:

> . . . despite all naturalistic considerations,
> Or in the end because of naturalistic considerations,
> We must believe in virtue. There is no
> Escape. No inland path around that rocky
> And spume-nagged promontory. There is no
> Escape: dead-fall on trail, noose on track, bear-trap

Under the carefully rearranged twigs. There is no
Escape, for virtue is
More dogged than Pinkerton, more scientific than the F.B.I.,
And that is why you wake sweating toward dawn.

(BTD, p. 29)

At the end Willie senses his own incompleteness and 'with the
potentials of indivisibility within his grasp, gives way to a fatal
yearning for absolute good, in violation of his intrinsic character and beliefs.'[22] Thus he is shot and killed by Adam Stanton,
the man of absolute virtue who will not allow his moral preserve to be infected by the man of fact. Stanton too is killed:
Beauty and the Beast both drown in the same dream.

Warren's politician 'was to be a man whose power was based
on the fact that somehow he could vicariously fulfill some secret
needs of the people around him.'[23] Willie Stark fills this rôle
for all the members of his retinue, but most of all for Jack
Burden whom Warren created to answer 'the necessity for a
character of a higher degree of self-consciousness than my
politician, a character to serve as a kind of commentator and
raissoneur and chorus' (AKM, p. vii). The parallel structure of
the first chapter (Willie and Jack both going home again)
prompts us to compare the two men and to ask what attracts
Jack to Willie. Without agreeing with E. R. Steinberg's view
that Willie does not 'develop understandably'[24]; his trans-
formation from dupe to demagogue is perfectly understandable; we can accept that the morally amorphous Jack is held
by the enigma of Willie's sheer self-certainty. This is more than
voyeurism: working for Willie becomes Jack's method of
investigating the mystery of selfhood, with special reference
to his own.

With Warren's consent the Cass Mastern episode, the mythic
sub-story of *All the King's Men*, was omitted from the first
British edition published by Eyre and Spottiswoode in 1948. In
the Introduction to the first unabridged British edition in 1974
Warren says that he nevertheless 'always felt that the section
is central to the novel'[25] and that it was devised as a method of
giving his story 'moral' and his narrator 'psychological'
dimension. As a student of history Jack Burden can grasp the
facts of the Cass Mastern story, but he evades the truth they

contain. Abandoning his research, he flees from 'the reproach implicit in the materials of the dissertation.'[26] The Cass Mastern material follows him around, an unopened parcel, like Jack himself. The story implicitly reproaches Jack for failing to recognise his involvement in 'the general human communion' (SE, p. 54). Throughout his life he has avoided responsibility, withdrawing into the false innocence of the Great Sleep, or into an abstracting idealism according to which nothing is real, or into the naturalistic philosophy of the Great Twitch by which people are reduced to amoral mechanisms. His failure to relate the realm of events to the realm of ideas is his failure to stay afloat in Conrad's 'destructive element': he attempts either to immerse himself in the fluidity of idealism or to withdraw to the dry land of naturalism. Jack cannot open the ineluctable parcel until the action of the novel brings home to him that he is a cause as well as an effect, a contributor to a web of morally ambiguous relationships. This realisation enables him at last to interpret the Cass Mastern story and to find in the lesson learned by Mastern the key to his own life.

The image of the spider web implies a tragic theory of human life as universal involvement and responsibility in shared complicity:

> Cass Mastern lived for a few years and in that time he learned that the world is all of one piece. He learned that the world is like an enormous spider web and if you touch it, however lightly, at any point, the vibration ripples to the remotest perimeter and the drowsy spider feels the tingle and is drowsy no more but springs out to fling the gossamer coils about you who have touched the web and then injects the black, numbing poison under your hide. It does not matter whether or not you meant to brush the web of things. Your happy foot or your gay wing may have brushed it ever so lightly, but what happens always happens and there is the spider, bearded black and with his great faceted eyes glittering like mirrors in the sun, or like God's eye, and the fangs dripping.
> (AKM, p. 200)

The idea that the world is all of a piece, a web in which man inevitably becomes entangled, is an unexceptionable proposition earned by the events of the novel and succinctly echoed by 'the flower-in-the-crannied-wall theory' a few pages later:

'I eat a persimmon and the teeth of a tinker in Tibet are put on edge' (AKM, p. 234). The suggestion that the entanglement is fatal makes the passage more complex and the image of the spider invests the account of man's situation with a horror that anticipates Corinthian McClardy's Campbellite picture of God as a great bear lunging at the tender throat of the lost fawn (WEAT, pp. 30–31). In Jack Burden's picture the chief fatality is presumably man's uninstructed sense of himself as innocent, the 'black, numbing poison' being a knowledge of evil, the spider itself ambiguously imaging God. The spider's eyes glitter 'like mirrors in the sun', sheets of light cruelly blinding to the viewer who had expected to see his own reflection in the mirrors. There is an Agrarian insistence on mystery here, an implicit criticism of the belief that a god can be solipsistically made or that the secrets of the world can ever be despoiled of their inscrutability. The eyes of the spider cheat man of the god he would make in his own image, burning into him instead a sense of his own radical imperfection.

Life teaches Jack how to face the truth contained in the Cass Mastern story which, in turn, helps him to see a pattern in the events he has lived through. The suicide of Judge Irwin especially carries the meaning of the story into his personal history. Before Mastern dies he rises out of his guilty self-preoccupation by recognising the virtue of the suffering soldiers around him: the parallel in Jack's progress involves the father-son relation. Jack's search for a spiritual father begins with the departure of Ellis Burden, and ends only with the deaths of his biological father (Judge Irwin), his surrogate father (Willie Stark), and the acceptance of his supposed father (Ellis Burden). This represents an interesting variation of the pattern of *At Heaven's Gate* in which Jerry Calhoun is led back from his surrogate father (Bogan Murdock) to his 'real' and biological father. Jack's acceptance of both biological and spiritual fathers signifies his ability now to reconcile the realm of fact with the realm of idea.

Jack's two essays in historical research enable him to understand himself, to appreciate the nature of the present and to entertain a disciplined hopefulness for the future. At the end of the novel Jack and Anne Stanton, now Mr and Mrs Burden,

make a Miltonic departure from an Eden of false hopes: they
have both suffered a fortunate fall, to be redeemed by a life
together lived by the knowledge that is now theirs. The novel's
main ideas, the interdependence of good and evil, human
freedom and human worth are finally summed up by Ellis
Burden who proposes that the existence of evil is a sign of
God's glory and power, the creation of good a sign of man's.
That Ellis Burden at least shares the status of Jack's 'real'
father with Judge Irwin is pointed by Jack's reflection on the
'scholarly attorney's' theologising: 'I was not certain but that
in my own way I did not agree with him' (AKM, p. 463). 'In my
own way' preserves Jack's detachment from the theological
dimension of Ellis Burden's formulation while identifying him
with its insistence on the need for human effort. This is Warren's
own position. His severe yet sustaining view of man's condition,
exemplified by this novel and maintained throughout his
career, is accurately expressed in the quotation from the
Confessions of Saint Augustine with which he concludes
Democracy and Poetry: 'There is a dim glimmering of light
unput-out in men; let them walk, let them walk that the darkness overtake them not.'[27]

Chapter Four — Notes

[1] Woodward, C. Vann, *The Burden of Southern History* (New York:
Random House, Vintage Books Edition), p. 53.

[2] Warren, Robert Penn, 'T. S. Stribling: a Paragraph in the History of
Critical Realism', *American Review*, 2 (Feb, 1934), 463–86.

[3] Curtiss, Mina, 'Tragedy of a Liberal', *Nation*, 148 (29 April, 1939),
507.

[4] Isherwood, Christopher, 'Tragic Liberal', *New Republic*, 99 (31,
May, 1939), 108.

[5] Wilson, Angus, 'The Fires of Violence', *Encounter*, 4 (May, 1955),
75–78.

[6] Wilson, p. 76.

[7] Cowley, Malcolm, (ed.), *Writers at Work: The Paris Review Interviews*
(London: Secker and Warburg, 1958), p. 171.

[8] Cowley, Malcolm, 'Luke Lea's Empire', *New Republic*, 109 (23 Aug,
1943), 258.

[9] AKM, Introduction, p. vii, footnote.

[10] Justus, James H., 'On the Politics of the Self-Created: *At Heaven's Gate*', *Sewanee Review*, **82** (1974), 284–99.

[11] Letter dated 16 Oct, 1943 from Frank Owsley to Robert Penn Warren, *Papers of Frank Owsley*, Tennessee State Library and Archives.

[12] In a book full of 'sons-of-bitches', Duckfoot Blake was one of the 'mountain peaks' of integrity for Owsley, the other being Ashby Wyndham. Letter from Owsley to Warren, 16 Oct, 1943.

[13] Cowley, Malcolm, *Writers at Work*, p. 171.

[14] Cowley, p. 168.

[15] Perhaps Bogan Murdock would have been able to survive his disgrace and the failure of his firm, capitalising on the public sympathy gained over Sue's death. The material fortunes of the Leas did not finally crash until 1967, when a Mrs J. Mauerman ordered the sale of Mr and Mrs Luke Lea Jr's personal property to satisfy in part a judgement of $137,735 against the Leas for default in payment of a $110,000 note. The sale was reported in *The Nashville Banner*, 21 Dec, 1967.

[16] Letter dated 25 Aug, 1946. *Papers of Frank Owsley*, Tennessee State Library and Archives.

[17] Bentley, Eric, 'The Meaning of Robert Penn Warren's Novels', *Kenyon Review*, **10** (Summer, 1948), 423.

[18] Cary, Joyce, *To Be a Pilgrim* (London, Michael Joseph: 1942), p. 198.

[19] For comment on Warren's dramatic versions see Casper, pp. 116–21, and William M. Schutte, 'The Dramatic Versions of the Willie Stark Story', *All the King's Men: A Symposium* (Pittsburgh: Carnegie Institute of Technology, 1957), pp. 75–90.

[20] For comment on these novels and surveys of the critical response to *All the King's Men* see Louis D. Rubin Jr., 'All the King's Meanings', *Georgia Review*, **8** (Winter, 1954), 422–34, and Robert B. Heilman, 'Melpomene as Wallflower; or, The Reading of Tragedy', *Sewanee Review*, **55** (1947), 154–66, reprinted in Longley, pp. 82–95.

[21] Williams, T. Harry, *Huey Long* (New York: Alfred A. Knopf Inc., 1969), p. x.

[22] Eisinger, Chester E., *Fiction of the Forties* (Chicago: University of Chicago Press, 1963), p. 215.

[23] Warren, Robert Penn, 'A note to *All the King's Men*', *Sewanee Review*, **61** (1953), p. 479. On these terms, Murray Guilfort, the corrupted lawyer in *Meet Me in the Green Glen*, is an inverted Willie Stark.

[24] Steinberg, Erwin R., 'The Enigma of Willlie Stark', in *All the King's Men: A Symposium*, p. 25.

[25] *All the King's Men* (London: Secker and Warburg, 1974), p. xiv.

[26] *All the King's Men* (London, 1974), p. xv.

[27] Warren, Robert Penn, *Democracy and Poetry, The 1974 Jefferson Lecture in the Humanities* (Cambridge, Mass.: Harvard University Press, 1975), p. 94.

5

Uses of History

Warren's first-hand experiences of the events forming the
background for *Night Rider* helped him early to a sense of the
vitality of Southern history and to feel that history as a
continuum in which he was himself involved. There were the
reminiscences of his grandfather about the battle of Shiloh:
'One hundred and sixty men we took in the first morning, son.
Muster the next night and it was sixteen answered' (*Segregation*,
p. 14). There was at the same time something almost on the
same scale in the young Warren's present itself—martial law
in Kentucky and an encampment of State Guards in Guthrie—
so that Warren could tell Ralph Ellison in 1957:

> I remember the troops coming in when martial law was declared
> in that part of Kentucky. When I wrote *Night Rider* I wasn't
> thinking of it as history. For one thing, the world it treated still,
> in a way, survived. You could still talk to the old men who had
> been involved. In the 1930's I remember going to see a judge
> down in Kentucky—he was an elderly man then, a man of the
> highest integrity and reputation—who had lived through that
> period and who by common repute had been mixed up in it—
> his father had been a tobacco grower. He got to talking about
> that period in Kentucky. He said, 'Well, I won't say who was and
> who wasn't mixed up in some of those things, but I will make one
> observation: I have noticed that the sons of those who were
> opposed to getting a fair price for tobacco ended up as either

bootleggers or brokers.' But he was an old-fashioned kind of guy, for whom bootlegging and brokerage looked very much alike. Such a man didn't look 'historical' thirty years ago. Now he looks like the thigh bone of a mastodon.[1]

History is never 'the thigh bone of a mastodon' for Warren. The 'historical' lives of Jeremiah Beaumont, the Lewis brothers, Amantha Starr, Adam Rosenzweig—even of John Brown— are as relevant to our own efforts to be human as the 'modern' life of Jack Burden or the various personal entrapments of *The Cave*. In his first three novels, Warren's feeling for history is part of his equipment for exploring the meanings of events in worlds he had known. *World Enough and Time*, set in early nineteenth-century Kentucky, is his first truly historical novel, although Warren does not care to use the term, referring to the book as simply 'a kind of historical job'.[2] In the long poem, *Brother to Dragons*, and the novels, *Band of Angels* and *Wilderness*, he turns again to nineteenth-century history for 'stories that seem to have issues in purer forms than they come to me ordinarily.'[3] One might sometimes wish Warren had more often turned away from the South for a broader stage on which to stretch his audacious talents; instead he confers space on his region by expanding it in the dimension of time.

In a review of *Band of Angels*[4] Leslie Fiedler describes the form Warren's fiction seemed to be developing as 'something not very different from nineteenth-century Italian opera: a *genre* full of conventional absurdities, lapses of good taste, strained and hectic plots—all aimed at becoming myth and melody.' Receptive to Warren's full-bloodedness, this appreciates the artistic daring of a writer who has declined merely to pick up a manner or become, like the novelist in Auden's poem, 'Encased in talent like a uniform.' Fiedler doubts 'that either the novel or the long poem intended to be read as a novel can stand such a metamorphosis,' but his notion of myth and musical analogy are generally apposite. Despite their poetic qualities, Warren's novels are realistic in style, but their sub-stories—Willie Proudfit's narrative, the Statement of Ashby Wyndham and the Cass Mastern episode— all strike a paradigmatic note for each novel. The Cass Mastern episode, for example, may be said to include the action of *All*

the King's Men within a single narrative phrase which har-
monises the meanings of the book. It is, as we have seen, Jack
Burden's myth. In the works considered in this chapter Warren
uses history, 'the big myth we live' (BTD, p. xii), to create
fictions that will work as mythic models for us all.

There is too much of the Grand Guignol in *World Enough and
Time* for Brendan Gill who wonders, in an early review of the
novel, 'why a writer of Mr Warren's stature had stooped to
what is, in our time, the showiest and least serious form of
fiction.'[5] Gill dismisses the book as commercial melodrama while
Leslie Fiedler hails it as a serious philosophical-historical novel.[6]
The seriousness of Warren's purpose is illuminated by the
differences between his story and the historical material from
which it derives. In 1944 when Warren was a Fellow of the
Library of Congress, Katherine Anne Porter, also a Fellow,
'came in one day with an old pamphlet, the trial of Beauchamp
for killing Colonel Sharp[7] . . . I read it in five minutes. But I
was six years making the book.'[8] During those years Warren
read the other documents of the 'Kentucky Tragedy'.[9] the
famous murder of 1825 which had already provided the basis
for drama and fiction by, among others, Thomas Holley
Chivers, Edgar Allan Poe and William Gilmore Simms. It is
easy to see why the story appealed to a writer of Warren's
philosophical and historical interests, but if the Beauchamp-
Sharp case presented him with an issue in purer form than usual,
he expanded and altered the story to develop what he took to
be its essential significance.

Jereboam Beachamp hears about Sharp's seduction of Ann
Cook from 'his acquaintances of the bar at Glasgow [Kentucky],
and those attending the courts there from Bowlinggreen.'[10]
He receives a glowing account of Ann Cook from 'a room mate
and bosom friend of mine, who had been intimately acquainted
with Miss Cooke, and much devoted to her.'[11] By combining
these two sources of information in the person of Wilkie Barron,
Warren establishes him as the manipulator of Jeremiah and
ironically undercuts Jeremiah's belief that he himself serves the
'pure idea' (WEAT, p. 62).

According to Ann Cook's letters, it is Colonel Sharp himself
who introduces Beauchamp to her: 'In one of his visits, he

brought with him, and introduced to me, a young man of an agreeable person, named B——p. He begged me to regard him as his friend, and to show him every attention in my power. I, who loved whatever he loved, and hated whatever he disliked, soon looked upon B——p with feelings of kindness and friendship.'[12] Warren's Jeremiah severs his connection with Colonel Fort before he meets Rachel Jordan. He suddenly apprehends his own destiny as he tells Fort, in his letter of rejection, that he is determined to 'turn from the face of the betrayer, and seek truth in the face of the betrayed' (WEAT, p. 68). Jeremiah arrives at the Jordan house a complete stranger, professing to be 'an intimate of a friend of Miss Jordan', by whom he means, presumably, Wilkie Barron. The historical documents conflict on this point: Ann Cook's account of her first meeting with Beauchamp is very different from Beauchamp's own. He writes: '. . . I resolved to intrude a visit upon her, however unwelcomely I anticipated she would receive it;—the more especially, if unaccompanied by an introduction from any friend, or acquaintance of hers . . . I introduced myself to her, and told her, that notwithstanding I had learned she was disinclined to make any acquaintances, or to receive the visits of any one, I had been impelled to obtrude a visit upon her.'[13] This clearly accords with Warren's fictional version. There is no corroborative evidence for either Beauchamp's or Ann Cook's account of their first meeting, but Warren's choice of Beauchamp's emphasises his focus on Jeremiah's abstract conception of Rachel Jordan and the force of will by which he creates 'the drama in which he played' (WEAT, p. 7) in terms of 'the deep truth of himself' (WEAT, p. 68).

The historical villain, Sharp, from being pro-Relief 'turned completely round in politics'[14] and the likelihood of the pro-Relief Beauchamp's guilt is grist to the political mill of the Anti-Relief party in their campaign for the success of the Old Court faction, but Jeremiah's involvement in the fight at Lumton and his standing for election as Relief candidate are of Warren's invention. Thus Jeremiah's character is fleshed out realistically while it is being drawn further into the tangle of world and idea, the philosophical issue with which Warren is chiefly concerned. Unlike Jeremiah, Beauchamp has no regrets about killing Sharp; there is no escape, no Grand' Bosse, no deliberate return to the world in the story as Warren found it. These are some of the additions whereby he transforms a piece of historical blood-and-thunder into 'myth and melody'.

Early in the novel we are told that Jeremiah Beaumont's life 'was a drama that he had prepared'; two pages later we read that 'perhaps the land and the history of the land devised Jeremiah Beaumont and the drama in which he played, and the scene is the action and speaks through the mouth of Jeremiah Beaumont as through a mask' (WEAT, pp. 5 and 7). Later again we are told that 'Jeremiah Beaumont had to create his world or be the victim of a world he did not create' (WEAT, p. 125), but as we watch him planning to kill Fort we learn that 'the obligation to kill Fort sprang from the depths of his nature' (WEAT, p. 132). Such superficially conflicting statements lead Harry M. Campbell to a view of Jeremiah as devised by his place and time rather than as the maker of his own drama and to conclude that the drift of Warren's philosophical speculations is towards a 'determinism not unlike that of Theodore Dreiser, although Warren is much more sophisticated and intellectual in considering all the angles than Dreiser'.[15] This suggests not only an inadequate understanding of Dreiser, but also an inability to see that the two kinds of statement made about Jeremiah's relation to his own drama are not mutually exclusive, and that the outcome of Warren's 'considering all the angles' is not conflict but harmony, a view of Jeremiah's life as the joint product of his heritage and environment on the one hand and, on the other, his capacity for self-creation in terms of an idea. The representative tragic doubleness of his condition is already implicit in the frontier background described in the opening pages: 'The dirk (of Spanish steel or made from a hunting knife or Revolutionary sword) and the Bible might lie side by side on the table, or Plato and the duelling pistols on the mantel shelf' (WEAT, pp. 6–7). The world imposes the need for dirk and pistols while man's nature as a follower of the idea may be said to impose the Bible and Plato. But this is far removed from Dreiser's determining 'chemisms' which are entirely at odds with the self-determining power of idea typically displayed by Warren's characters. Warren's own reading of the Frank Cowperwood trilogy further invalidates Harry M. Campbell's recourse to Dreiser's 'determinism' for a likely parallel to the philosophy of *World Enough and Time*: "Dreiser, though seeing man caught in the great machine of nature, does allow him the dignity of the 'terror and wonder of individuality' . . . Dreiser is not quite ready to say with Margoth, the brutal geologist in Melville's *Clarel*, that 'All is Chymistry' " (*Homage to Theodore Dreiser*, pp. 153–54).

Naturalism, as we have seen, had much appeal for Warren in his earlier years and never ceases to be an issue in his work; but by the time of *World Enough and Time* he was far from a simple view of man as 'caught in the great machine of nature'. The success of any life, in Warren's mature view, depends as much on a right regard for nature as it does on the conception and maintenance of an idea: there must be a proper balance between dirk and Bible. In *World Enough and Time* Jeremiah's perverse idealism involves him and nature in a relationship degrading to both. Unconsciously resisting the Campbellite grimness of Corinthian McClardy's sermon, Jeremiah is so pantheistically drawn to a shining, ice-covered tree that his 'substance seemed to pass beyond the tree and into all the land around that spread in the sunlight, and into the sunlight itself' (WEAT, pp. 31–32). While this Wordsworthian naturalism seems harmless enough, it marks Jeremiah's readiness for the descent into nature which begins with his murder of Fort and leads to the depravities of La Grand' Bosse's diseased kingdom. Jeremiah is profoundly deaf to the warning that 'he should not enter into nature, for the Kingdom is not of this world' (WEAT, p. 32). His ecstatic participation in the tree and its context is recalled as he waits in the night to murder Colonel Fort:

> He had the fancy that he was growing into the ground, was setting root like the plants of the thicket, was one of them groping deeper and deeper into the cold, damp earth with fingers of root and tentacles like hair. He let his cheek rest against a thick, dry stalk of lilac, but the silk of the mask came between. So he raised the silk to give his cheek that companionship. And he remembered

how, on the morning of the great and glittering frost years before, when he had been but a boy, the morning when all the world was covered with brilliant ice in the sun, he had touched the bough of the ice-ridden beech and had felt his being flow out into the shining tree, as though the bough were a conduit, and into the sunlight from every lifted twig, and down the trunk into the secret earth so that he was part of everything.

(WEAT, p. 259)

The memory of the radiant beech seems to endorse the killing of Fort as a logical consequence of all Jeremiah has been and done. Thus nature, perversely strengthening him in the performance of his crime, is a corrupting influence which further clouds his vision and carries him deeper into his tragically contaminating idea. He remembers the beech again as he lies in the dark of his cell (WEAT, p. 343), where his final stage of error begins in frenetic sex with Rachel as he strives naturalistically to affirm his vitality. In his final plunge into the nature of La Grand' Bosse's nightmare Kingdom he seeks 'communion only in the blank cup of nature, and innocence there' (WEAT, p. 506). The innocence he finds, however, is not the moral neutrality of nature but the animality of man dehumanised.

Jeremiah's final decision is to give up the false peace of animal innocence and to return East so that he may suffer in the terms of civilisation for 'the crime of self, the crime of life' (WEAT, p. 505). Like Jack Burden he comes to realise that man cannot live wholly either in the realm of the ideal or in the realm of nature, that to be human and responsible involves living in both. 'Innocence,' Jeremiah says, 'is what man cannot endure and be man' (WEAT, p. 506); thus he flees from the naturalistic realm of La Grand' Bosse toward both his guilt and his own humanity. There is a close parallel between Jeremiah's ending and that of Joe Christmas in Faulkner's *Light in August*. During his flight after the murder of Joanna Burden, Christmas feels himself beyond time and achieves a transcendent state in which he finds himself at last. Although he knows he will be put to death for Miss Burden's murder, he deliberately re-enters human time and community because only within their framework will his life have meaning.

Before Jeremiah murders him, Fort refers to a plan to

'reconcile all in justice', by 'all' meaning, in the narrator's words, 'the world and . . . the idea, the flesh and . . . the word, the Old Court . . . and the New' (WEAT, p. 510). In his letter to Rachel, Fort describes his own effort to achieve a redemptive pattern of life which echoes the sequence required for self-definition given in Warren's essay on 'Knowledge and the Image of Man'. After his spell outside 'the world' with Rachel, he 'came back into the world, and hope to do my duty still, whatever it may be and bear with fortitude the ills and losses' (WEAT, p. 147). This is not simply a reflection of Fort's stoicism but of his attempt to reconcile the dream of his private world with the demands of the public world. The movement of his life is eventually mirrored by Jeremiah's: like surrogate father, spiritual son (Appendix, pp. 249–50).

It is a danger, in a discussion of such a novel, that Warren the philosopher will be over-emphasised at the expense of Warren the artist. One must be struck by the felicity of detail with which Warren concretises his historical period and his themes. We are given a meticulous account of Jeremiah's Kentucky background, of his parentage and of influences that prove formative, from the apocalyptic austerities of Corinthian McClardy's preaching and the crude arrogance of grandfather Marcher to the books in which the young Jeremiah searches 'for what truth might be beyond the bustle of the hour and the empty lusts of time' (WEAT, p. 26), the 'book of the Martyrs' chief among them. There are the shabby, bitter figures of Timothy and Maria Jordan, Munn Short's tale of conversion— a brief sub-story reminiscent of Ashby Wyndham's statement —and the bizarre career of La Grand' Bosse, personification of original sin. There is the vivid account of the election-day brawl at Lumton in Chapter 3. Richmond C. Beatty cites the conversation between Jeremiah and the vigilantes at the beginning of Chapter 7 (WEAT, pp. 276–78) as an illustration of the book's 'convincing particularity'.[16]

The nature-motif of the beech tree illustrates Warren's use of imagery to substantialise his argument. There are many other examples, like the keelboat with its fiddler and bugle-call which come back to Jeremiah 'as an image for whatever had summoned him to plunge into a stream stained darker than the

H

Kentucky River ever was at flood' (WEAT, pp. 21 and 453). A benign nature pulls Jeremiah back from his pursuit of the idea in the figure of Rachel on her knees, begging him not to go to Fort because she is to have a child; but the force of this appeal is challenged by a nature of different aspect as the image of Rachel 'somehow merged with the foul dark-faced female creature in the woods beyond McClardy's Meadow clutching at his knees and whimpering before he struck her to snatch free and plunge toward the sound of healing waters' (WEAT, p. 227). The theme of historical continuity is ironically pointed by the comfortable ignorance of the 'most respectable descendants' of La Grand' Bosse, 'who did not know him and would have denied him with shame', but who 'still carried under their pink scrubbed hides and double-breasted sack suits (cunningly cut to redeem the sagging paunch) the mire-thick blood of his veins and the old coiling darkness of his heart' (WEAT, p. 476). The tailoring of the sack suits recalls La Grand' Bosse's British officer's jacket, cut to accommodate his hump. After despatching Jeremiah in the wilderness, One-eye Jenkins brings his head back to Frankfort with the neck encased in clay (WEAT, p. 508). Death has brought the resolution that eluded Jeremiah while he lived: he is now both head (idea) and clay (the dust of the world). Stated baldly, this may seem what Melville would have called 'hideous and intolerable allegory', but it is perfectly acceptable and effective here not merely because it fits Warren's argument, but because One-eye Jenkins' action is credible in terms of the need for proof if he is to claim the reward offered for Jeremiah and because the use of clay as sealant and preservative is practical before it is symbolic. *World Enough and Time* succeeds as a philosophical novel of high distinction because of Warren's ability to flesh out his argument, amplifying his image of man through the media of a dazzling plot, richly imagined characters and vivid scenes.

II

In 1811, which came to be known as the *Annus Mirabilis* of the

West (BTD, p. 218), a great comet appeared in the northern sky and there were violent floods throughout the Ohio River bottom lands. On September 17 there was an almost total eclipse of the sun and on the night of December 15 came the New Madrid earthquake, first of a series of earthquakes that shook the Mississippi Valley for months. Against this background two nephews of former President Thomas Jefferson butchered a seventeen-year-old slave named George on their plantation in Livingston County, West Kentucky. The Lewis brothers herded their slaves into a kitchen cabin and bolted the door. Lilburn, enraged because George had broken a pitcher which supposedly had belonged to the late Mrs Lewis, sank an axe into the slave's neck and ordered another slave to dismember the body. While Lilburn sermonised his petrified slaves on obedience—and silence—George's remains were thrown on a fire to destroy the evidence. An earthquake destroyed the kitchen chimney before the body was totally cremated. A neighbour noticed a dog gnawing a strange object: George's skull signalled a *corpus delecti*. Indicted for murder, Lilburn and Isham Lewis were released on bail, formed a suicide pact and prepared to shoot each other in the family graveyard. While Lilburn was showing his brother how to hold the muzzle of his rifle to his chest and press the trigger with a stick, the gun went off and killed Lilburn. Isham was jailed, sentenced to be hanged, but escaped before trial and disappeared, although, as Warren's Foreword tells us: 'when the local militiamen, after service with Andrew Jackson at New Orleans, returned to Livingston County, they reported that they had seen and talked with Isham at the battle and that he had been killed there by a British musket-ball' (BTD, p. x).

As reconstructed in an exemplary study of the case by Boynton Merrill, Jr. the murder seems to have had no motive, only psychological plausibility. Frontier reaction to pressure was often violent: Lilburn 'was under constant stress from money troubles'; in under two years his first wife, his older brother and his mother had all died; he was now married to a beautiful but 'cold, proud, scornful, young wife'. The morally corrosive institution of slavery provided Lilburn with workers who ran away from his cruelty; it also provided a scapegoat for his rage against a malevolent fate. Liquor, probably, did the rest.[17] Warren focuses on the murderers' relationship to Thomas Jefferson and probes through the lurid surface of the case to find another illustration of 'the disparity in man between beatific vision and the ubiquitous evil which blights it.'[18] The crime and its implications are revealed as the dark underside of Jefferson's bright rationalism.

Early in the poem R.P.W. tells us that he once intended to make a ballad out of the Lewis story:

> . . . but the form
> Was not adequate: the facile imitation
> Of a folk simplicity would never serve,
> For the beauty of such simplicity is only
> That the action is always and perfectly self-contained,
> And is an image that comes as its own perfect explanation
> In shock or sweetness to the innocent heart.
>
> (BTD, p. 43)

The story of Billie Potts had precisely the beauty of such folk simplicity, being 'perfectly self-contained' in its morally primitive logic of sin and retribution. It could, therefore, be appropriately contained in ballad form to give the coherent basis for the poet's elaborate commentary. The story of *Brother to Dragons* does not have this instant self-sufficiency, but evolves as the characters speak, often contradicting each other, and as R.P.W., arbitrating between their perspectives, brings it home to us that

> . . . the action is not self-contained, but contains
> Us too, and is contained by us, and is
> Only an image of the issue of our most distressful self-definition.
>
> (BTD, p. 43)

This blatantly artificial form succeeds through Warren's readiness not only to declare but to take advantage of it. For Randall Jarrell, reviewing the work in 1953, it was 'an event, a great one', and 'Robert Penn Warren's best book'.[19]

The blank verse, often Eliotesque in its rhythm and cadences, is regular enough to sustain the flow of high feeling, but loose enough to preserve the spontaneity of narrative action and energetic argument, accommodating the colloquial speech of

Aunt Cat, the Brother and Isham Lewis as well as the tense
brooding of Thomas Jefferson. 'Warren has managed to
convey', as Charles H. Bohner puts it, 'the unique flavour and
slant of each character's speech while maintaining the unity of
tone of the poem as a whole.'[20] There are some strained passages and some bad lines, like Jefferson's over-alliterative
description of the men who attended the First Continental
Congress as 'Marmosets in mantles, beasts in boots, parrots in
pantaloons' (BTD, p. 6), which recalls the mannered verse of
Warren's early Fugitive period. There are moments of over-
insistence and sudden false notes:

> . . . And there's always and forever
> Enough of guilt to rise and coil like miasma
> From the fat sump and cess of common consciousness
> To make any particular hour seem most appropriate
> For Gabriel's big tootle.

> (BTD, p. 64)

Such lapses hardly matter in 'a work which is most remarkable
as a sustained whole'[21] and in which the narrative carries the
reader swiftly past brief infelicities.

Warren's verse exemplifies to a remarkable degree in so long
a poem the ideal language described by Eliot in the fifth movement of 'Little Gidding':

> The word neither diffident nor ostentatious,
> An easy commerce of the old and the new,
> The common word exact without vulgarity,
> The formal word precise but not pedantic,
> The complete consort dancing together.

If there is a kind of ostentation in the mock-heroic of 'Marmosets in mantles' and 'Gabriel's big tootle', it is Warren's mastery
of 'the complete consort' that most impresses in the language of
Brother to Dragons. The aptly common word sharpens our
sense of the tale's contemporary relevance in R.P.W.'s account
of his journey to Smithland:

> Up Highway 109 from Hopkinsville,
> To Dawson Springs, then west on 62,
> Across Kentucky at the narrow neck,

Two hours now, not more, for the road's fair.
We ripped the July dazzle on the slab—
July of '46—ripped through the sun-bit land.

(BTD, p. 15)

The formal word appears not only in the soul-searchings of
Thomas Jefferson and the speculations of R.P.W. but, for
example, in the invocation to a ritual analogous to Wovoka's
Indian Ghost Dance by which Jefferson expresses his spiritual
rehabilitation. Through the enlightenment provided by Meriwether Lewis's tragic ending and Lucy Lewis's intuitive sense
of truth, he has passed from a restrictive idealism through
complete despair to acceptance of human nature and a new
faith in man's effort to create, after all, the 'gleaming West
anew':

Dance back the buffalo, the shining land!
Our grander Ghost Dance dance now, and shake the feather.
Dance back the morning and the eagle's cry.
Dance back the Shining Mountains, let them shine!
Dance into morning and the lifted eye.
Dance into morning past the morning star,
And dance the heart by which we have lived and died.
My Louisiana, I would dance you, though afar!

(BTD, p. 195)

Warren has described *Brother to Dragons* as a "communal
nightmare. People from the past are caught in a terrible dream
that must be re-enacted, over and over, for ever—or until they
can resolve it, by coming to an understanding that will let
them 'die' into peace. Sometimes they relive the past, sometimes they speak bits of narrative, sometimes they probe at
some fragment of meaning discovered for the first time. Always
they are struggling for the escape."[22] The issue which Warren's
tormented characters are compelled to discuss and from which
they long to escape arises when the spiritual father of America
faces the fact of human evil in the crime of his nephew. In
All the King's Men the historical figure of Huey Long prompted
Warren to a meditation on the moral life of man in a political
context, which he conducts by means of a story about a man
like Long. Whether the story illuminates the career of the real

Kingfish is for the historian to say and is, in any case, strictly accidental. In *Brother to Dragons*, however, while he has 'no compunction about tampering with facts', Warren scrupulously grounds his tale in the evoked past and in the actual character of Jefferson as history presents them. As he says in the Foreword: '. . . a poem dealing with history is no more at liberty to violate what the writer takes to be the spirit of his history than it is at liberty to violate what the writer takes to be the nature of the human heart. What he takes those things to be is, of course, his ultimate gamble.' (BTD, p. xii).

Warren protects both his gamble and the character of Jefferson from accusations of naivety. Although he admits that he once thought man, the 'master-monster' was 'innocent', Jefferson is allowed to put the notion of innocence into a defining context:

> . . . even then I was no fool,
> And knew that if you open the door of the cupboard
> There are wood-violet and shanker, merd and magnolia,
>   side by side.
> And if I thought the housekeeping of Great Nature
> Was wasteless and took all to beneficent use,
> And decomposition and recomposition are but twin syllables
>   on the same sweet tongue
> And two vibrations of the same string stung to joy,
> I scarcely held that meditation on the nurture of roses
> Is much comfort to a man who had just stepped in dung,
> And philosophy has never raised a crop of hair
> Where the scalping knife has once done the scythe-work.
>
>   (BTD, p. 37)

Jefferson, nevertheless, resolutely believed in man's essential innocence and in his power to redeem nature according to the values of plainness, order and harmony symbolised by the Maison Quarré at Nîmes which stood in such contrast to the depraved, bestial carvings of the Gothic imagination (BTD, pp. 38–39). Reminding us of Hawthorne's 'Young Goodman Brown', Jefferson's first reaction to the bestiality of his nephew is to reject Lilburn and to lapse into a cynical view of human ideals. The purpose of the book is to compel the imagined

Jefferson to recognise his spiritual as well as his blood kinship
to Lilburn and to accept the connection between ideal social
vision and recalcitrant individual reality.

At the beginning of Warren's tale Jefferson is the bitterly
disillusioned idealist, his absolute and abstract vision of the new
society radically violated by Lilburn's murder of George.
Recreation of the events which led to the murder issues in the
view that, however indefensible the crime, it was nevertheless
'but the sum of all the defensible hours / We have lived through'
(BTD, p. 111). This paradox is developed and explained by the
career of the murderous Lilburn. Lucy Lewis loved Lilburn
but deprived him of love by willing her own death in a recoil
from human involvement. Lilburn repeats the pattern of
deprivation by abusing his wife so that she withholds her love
from him. A scapegoat must be found and George is manipulated into the rôle. Now Lilburn has provided himself with a
pretext for the act whereby he may conclusively define himself
in terms of the sanctity of his mother's memory. George has
broken Lucy's pitcher; the loving son avenges the violation.
In the logic of his need he has earned, at last, his mother's
love. Morally, the Lewis family's early nineteenth-century
Kentucky is clearly an extension of Percy Munn's Tennessee,
Willie Stark's Louisiana and the 'dark and bloody ground'
of *World Enough and Time*. By presenting the murder as an
evil act but one performed in the name of an ideal, however
sentimental, Warren implicates us all in a criminality which
bears shocking relation to Jefferson's ideal of human perfectibility.

The title of the book establishes Jefferson as Job-like in his
bitterness and hurt pride. Job complains that he has become 'a
brother to dragons and a companion to owls' (Job, 30: 29).
Not only is Jefferson made to face the fact that he is an uncle
to dragons, but he must also learn how treacherously the
dragon-seed of his ideas sprouted in the life of Meriwether
Lewis who experiences such savagery both in the idealised
West and during his Governorship of the Louisiana Territory
that he despairs of man to the point of suicide. The ghostly
Meriweather accuses Jefferson of making his 'sweet lie' out of
vanity:

. . . I would honour more the axe in the meat-house,
As more honest at least, than your special lie
Concocted, though out of nobleness—oh, yes,
It was noble, but was concocted for your comfort
To prove yourself nobler in man's nobleness.
Yes, in man's nobleness, you'd be the noble Jefferson.

(BTD, p. 186)

Whereas the murder of George is an inverse function of Lilburn's primitive virtue, Jefferson's ideal conception of man is shown to be a function of his own guilt. His sister, Lucy Jefferson Lewis, endorses Meriwether's perception that her brother's belief allowed him indirectly to assert his own nobility, denying his natural capacity for evil. Thus she leads Jefferson out of his new vanity of alienation, and, in his last speech, he invokes reason not 'as a given condition of man', not as natural, but as something to be created out of man's acknowledged imperfections:

. . . if there is to be reason, we must
Create the possibility
Of reason, and we can create it only
From the circumstances of our most evil despair.
We must strike the steel of wrath on the stone of guilt,
And hope to provoke, thus, in the midst of our coiling darkness
The incandescence of the heart's great flare.

(BTD, pp. 194–95)

Brother to Dragons is as thoroughly philosophical a poem as any in the language, but as in all Warren's best work, 'the abstract, the general, the universal is always related forcibly, even violently to the concrete, the particular, the local.'[23] Warren keeps the reader in the company of flesh and blood through his own participation in the poem—'Red-headed, freckled, lean, a little stooped' (BTD, p. 26)—and by embodying philosophical points in sharply appropriate imagery. On his first visit to the ruined Lewis place R.P.W.'s difficulty in penetrating the undergrowth of history and the ambiguities of the human heart is symbolised by the difficulty of the climb and Mr Boyle's scepticism:

. . . I did it too,
And just like Boyle had said, I was a fool,
A god-damned fool, and all that brush to fight.
Saw-vine and sassafras, love-vine, wild rose,
But the roses gone, and the tangled passion-vine,
And blackberry man-high and tangled like a dream,
And up the bluff, where cedar clambered rock,
The tall, hot gloom of oak and ironwood,
Canted and crazed but tall, and from their boughs
The great grapevine, a century old, hung in its jungle horror,
Swayed in its shagged and visceral delight,
Convolved from bough to bough, hawser and halyard,
Like rotten rigging of that foundered hill.

(BTD, p. 31)

R.P.W.'s account of this first visit is dominated by the appearance of a huge black snake, an early instance of what Victor H. Strandberg regards as 'the poem's master metaphor—the beast image.'[24] At first terrified as by a vision of archetypal evil, R.P.W. goes on to insist that 'the manifestation was only natural' (BTD, p. 34) and after the initial shock has worn off the snake seems:

. . . benevolent and sad and sage,
As though it understood our human pitifulness
And forgave all, and asked forgiveness, too.

(BTD, p. 35)

R.P.W.'s initial reaction to 'old *obsoleta*' establishes the snake also as an image that mirrors the human self. Morally neutral, a purely 'natural' creature, the snake evokes at first a response from R.P.W. in terms of the capacity for evil that is part of his moral nature as a man, but later it reflects the opposite human potentialities for benevolence, wisdom, pity. Equally, the catfish sleeps in its element of Mississippi water, 'at one with God'; it only shows 'the brute face . . . of the last torturer' (BTD, p. 94) to the subjectively creating eye of man who sees reflected in the catfish merely that aspect of his mixed being which the early Jefferson chose to ignore.

R.P.W.'s second visit to Rocky Hill emphasises the continuing relevance of the story. The issue is resolved, the communal nightmare over. The ghostly characters of the tale may now 'die' into peace and R.P.W. rejoins his father in the waiting car. We are back in a present which R.P.W. has expanded by his elucidation of the past which it contains.

III

Warren's least successful novels are *Band of Angels* and *Wilderness*, both 'historical' jobs. 'Fiction', he says, 'may be said to have two poles, history and idea, and the emphasis may be shifted very far in either direction' (SE, p. 168). The failure of *Band of Angels* is partly due to his shifting the emphasis too far towards the pole of history and partly to the technical inadequacy of his heroine. The problem is not merely that, as Charles H. Bohner puts it, so much 'attention has been lavished on the novel's interior decoration',[25] but that the passive Amantha is so easily overshadowed. 'At times', says Bohner, 'there is such a clutter of detail, such an insistence on background authenticity, that the reader may feel—as does the visitor to some widely heralded Historical Restoration—that the scene has everything but the breath of life.'[26] After such profusion, *Wilderness* is surprisingly compact, closer to the compressions of *Brother to Dragons* or *Audubon*; but this time Warren shifts the emphasis too far towards the pole of idea. The stages of Adam Rosenzweig's moral progress are clear enough, but they are seldom persuasively attached to his character or to the events that mark them.

As Warren says himself, both books are impaired by his failure to bring their protagonists alive (Appendix, pp. 253–54). In *Band of Angels* there is a persistent gap between Manty's reflections on herself and her character as revealed in action. She is, for example, 'incredibly articulate':[27] in the first few pages we are improbably given a bird calling in 'melancholy iteration', family portraits 'limned by the brush of a maestro', and a confession of 'infantile ineptitudes'. Until the book's final section boosts her reality as well as Tobias's, she has little substance. In *Wilderness*, as Warren concedes, 'You have the strange effect of a central hollowness with a rich context, with the central character as an observer, that is a *mere* observer. He's involved intellectually, but *only* intellectually. The story is never fleshed out in enough depth so that the world of context is related to his experience in the right way'. (Appendix, p. 254). *Wilderness* is an insecure combination of blatantly philosophical design and sketchily portrayed reality. The overall effect is of an attenuated mythic sub-story which has mutinied in a bid to become the novel of which it was intended to be only a part.[28]

Manty abruptly sounds the two main themes of her story on its first page: 'Oh, who am I? . . . If I could only be free' (BOA, p. 3), and the reader may be forgiven for thinking it too early for a heroine to be so summarily plunged into aria. It is rather as though, the curtain just up, Tosca or Brünnhilde were displayed at full throttle before the audience had been given time to settle itself or gain an inkling of what the fuss was about. To be sure, nearly all the main characters in the novel attempt to achieve identity and freedom during a period of American history which made these matters crucial for the generality of men. Manty's peristaltic effort ends in the low-keyed comedy of the novel's closing pages in which, after all the operatic clangour has died away, she and Tobias Sears truly meet at last and enter into the awful responsibilities of ordinary, prosaic living.

Her half-caste status means that Manty cannot define herself by identifying with either black or white. As Leslie Fiedler says, the abolitionist clichés of Oberlin are 'as useless to her in understanding the realities of slavery and being a Negro as are the opposite clichés of the Southern slave-holders.'[29] She can never bring herself to say, 'I am a Negro', and she knows she is not white; thus, like Faulkner's Joe Christmas, she is nothing in a category-oriented world. Fiedler says that she is equally incapable of declaring herself white.[30] This is not strictly true: she says 'I'm white', in order to dissociate herself from Rau-Ru (BOA, p. 332). In this context, however, whiteness is asserted as disguise rather than as self-definition. Manty evades the obligation to define herself, using a mechanistic view of history to the same purpose as Jack Burden uses his Great Twitch. As long as she believes that '. . . what you are is an expression

of History, and you do not live your life, but, somehow, your
life lives you, and you are, therefore, only what History does
to you' (BOA, p. 134), she can abrogate responsibility, blaming
others for what she does.

The others in question—in particular her father, Hamish
Bond and Tobias Sears—are made to feel that they have
wronged her and are, therefore, responsible for her. It is Manty's
pious attack on her father as slave-holder which leads to the
scene in the Cincinnati restaurant, but her father, out of his
general guilt towards her, apologises for the embarrassment she
feels when he defends her from 'the mean snicker of the un-
redeemed world' (BOA, p. 30) and the resulting sense of her own
failure. Manty remembers seizing the opportunity to transfer
all responsibility to her father: '. . . there came to me some hard
sense of an advantage just gained, not to be exploited yet but
held in reserve' (BOA, p. 32). While she is capable of positive
emotional action in making the most of such opportunities,
Manty is, basically, a negative character, habitually in flight.
Her inability to accept the legal freedom offered by Bond
expresses her dependence on him and her incapacity for self-
determination.

Manty is in flight from the problem indicated by the quotation from Housman which provides the book's epigraph. The
lines come from the last stanza of poem 28 in *A Shropshire Lad*,
'High the vanes of Shrewsbury gleam', a lament by a girl
forcibly begotten on her 'slave' mother by a conquering
Saxon:

When shall I be dead and rid
Of the wrong my father did?

It is the problem of origin again, familiar to us from 'Original
Sin: A Short Story', 'The Ballad of Billie Potts', the repudiations of Jerry Calhoun, Jason Sweetwater and Sue Murdock
and the vexed visits home of Jack Burden and Willie Stark.
Warren's answer, of course, is that one only begins to live
authentically by accepting the past and whatever wrong one's
father did. In Manty's past lies the fact that her father, loving
her, did her the wrong of never drawing up the manumission
papers that could have separated her from him. Her father

had thus left her undefined, free to create herself. Finally, she realises that 'Nobody can set you free . . . except yourself' (BOA, pp. 363–64).

None of the characters on whom Manty especially depends finds either freedom or the desired identity. Throughout his life Hamish Bond blames his parents and others for his ignominious career as a slave-trader: like Manty, he refuses the onus of self-determination. At his death he finds himself, ironically, 'ass-deep in niggers' (BOA, p. 324), as he had sardonically promised his mother he one day would. Rau-Ru's freedom leads nowhere. Seth Parton seeks absolute purity, but with theology abandoned for the stock market and married to the fleshly Miss Idell, ends on better terms with impurity. Tobias Sears, philosophically the most interesting of the supporting characters, does, surprisingly, achieve Warrenesque redemption, though not in a way he could have foreseen.

Demoralised by the war, Tobias concludes in despair that '. . . we undertook to do good in the world, but we had not purged our own soul' (BOA, p. 294). Focusing on his own soul, he reveals his egoism in poetry which dramatises himself 'dying always into the beauty of Idea, into the nobility of Truth, dying into the undefiled whiteness of some self-image' (BOA, p. 346). The indulgently idealistic tragic posture proclaims him sinner indeed in the Warren world. Manty recognises a fellow escape-artist. In Warren's proleptic west Tobias is reconstituted not in terms of the romantic ideal but of the 'Thingism' which he had previously condemned. The fervour of his materialism, however, is undercut by a sardonic realisation of the depths to which he has fallen. This protective yet demeaning self-satire defines him until the last section of the novel.

Some readers flinch from the comedy of the Josh Lounberry story, perhaps because it seems an afterthought, like the Willie Proudfit section of *Night Rider*, or because it reads more like an epilogue than the climax expected. John M. Bradbury, for example, has little enthusiam for it:

> The epilogue of rehabilitation, however, like that of Dostoevsky's *Crime and Punishment*, seems forced and gratuitous. Perhaps this is the inevitable fate of 'resolved' fiction in an unresolved world.

Logically we may accept the resolution, but humanly we cannot.[31]

This is hardly a matter susceptible to critical proof, and Bradbury's distinction between 'logical' and 'human' is obscure. The novel's scaling down from an operatic to a domestic level may lead the reader to feel that the last phase of the story is loosely tacked on to complete Warren's philosophical design. Yet, whatever Manty's deficiencies as narrator, there is no reason why we should question her selection of significant detail or the pace with which she conveys us from New Orleans westward to Halesburg, Kansas for the display of final meanings. The closing movement of *Band of Angels* is not only its most audacious section artistically, but the one part of the novel in which Warren closes the gap between image and idea.

After the melodrama that has gone before, we see Manty and Tobias in the 'commonness of the world' (WEAT, p. 355), fumbling towards a routine life together, unstimulated and unsupported by grand pains and postures. Warren is not devaluing their past struggles, but his shift to a minor key is a way of saying that it is in the quotidian world of prose and imperfection that ideas must live to prove their value. For the first time, in these closing pages, we are in the presence of two people relating openly to one another in credible direct speech. They are both done with evasions. If Tobias 'had been, long ago, the liberator, the bearer of freedom, and had risked his very life in heroism', Manty realises that 'he had not been involved in that community of weakness and rejection, he had merely leaned down from his height, had inclined his white hieratic head that glimmered like a statue' (BOA, p. 372). Drawn into involvement with Josh Lounberry and his father, Uncle Slop, Tobias's sensibility expands to accommodate both the sheer human values in the case and the comic irony of his being 'a Jehu to coons'. The idealist has come down from his height and feels better for it. Manty in her turn is freed from false images of herself through the agency of Mr Lounberry whose ability to honour the father who had rejected him brings home to her that her father had loved her. Accident certainly plays a considerable part in the development of Manty and Tobias, but they do, at last, earn the reality of themselves. *Band of Angels* is a flawed work of fiction, but it makes eloquent sense in its ending.

IV

In *Band of Angels* the shortcomings of his heroine do not prevent Warren from projecting the abundant world that contains her into credible orbit. In *Wilderness*, despite the given reality of its historical framework, the hollowness of Adam Rosenzweig and the distance between him and the events in which he is involved impart an abstract quality even to narrative and descriptive passages. Warren's power as a fabulist owes much to the clarity with which his characters are visualised. He is not, typically, the kind of novelist Henry James has in mind in the Preface to *The Portrait of a Lady* where, with crushing tolerance, he refers to 'the imaginative writer so constituted as to see his fable first and to make out its agents afterwards.' In *Wilderness*, however, the fable is too much with us and its agents remain dim.

In terms of psychology and theme, that is, of Adam's education in the real and illusory aspects of the new Eden, the vicious confusion of New York in Chapter 4 is a functional contrast to the ideal image of boy and dog seen from the *Elmyra*. As a projection of Adam's experience, however, the chapter is little more than a sketch. The derelict children, the old man at the Bavarian wayside shrine, the Negro hanging, a black Christ, from the lamp post and the mob that almost engulfs Adam in the draft riots of 1863 are as obviously contrived as the cardboard character of Aaron Blaustein. The impediment of Adam's foot becomes a wearisome symbol, although it can occasion affecting moments, like Mose Talbutt's shrewd, half-affectionate refusal to grant Adam the dignity of his archetypal name, calling him 'Slewfoot' instead (W, p. 92).

Warren's method in *Wilderness* replaces the operatic fullness of *World Enough and Time* or *Band of Angels* with an uneasy oscillation between a kind of realistic impressionism and Bunyanesque allegory. There is a rough correlation between Bunyan's Mr Legality and Adam's uncle, and an obvious parallel between the testing of Adam's faith in man and Bunyan's in God. Adam, like Christian, sees terrible sights, meets a selection of bad characters and is repeatedly tempted. After he has resisted the appeal of Aaron Blaustein, another of Warren's false fathers, he is tempted by Maran Meyerhof. She tempts his pride as well as his flesh and, more subtly, his human disposition to live naturally in the satisfactions of agrarian employment. For Adam to end his journey here would mean a loss of his defining humanness like Jeremiah Beaumont's relinquishing of himself in the 'blank cup of nature' (WEAT, p. 506). The temptations of pride and hypocrisy are central to Adam's evolving relationship to Mose Talbutt. In a development of the early blow to his idealism in his revulsion from the dead Negro in Chapter 4, Adam is repelled by Mose. His kindness to Mose is paternalism: morally as well as physically he is still 'Slew-foot'.

Occasionally Warren succeeds in infusing an imagined historical moment with reality as well as significance. In Chapter 15 Adam is drawn into the tawdry violence of the War and shoots a man not in the name of his abstract dream of freedom, but because of an immediately felt 'sharp access of moral repugnance' towards dirty fighting (W, p. 297). The reader is still aware of the author's philosophical designs, but the vicious ballet of the 'eight maniacal scarecrows' and the men in blue is so precisely rendered from the dazed and wondering Adam's point of view that meanings are firmly supported by the realism of the presentation.

Like Jefferson in *Brother to Dragons*, Adam learns that freedom depends on man's recognition of his own nature. Man must hold to the possibility of virtue while accepting his propensity for evil and the embroiling causalities of history. In his sadness and his hope Adam is freed at last from the beguiling but treacherously simple categories symbolised by the glittering white of the Zelzsteinberg and the blue-black of the Bavarian forest (W, p. 3). All this appears sentimental because Adam has never been made sufficiently real.[32] His final state of mind

I

is an imposition by the author instead of the earned evolution of a substantiated character.

It is, therefore, surprising to find as expert a reader as Charles H. Bohner praising *Wilderness* for its 'economy of means'.[33] Despite the overtones of Bunyan, the book lacks the resonance as well as the immediacy of Warren's best fictions and few of the characters are more than ciphers. Philosophically it reiterates the message of *Brother to Dragons*, but there is little in Adam Rosenzweig or in what Henry James would have called 'the concrete terms' of the novel to allay the reader's disappointment in Warren's failure to make another 'little myth' out of 'the big myth we live'.

Chapter Five—Notes

[1] Cowley, *Writers at Work*, p. 169.

[2] Letter to Frank Owsley, dated 31 Jan, 1950. *Papers of Frank Owsley*, Tennessee State Library and Archives.

[3] Cowley, p. 169.

[4] Fiedler, Leslie, 'Romance in the Operatic Manner,' *New Republic*, **133** (Sept, 1955) 28–30; rpt. in *No! in Thunder: Essays on Myth and Literature* (London: Eyre and Spottiswoode, 1963), pp. 131–33.

[5] Gill, Brendan, 'One Bourbon on the Rocks, One Gin and Tonic', *New Yorker*, **26** (24 June, 1950), 89.

[6] Fiedler, Leslie, 'On Two Frontiers', *Partisan Review*, **17** (Sept.–Oct., 1950), 742; rpt. in *No! in Thunder*, pp. 119–26.

[7] *Beauchamp's Trial, A Report of the Trial of Jereboam O. Beauchamp, before the Franklin Circuit Court, in May 1826, upon an Indictment for the Murder of Col. Solomon P. Sharp, a Member of the House of Representatives, and late Attorney General of Kentucky* (Albert G. Hodges: Frankfort, Ky, 1826).

[8] Cowley, p. 176.

[9] These are: *The Confession of Jereboam O. Beauchamp* (Bloomfield, Ky, 1826); *Letters of Ann Cook, Late Mrs Beauchamp, to her Friend in Maryland* (Washington, 1826); L. J. Sharp, *Vindication of the Character of the Late Col. Solomon P. Sharp, From the Calumnies Published against Him since his Murder, by Partick Darby and Jereboam O. Beauchamp* (Frankfort, Ky, 1827). The documents are collected in Loren J. Kallsen, ed., *The Kentucky Tragedy, A Problem in Romantic Attitudes* (Indianapolis: The Bobbs-Merrill Co., Inc., 1963).

[10] Kallsen, p. 6.

[11] Kallsen, p. 7.

[12] Kallsen, p. 148.

[13] Kallsen, pp. 8–9.

[14] Kallsen, p. 21.

[15] Campbell, Harry M., 'Warren as Philosopher', in *World Enough and Time, Hopkins Review*, **6** (Winter, 1953), 114. Repr. in *Southern Renascence: The Literature of the Modern South*, ed. Louis D. Rubin Jr., and Robert D. Jacobs (Baltimore: Johns Hopkins Press, 1953), p. 253.

[16] Beatty, Richmond C., 'The Poetry and Novels of Robert Penn Warren', in *Vanderbilt Studies in the Humanities*, **I**, ed. R. C. Beatty, J. P. Hyatt and Monroe K. Spears (Nashville: Vanderbilt University Press, 1951), p. 157.

[17] Merrill, Jr, Boynton, *Jefferson's Nephews: A Frontier Tragedy* (Princeton: Princeton University Press, 1977), pp. 256–265; 329–335.

[18] McDowell, Frederick P. W., 'Psychology and Theme' in *Brother to Dragons*, *PMLA*, **70** (Sept, 1955), 565. Repr. Longley, p. 197.

[19] Jarrell, Randall, 'On the Underside of the Stone', *New York Times Book Review*, **23** Aug, 1953, p. 6.

[20] Bohner, p. 127.

[21] Schwartz, Delmore, 'The Dragon of Guilt', *New Republic*, (14 Sept, 1953), p. 15.

[22] 'Notes on Action and Stage' for a projected dramatic version of the poem, in an unpublished MS given to the writer by Mr Warren.

[23] McDowell, 'Psychology and Theme', Longley, p. 197.

[24] Strandberg, p. 140. In his determination to stress the theme of the unconscious self Strandberg stops short of noticing what the various beast images in the poem imply about the nature of that self as revealed in particular acts of perception.

[25] Bohner, p. 128.

[26] *Ibid.*

[27] Martin, Terence, '*Band of Angels:* The Definition of Self-Definition', *Folio*, **21** (Winter, 1956), 31.

[28] Charles Thomas Samuels has characterised the book along similar lines. See, 'In the Wilderness', *Critique: Studies in Modern Fiction*, **5** (Fall, 1962), 46–57.

[29] Fiedler, Leslie, *Love and Death in the American Novel*, second edition (London: Jonathan Cape, 1967), p. 411.

[30] Fiedler, p. 411.

[31] Bradbury, John M., *The Fugitives*, p. 228.

[32] Samuels, Charles Thomas, 'In the Wilderness', p. 56.

[33] Bohner, p. 158.

The Human Bond and a New Sense of Poetry

All the King's Men gained Warren his first Pulitzer Prize in 1947. He won his second in 1958 with *Promises: Poems, 1954–1956*, his first book of poems since *Selected Poems, 1923–1943*. *Promises* was also awarded the Edna St Vincent Millay Prize of the Poetry Society of America and the National Book Award. James Dickey hailed the book vigorously: 'When he is good, and often when he is bad, you had as soon read Warren as live.'[1] Warren says that during the years between the first *Selected Poems* and the new book he found himself unable to finish a short poem: 'I wrote, started many over that period of years. I never finished one . . . I'd write five lines, ten lines, twenty lines—it would die on me' (Appendix, p. 255). The personal quality of the poems in *Promises* suggests that the 'whole new sense of poetry' that came to him some time after he had finished *Brother to Dragons* was directly connected with his divorce from Emma Brescia in 1951, his marriage to Eleanor Clark in 1952 and the birth of their two children, Rosanna and Gabriel. In 1954, when Rosanna was one year old, the Warrens spent the summer at Port Ercole on the Italian coast about a hundred miles north of Rome. The experience revitalised Warren's lyric gift: 'the place and the events all tie together in the sense of a new way into poetry' (Appendix, p. 255).

'To a Little Girl, One Year Old, in a Ruined Fortress'

consists of five poems centred on Rosanna with her parents at
Port Ercole. The old fortification, 'Rocca: fortress, hawk-heel,
lion paw, clamped on a hill', and the nearby hunchback with
his deformed child symbolise the spent civilisation of the
Old World, 'the malfeasance of nature' and 'the filth of fate'.
Juxtaposed with these images is the innocent, golden-haired
Rosanna, emblem of renewal and promise. In 'Sirocco' (SP,
p. 219) the poet contemplates the incongrouous mixture of
images which he has himself created by introducing his
daughter to such a place. The opening lines' tone of wonder at
the juxtaposition he has made—'To a place of ruined stone we
brought you, and sea-reaches'—is sustained throughout the
poem, pointed by the repetition, 'We have brought you'. Like
the poet himself, the reader will look beneath the surface of the
images to find their inner relations, but the poem's keynote is
its wonder and the heart-ache which the imagery evokes in the
poet and which reminds us of the impact of natural beauty
on Adam Rosenzweig in the opening pages of *Wilderness* or of
Jeremiah Beaumont's delight in the beech tree. In this first
of the five poems Warren is content to allow the scene to
vibrate in his imagination without intellectually probing his
apprehension of it. His feelings deepen in the second and third
poems while intellect gradually takes hold of the data brought
to it by intuitive perception. In the fourth and fifth poems of
the sequence the poet achieves understanding of his experience
through the revelation of meaning in his daughter's pleasure in
her flower and, finally, as he surveys the landscape from a
shaded enclave of rock high on the mountain.

Animated by the sirocco, the images of the first poem do, of
course, suggest a typically Warrenesque world of oppositions
and ironies. The innocent girl is a foil to the world of experience
symbolised by the fortress with its implications of vanished
power and of the enduring realities of a world in which might
is right and ideals must be defended by calculated force. The
realistic principle endures just as the 'geometry of a military
rigour' survives 'as a reminder of the Spaniard's most fastidious
mathematic and skill', although Philip's world is now ruined.
Ironically, although he loved God, espousing the right dream
for his epoch, he did not prosper while living and now, like

Ozymandias' shattered visage, his scutcheon lies broken and derelict. Is this what life promises? Are we to look on Philip's works and despair? Is the innocent laughter of the little girl mocked by this tale of time? We can see that these are the questions posed by the poem, although the poet is so struck by the objects of his apprehension that he does not himself move from contemplation to deliberate analysis until later in the sequence. It is the intensity of feeling conveyed by the poem's imagery that makes the answers to these questions moving and substantial instead of merely banal.

The garbage under which the arrogance of *'Philipus me fecit'* has for so long lain buried is countered by the beauty of 'rosemary with blue, thistle with gold bloom.' It is human to desire perfection—a world without garbage: 'Far hangs Giannutri in blue air. Far to that blueness the heart aches' in yearning for the absolute image that transcends the opposed poles of ruin and natural beauty. The pleasure in such beauty and the heart-ache itself are alternatives to despair. The sun's regilding of the girl's hair aligns her with the natural gold of the thistle and her beautiful innocence is therefore included in the *sic transit gloria* of the last line: 'And on the exposed approaches the last gold of gorse bloom, in the sirocco, shakes.' Here the sirocco symbolises time, to whose operation bloom and girl are as subject as the works of the anguished Philip. Yet the bloom will return with the next season, the girl will survive this sirocco, it is still remembered that Philip loved God and his ruin endures as a token of his earthly effort.

In the second and third poems of the sequence the poet finds that a view of the world based on his joy in his daughter is severely threatened by the dark side of life. If the sirocco represents time in the first poem, it also imparts the breath of life to the scene, but in 'Gull's Cry' (SP, p. 220) a static scene is dominated by the goat droppings that await the prospecting beetle, by the motionless gull, and the *gobbo's* wife, mother of the defective child, sunk in her suffering. The immobility of most of the elements in the scene suggests a world fixed on a plane of unmeaning naturalism, like the gull stuck on its shelf of air. There is activity beneath the surface of things, but it is only the 'molecular dance'. Victor H. Strandberg explains the

meaning of the gull image by referring to the description of
another gull in the ninth poem of 'Promises', the volume's
second sequence: 'And agleam in imperial ease, at sky-height, /
One gull hangs white in contempt of our human heart, and the
night' (SP, p. 244).[2] Freedom of flight and 'outcry' against the
night, if not contempt for it, do partly characterise the gull in
the closing lines of 'The Flower' (SP, p. 224). but Strandberg's
determination to find consistent patterns of imagery in
Promises leads him into the error of confining this image to a
single meaning. In 'Gull's Cry' the bird is merely seen as another
creature subject to naturalistic limitations. 'The gull, at an
eye-blink, will, into the astonishing statement of sun, pass',
but this deprives the gull of expected grace, converting its
flight into the mechanistic behaviour of the human eye which
one moment sees the bird and the next does not. The gull's
struggle to achieve freedom of flight symbolises the poet's
desire to rise above the naturalistic level, but its efforts in the
'anguish of air'—by which phrase Warren implies that the
bird's very element of existence is its torment—are 'irrelevant'
because they are futile.[3] It is the quality of life under the sun
which makes its 'statement' appear 'astonishing'. Strandberg
is reminded of the 'gaze blank and pitiless as the sun' attributed
by Yeats to his 'vast image' in 'The Second Coming': 'This
seems to be a naturalistic sun, which carelessly brought forth
life—such as the beetle, the goat, the hunchback and the
defective child—and which presides with mechanical indifference over the dissolution under its reign.'[4] Warren's point,
however, is that the sun presides with mechanical impartiality
over *everything*, from goat, beetle, gull and defective child to
the poet and his daughter. Natural creatures and oppressed
humans toil and suffer, but the girl's laughter and the poet's
joy in her are real too, implying possibilities unrealised by the
other constituents of the scene. Awareness of such possibilities
carries the obligation to assert a view of life as meaningful after
all, and the girl's laughter becomes an affirming cry answering
the frustrated cry of the gull and bringing 'all' into unity:

> But at your laughter let the molecular dance of the stone-dark
>   glimmer like joy in the stone's dream,

And in that moment of possibility, let *gobbo, gobbo's* wife,
and us, and all, take hands and sing: *redeem, redeem*!

If the reader is inclined to judge the concluding affirmation of
'Gull's Cry' facile, that is precisely the charge the poet himself
levels at it by focusing on the most recalcitrant example of
nature's 'malfeasance' in 'The Child Next Door' (SP, pp. 220–
21). His seizure of something close to hatred[5] towards the
defective child's sister is a momentary recoil from her inadequate perspective:

> . . . Fool, doesn't she know that the process
> Is not that joyous or simple, to bless, or unbless,
> The malfeasance of nature or the filth of fate?

If the sister's 'pure love, calm eyes' and saintly patience strike
him as offensively innocent in a world that includes such
monstrosity, must he not abandon the affirmation of 'Gull's
Cry' as an even more culpable instance of wilful innocence in
himself? It is at this point in the sequence that the poet
consciously brings his intellect to bear on the matters which
have been working so powerfully on his feelings. His questions,
however, instruct him in the need for faith:

> Can it bind or loose, that beauty in that kind,
> Beauty of benediction? We must trust our hope to prevail
> That heart-joy in beauty be wisdom, before beauty fail
> And be gathered like air in the ruck of the world's wind!

The poet's question here is somewhat obscure—a slight blemish
on an almost perfect poem. He appears to ask whether the
sister's 'beauty of benediction' can hold us all together in joy—
as the 'all' of 'Gull's Cry' are imagined holding hands and
singing—or whether such beauty can 'loose' or liberate us from
a mordant view of life based on the tragedy of the defective
child. His answer is that 'our hope to prevail', as much a fact of
human experience as 'this monstrous other', demands that we
believe in the cognitive value of the joy which underlies the
sister's attitude to life and which the poet knows himself
through the 'goldness' of his daughter. The determined affirmation of 'Gull's Cry' is tempered to a more reflective, balanced
vision of the world as the poet thinks not only of his daughter—

at once foil to the defective child and an extension of the beautiful sister—but also of the dissolutions wrought by time and the mysterious chaos of the universe, 'how empires grind, stars are hurled'.

Now, with an effort, the poet can respond to the '*ciao*' of the defective child, which is both a sign that he recognises a connection between the child and himself and an acceptance of the attitude of the sister because it is she who has taught the child to make the greeting. 'We're all one Flesh, at last', we are told in 'Go it, Granny—Go it, Hog!' (SP, p. 262), and the poet's response to the child's greeting shows his awareness of how we are indeed bound together in joy and in limitation. Strandberg is at his most perceptive in his interpretation of the last lines of this poem:

> It is a brilliant touch on Warren's part to indicate by the simple repetition of the child's greeting a major shift in the narrator's perspective, from an external attitude of pity to an internalized identification of the narrator with the defective child. This is the culmination of the ritual of brotherhood. In the ultimate view of things, considered from a spiritual perspective, the child and the narrator are one: both are tragically defective through an inadequate inheritance, both communicate only imperfectly, both are bounded by insuperable limitations and subject to the caprices of the 'world's wind'.[6]

Warren is not specifically concerned with the adequacy or otherwise of his inheritance until 'Promises', the volume's second sequence of poems, and he would almost certainly dislike Strandberg's tendency to reduce the defective child from a real 'monster' in 'that purlieu of dirt' to a pre-emptively symbolic rôle. In *Incarnations*, the seventh poem of the sequence called 'Internal Injuries' announces, 'The world / Is a parable and we are / The meaning' (SP, p. 133), but the title of the sequence indicates that to hold such a view is to be metaphysically wounded. Warren's world constantly denies the proposition that 'only Nothingness is real' (SP, p. 133). His landscapes seldom function in the way of the *paysage moralizé*[7] W. H. Auden defines as a confected 'inner space of private ownership'.[8] 'The Child Next Door' ends with the statement, '*This is the world'*, just as the boy in 'Court-Martial' concludes his memoir with the insistence, 'The world is real. It is there' (SP, p. 232). Nevertheless, Strandberg's comment points the degree to which the process of the Rosanna sequence has now become intellectual as well as emotional. In the fourth poem the image of the flower is used like a metaphysical conceit and the fifth is openly concerned with the problem of interpretation.

'The Flower' (SP, pp. 221–24) is the sequence's least successful poem not because of 'the rambling, inconclusive organisation and thinking' which John L. Stewart finds in it—organisation and thought are kept in shape by the poet's focus on his daughter and her daily flower—but because Warren seems unable to achieve the sustained tautness of expression that characterises the first three poems. The reason would appear to be largely technical: whether rhymed or not, the short line needs more thrust or wit than this.[9] Warren displays these qualities in 'Court-Martial', 'Dark Night of the Soul', in much of the verse of *Incarnations* and in the 'Interjections' that break into the sequence of *Or Else*, but the short lines of 'The Flower' are at odds with the poem's uneasy combination of narrative and meditation. The statements are often flat and monotonous, the movement jerky, the rhymes limp as in the third section, in which the poet tells how he carries his daughter up the hill to her favourite spot:

> We approach your special place,
> And I am watching your face
> To see the sweet puzzlement grow,
> And then recognition glow.
> Recognition explodes in delight.
> You leap like spray, or like light.
> Despite my arm's tightness,
> You leap in gold-glitter and brightness.
> You leap like a fish-flash in bright air,
> And reach out. Yes, I'm well aware
> That this is the spot, and hour,
> For you to demand your flower.

Warren recovers grip of his medium in the longer, richer lines of the poem which ends the sequence. If the girl's leap of joy in the above lines is unpersuasive, a similar moment is beautifully rendered in stanzas four to six of 'Colder Fire' (SP, p. 225). Here the poet not only speaks of his daughter's delight in the butterflies but compactly associates her beauty and innocence with their fragility, their shortness of flight and the transience of ecstasy:

> You leap on my knee, you exclaim at the sun-stung gyration.
> And the upper stirs, as though the vast stillness of sky
> Had stirred in its sunlit sleep and made suspiration,
> A luxurious languor of breath, as after love, there is a sigh.
> But enough, for the highest sun-scintillant pair are gone
> Seaward, past rampart and cliff borne, over blue sea-gleam.
> Close to my chair, to a thistle, a butterfly sinks now, flight done.
> By the gold bloom of thistle, white wings pulse under the sky's
> dream.

With the waning of the season in 'The Flower' the day comes when there is no bloom 'worthily white' for the poet's daughter. Her pleasure in a 'ruined' flower prompts the poet to rise above his own need for perfection and to accept the flux and change of the world, seeing, rather sentimentally, in the image of his daughter and her flower an intimation of the transcendent unity of life:

> Yes, in that image let
> Both past and future forget,
> In clasped communal ease,
> Their brute identities.

Charles H. Bohner's evaluation of 'The Flower' as 'the finest poem of the series' appears to be based on the fact that the above lines express 'the controlling idea' of the volume,[10] but a strong theme—even when it is restated elsewhere—does not necessarily make a strong poem. The same 'controlling idea' of the unity of life emerges much more dramatically at the end of 'Gull's Cry', becomes more movingly explicit in 'The Child Next Door' and grows again out of the particularities of experience in 'Colder Fire' to ring out in the climax of this flawed but impressive sequence.

At the beginning of 'Colder Fire' (SP, pp. 225–26) the poet admits that the despondency induced in his wife and himself

by 'defection of season' is wrong. Man should not be so affected
by mere nature. As he pulls out of his mood he realises that
nature affords not only butterflies for his daughter and himself
to delight in but also an analogy between the delicate, ephe-
meral vitality of the butterflies and his daughter's mortality.
As it is the butterflies' nature to mount light, 'As though that
tall light were eternal indeed, not merely the summer's re-
prieve', so it is incumbent on man to seek to rise above his
earthbound state, and the poet raises his eyes to the mountain,
remembering the place where he and his wife experienced a
transcendent sense of things. The effort involved in the ascent
of the spirit to a point of adequate perspective is dramatised by
the catalogue of mountain paths, terraces, trees and scarps.
The 'deep recess . . . benched and withdrawn in the mountain-
mass' expresses once again Warren's definition of man as both
a natural and idealising being, for here the poet and his wife
were embedded in the nature of rock and tree and at the same
time above nature as they looked out over sea and land.
Warren then skilfully encloses his point of vantage and its
implications within two natural images which suggest the
relation of beauty to evanescence, fulfilment to mortality:
close by him the 'time-tattered butterflies' still dance, though
now 'disarrayed', no longer in formation 'pair by pair', and
on the branches of the pines in his remembered enclave of rock
'Condensed moisture gathers at a needle-tip. It glitters, will
fall.' The poet's acceptance of the life cycle of a butterfly, even
of a bead of condensation's, is a sign of that transcendent
awareness of the nature of the world which is the 'colder fire'
within which particular joys may flame.

Addressing his daughter in the second last stanza, the poet
admits the limiting subjectivity of his language and his vision.
It is an Eliotesque gambit, like saying, 'That was a way of
putting it—not very satisfactory', as Eliot does in Part Two of
'East Coker', before he authoritatively looses his images and
ideas on the reader. Warren recognises that his daughter will
create the language appropriate to defining the experience
that will be uniquely hers, just as he has used here the language
appropriate to his experience and to the truth he sees. Thus the
poet tactfully concedes the personal quality of his own lan-

guage before the last stanza in which, with absolute conviction, he defines the meaning to which he has been led by the experience recounted in the poem:

> For fire flames but in the heart of a colder fire.
> All voice is but echo caught from a soundless voice.
> Height is not deprivation of valley, nor defect of desire,
> But defines, for the fortunate, that joy in which all joys
> > should rejoice.

Thus Warren ends the poem with a statement of what Bohner regards as the sequence's 'controlling idea', the unity of life, elaborating that idea into an assertion of the need for a comprehensiveness of vision that embraces all opposing categories of experience and value, both height and valley, defect of desire as well as desire itself. It is Warren's way of saying what Melville tells us in the whiteness of his whale. (See Appendix, pp. 247–48).

With the exception of 'The Flower', the first sequence of *Promises* is equal to the best of Warren's poetry. It demands the kind of close reading required by 'Kentucky Mountain Farm', and *Eleven Poems on the Same Theme*. The most successful poems in the longer sequence dedicated to Gabriel are of a different kind, more open, usually narrower in focus and in many cases employing the method of verse narrative so effectively used in 'The Ballad of Billie Potts'. Some of the poems, such as 'Foreign Shore, Old Woman, Slaughter of Octopus', 'Moonlight observed from Ruined Fortress' and 'Mad Young Aristocrat on Beach' have Italian settings linking them to the first sequence, but most are set in the South of the poet's youth. The real connection between the Italian context and the Southern characters and images that populate most of the poems is established in 'Lullaby: Moonlight Lingers' (SP, pp. 255–56). Watching his son sleeping, surrounded by the moonlit Italian landscape, the poet remembers an image from his own past:

> Now I close my eyes and see
> Moonlight white on a certain tree.
> It was a big white oak near a door

Familiar, long back, to me,
But now years unseen, and my foot enters there no more.

Contemplating his son and speculating on the nature of the world in which the boy will pass to 'high pride of unillusioned manhood' (SP, p. 249), the poet feels a need to define the world of his own youth, the types and symbols which instructed him in his maturing. The underlying reason for this need is a sense of the continuity of life: 'Moonlight falls on sleeping faces. / It fell in far times and other places' (SP, p. 256). The 'other places' include a recognisable, just slightly poeticised Guthrie, Kentucky, which the poet revisits in 'Walk by Moonlight in Small Town' (SP, pp. 253–54). Here 'each street and building holds some memory, some scrap of the past; and the poet yearns to know their meaning, to realise an ideal forever beyond the human world of imperfection.'[11]

Might a man but know his Truth, and might
He live so that life, by moon or sun,
In dusk or dawn, would be all one—
Then never on a summer night
Need he stand and shake in that cold blaze of Platonic light.

What the poet yearns for is, as Cleanth Brooks observes, strictly impossible: 'Man can never know his truth so thoroughly that he will not need to shake in the cold blaze of the light of the idea.'[12] Man must, however, keep on trying, and in this sequence of poems the human bond and the continuity of life are the truths which the poet finds especially crucial to his own vision and which he therefore wishes to pass on to his son.

The last of the sequence's three 'Lullabies' suggests that, as water 'moves under starlight, / Before it finds that dark of its own deepest knowledge' (SP, p. 268), so his son will find his deepest knowledge in sleep. This idea, part Freudian, part fanciful, helps us to understand what the poet means when he says in 'Lullaby: Smile in Sleep' that the boy 'dreams Reality' (SP, p. 252). There is an assertive sentimentality about all this, but the statement that 'all that flows finds end but in its own source' (SP, p. 268) has significance for the whole sequence. The source of all that flows in the boy is not only the poet himself, but also the poet's parents, the Ruth and Robert of the first poem, his grandfather—unwitting agent of revelation in 'Court-Martial'—the ghostly 'field full of folk' which the poet imagines behind him in the first part of 'Dark Woods' (SP, p. 234) and all the idealistic, studious, lusty, materialistic and pioneering men of 'Founding Fathers, Nineteenth-Century Style, Southeast U.S.A.': 'For we are their children in the light of humanness, and under the shadow of God's closing hand' (SP, p. 243).

The 'you' of 'What Was the Promise that Smiled from the Maples at Evening?' is the boyhood self of the poet who remembers his impulsive retreat into the darkness away from the love and security proffered by his parents. The poet assures his son that the men and women of the past died for the purpose expressed in the last line: 'We died only that every promise might be fulfilled' (SP, p. 228). The fulfilment available to any age involves the passing of the preceding one and the boy's withdrawal from what his parents can provide is a natural recoil which foreshadows the image in the first part of 'Infant Boy at Midcentury' of the 'rosy heel' of the poet's son learning 'to spurn / Us, and our works and days' (SP, p. 249). Just as the mature poet has developed a tender respect for his parents— 'their bones in a phosphorous of glory agleam, there they lay' (SP, p. 228)—and an appreciation of the relevance of their earthly effort, so he speaks to his son of the continuity of the human condition, suggesting he remember, as he advances into his 'fair time', that 'many among us wish you well' (SP, p. 250). There will be 'modification of landscape', but it is realism, not envy of the opportunities lying open to the young, to suggest that 'The new age will need the old lies' as it strives in the continuing process of 'accommodating flesh to idea' (SP, p. 250). The poet has, after all, been reminded in 'Foreign Shore, Old Woman, Slaughter of Octopus' of the continuity of the human heart, 'that what came will recur' (SP, p. 244). If the verse of the first part of 'Infant Boy at Midcentury' is forced, even raucous, the second and third parts impress by precision of thought and quiet-toned expression. This is sentiment as distinct from the sentimentality of the 'Lullabies'. These poems expand the idea of life's connections beyond the scope of the family's generations and in 'Mad Young Aristocrat on Beach' (SP, pp. 257–58) Warren reminds us once more that the unity of life is broader than the chronological line. The poet recognises a common human predicament in the figure of the young man, maddened by his memories and disappointments. Therefore:

> We should love him, because his flesh suffers for you and for me,
> As our own flesh should suffer for him, and for all
> Who will never come to the title, and be loved for themselves, at innocent nightfall.

If this is cumbersome writing, the poem does achieve a cumulative effect, engaging our interest in the strange young man so that we follow his tormented fluctuations of mood until Warren's concluding point is upon us. The point itself echoes the poet's recognition of the bond between himself and the defective child in 'The Child Next Door' and anticipates many of the poems of *Incarnations* as well as the first of its epigraphs: 'Yet now our flesh is as the flesh of our brethren (Nehemiah, 5:5).

Recalling his discovery in 1954 of a new feeling for poetry, Warren says: 'The narrative sense began to enter the short poem . . . as a germ, that is' (Appendix, p. 255). Warren's rhetoric usually benefits from the restraints imposed by the need to keep even a slight story going. The exception in 'Promises' is 'Dark Night of the Soul' (SP, pp. 245–48), a variation of the story told in 'Blackberry Winter'. The poem tells its tale skilfully, developing the situation to the point at which the tramp looks up into the boy's face to be held, Donne-like, by 'the single thread / Of the human entrapment' (SP, p. 247). The tramp jerks away and the boy, now a man, follows him in imagination to the moment of the old man's asserted illumination. This strikes the reader as presumptuous because no reason is given, or is even deducible, for the joy which we are told the tramp finds. It is another instance of sentimentality. No such charge can be made against 'Court-Martial' (SP, pp. 228–32) in which Warren develops the relationship between a boy and his grandfather further than he had taken it in 'When the Light Gets Green', dramatising the boy's awakening to violence and guilt. Manoeuvring his toy soldiers through reproductions of the campaigns described by the old man, the boy idealistically undertakes 'to repair / The mistakes of his old war' (SP, p. 229). As he plays, he elicits from his grandfather an account of the summary lynching of bushwhackers during the Civil War: '*Brevitatem justitia amat.* / Time is short—hell, a rope is—that's that' (SP, p. 230). The boy passes judgement on his grandfather and Warren describes exactly how the old man's savour of his memories turns for a moment, as he feels the boy's eyes on him, into an involuntary pang of conscience under cover of protest:

'By God—' and he jerked up his head.
'By God, they deserved it,' he said.
'Don't look at me that way,' he said.
'By God—' and the old eyes glared red.
Then shut in the cedar shade.

The old man falls asleep and the boy is left with 'ruined lawn' and 'raw house' in a real, fallen world, no longer populated by toy soldiers or by the ideals for which his grandfather stood before the afternoon's revelation.

'Country Burying' (SP, pp. 237–38) contrasts the poet's youthful and mature responses to the locale of his boyhood. Taking his mother to town to bury an acquaintance whose name he does not even bother to ask was merely the loss of 'a boy's afternoon', but life away from the familiar things of his childhood has taught him a need for the place that formed his 'centre.' He imagines himself returning to enter the little white church whose stillness is broken by the buzzing of a fly. The italicised last line indicates that there is a real fly buzzing in the present from which the poet looks back on his small town: '*Why doesn't that fly stop buzzing—stop buzzing up there?*' (SP, p. 238). The poet's irritation with the fly neatly points the new reverence he feels for his place of origin and his need to contemplate its meaning.

There are three shockers among the verse narratives: 'School Lesson Based on Word of Tragic Death of Entire Gillum Family', 'Dragon Country: To Jacob Boehme', and 'Ballad of a Sweet Dream of Peace'. The 'Ballad' (SP, pp. 260–64),

K

hyperbolically admired by Strandberg for displaying 'all the visionary power that poetry is capable of',[13] is the most ambitious but the least succesful of these. John L. Stewart dismisses it as 'a queer sequence of nightmares of sexual fear and guilt.'[14] Broader concerns are discernible through the irritating opacities of the poem: a basic allegory offers the figure of Granny as representative of the human condition, the Purchaser of Part Seven as God and the hogs as devouring time itself whose remorseless appetite has us all lined up for consumption however we may protest. The poem's superficial brilliance does not, however, compensate for its mixture of crude effects and sheer obliquity. Both 'School Lesson' and 'Dragon Country' succeed him much better in using a colloquial manner to express by way of violent action the natural and supernatural mystery of life. Warren describes the uncouth Gillums in 'the real language of men' as spoken in rural Kentucky:

> In town, Gillum stopped you, he'd say: 'Say, mister,
>   I'll name you what's true fer folks, ever-one.
> Human-man ain't much more'n a big blood blister.
>   All red and proud-swole, but one good squeeze and he's gone.
> 'Take me, ain't wuth lead and powder to perish,
>   Just some spindle bone stuck in a pair of pants,
> But a man's got his chaps to love and to cherish,
>   And raise up and larn 'em so they kin git their chance.'
>
> (SP, p. 239)

There is no way of knowing why Old Gillum turns from cherishing to mayhem; his homespun certainties contrast with the riddle he bequeaths to his children's classmates who are left 'studying the arithmetic of losses'—the facts of the event—but are too young to take up 'the lesson of the sudden madness there is in things.'[15] The poet himself takes up the lesson in the fable of 'Dragon Country: To Jacob Boehme' (SP, pp. 258–60) in which a dragon has appeared to lay waste the state of Kentucky. The people are not prepared to accept the presence of mystery in their lives: when a man inexplicably disappears, his family pretends that he has 'gone to Akron, or up to Ford, in Detroit', and Jebb Johnson's mother refuses to identify what is left of a leg inside his boot as the remains of her son. But the poem's biggest surprise is kept until the last two stanzas in which the poet expresses contempt for the efforts of religion to deal with the danger that terrorises the land and even suggests that 'the Beast' is somehow necessary:

> But if the Beast were withdrawn now, life might dwindle again
> To the ennui, the pleasure, and the night sweat, known in the time before
> Necessity of truth had trodden the land, and our hearts, to pain,
> And left, in darkness, the fearful glimmer of joy, like a spoor.

Warren's addressing his poem to Jacob Boehme prepares us for a connection between it and Boehme's philosophy of the world as involving two opposing principles, good and evil, light and darkness, both of which are aspects of God. A reading of the last stanza in terms of Boehme's belief in the necessity of antithesis might lead the reader to conclude that Warren is celebrating evil as the necessary counterpart of good. Warren's point, however, as Cleanth Brooks defines it, offers not a mere echo of Boehme's philosophy but a subtle and humane variation of it for which we have been prepared by the lesson of *Brother to Dragons*. "The 'joy' of which a 'fearful glimmer' glows in the last line comes not from evil as such but from an acceptance of the 'necessity of truth'. If one admits the element of horror in life, if he concedes the necessary mystery, if he faces the terrifying truth about it, if he admits the existence of the dragon of evil, that very facing of the truth constitutes the promise—and the only promise—of ultimate joy."[16]

George P. Garrett sees *Promises* as belonging to 'what might be called the grand tradition of southern writing'. The ingredients of this tradition include: 'a love of the land . . . a sense of its history, a strong bond of family, a sense of humour . . . and a way with language.'[17] Warren's love of the land and the people of the South inspires, for example, 'Country Burying', 'School Lesson', 'Walk by Moonlight in Small Town' and the short sequence, 'Boy's Will, Joyful Labour Without Pay, and Harvest Home (1918)'. There is great love of region behind the accuracy with which he records the exact quality of light when the storm gathers in the third stanza of 'Summer

Storm (Circa 1916) and, God's Grace' (SP, pp. 240–41) and a tender respect for the objects that belong to the region's way of life vivifies the description of the end of a working day on the farm in 'Hands are Paid':

> The springs of the bed creak now, and settle.
> The overalls hang on the back of a chair
> To stiffen, slow, as the sweat gets drier.
> Far, under a cedar, the tractor's metal
> Surrenders last heat to the night air.
> In the cedar dark a white moth drifts.
> The mule's head, at the barn-lot bar,
> Droops sad and saurian under night's splendour.
> In the star-pale field, the propped pitchfork lifts
> Its burden, hung black, to the white star.
>
> (SP, p. 267)

In the first edition of *Promises* this poem is followed by the third 'Lullaby' to the poet's son, then by a cryptic final poem called 'The Necessity for Belief' which Warren omitted both from *Selected Poems: New and Old. 1923–1966* and from *Selected Poems, 1923–1975*:

> The sun is red, and the sky does not scream.
> The sun is red, and the sky does not scream.
> There is much that is scarcely to be believed.
> The moon is in the sky, and there is no weeping.
> The moon is in the sky, and there is no weeping.
> Much is told that is scarcely to be believed.
>
> (*Promises*, p. 84)

Warren's dropping 'The Necessity of Belief' from the later collections is consistent with his insistence on the earned vision. One can imagine his reproaching himself with the thought that, while there might be 'no weeping' for him at the moment in which he conceived the poem, the defective child lived on in Port Ercole and terrible things were still happening in Kentucky. But the concluding juxtaposition of pieces in the original edition is suggestive, for one feels that the spirit of hope in this outstanding volume arises from a new delight drawn from the simplest of things as well as from the challenging joys of fatherhood.

II

You, Emperors, and Others: Poems, 1957–1960 takes its title poem from the book's two opening groups of poems, the first addressed to 'You', the second dealing with Roman emperors. The latter group proclaims no mere antiquarian interest, however, as 'Apology for Domitian' (SP, pp. 199–200) makes plain: 'Let's stop horsing around—it's not Domitian, it's you / We mean.' In 'The Letter About Money, Love or Other Comfort, if Any' (SP, pp. 192–95) the speaker confesses to 'a passion, like a disease, for Truth' and in the poems of this volume the search for truth often focuses on the problem of identity.

'The Letter About Money' tells of a mysterious stanger who gives the speaker in his youth a letter to be delivered 'by hand only' to another stranger, the 'you' of the poem. Pursuing the addressee across the world, the speaker finally leaves the letter under a pile of stones near the supposed retreat of the 'you', who appears to have been hunted 'to the upper altitudes' to live as an outcast from society, 'for you are said to be capable now of all bestiality, and only your age / makes you less dangerous.' Like the nightmare figure of 'Original Sin: A Short Story', the stranger to whom the letter must be delivered is invested with pitiful and repellent characteristics, yet the mysterious commission must be discharged. The speaker's concluding hope for a vision of truth and his 'peace with God' evidently depends on his keeping faith with the shadowy stranger. The final implication of the poem, which makes it a variation on the theme common to 'Original Sin', 'Pursuit' and 'Crime', is that the speaker has been charged to track his own deeper self. His 'metaphysical runaround' is a journey into the mirror of 'Clearly About You' (SP, p. 191) to find the undiscovered self who holds the secret of identity. The 'you' of the group of poems entitled 'Garland For You' is face in the mirror at which we stare with incomprehension, or it may be the stranger within us who seems alien to the image we cherish of ourselves. The truth about this 'you' may be reflected back at us by the remote figures of Domitian and Tiberius, by the 'Roman citizen of no historical importance' who furnishes the epigraph for 'Clearly About You', or by the two dead Civil War soldiers whose monologues comprise the 'Two Studies in Idealism' (SP, pp. 215–16) that provide Warren's 'Short Survey of American, and Human, History', illustrating man's abiding need to 'know what he lives for' in the midst of 'life's awful illogic and the world's stew'. Thus the theme of identity is involved with the theme of continuity, the human bond in time.

'The Letter About Money', written in one breathless if not incontinent sentence held in shape by a complex but strict rhyme scheme, is a technical *tour de force* with undeniable cumulative power. It typifies the experimental quality of *You, Emperors, and Others*. The risks Warren takes in this volume were not to the taste of the book's early reviewers. Dudley Fitts damned it with condescension: 'All in all, and in spite of a handful of poems that seem to be clear about the point they want to make, Mr Warren's new book is an exercise in metrical high jinks. Fairly high jinks. There's no law against a poet's taking an artistic vacation, and this binge was obviously fun.'[18] John Edward Hardy accused Warren of 'stale and unconvincing posturings, assumptions of worn-out disguises' in the production of 'seventy-nine pages of poems largely about nothing in the world, except a desperate striving for significance. Or, striving for You.'[19] The basis for Hardy's aversion to the book is his belief that Warren 'does not know . . . or indeed, I suspect, care . . . anything about mice, travelling salesmen, ladies with cancer, or you. He has written a book, apparently, out of some obscure feeling that he *ought* to know and care, of regret that he doesn't.'[20]

Especially coming after *Promises*, *You, Emperors, and Others* is a disappointment. No responsible critic would question Hardy's right to find fault with many of the poems in the book; but no reader responsive to Warren's work as a whole could accept the particular form of moral condemnation implicit in what Hardy says about Warren's not caring about his fellow creatures. Everything of Warren's prior to this volume testifies to a profound and energetic involvement in 'the lonely /

Fact of humanness we share' (YEO, p. 6). Hardy's comments overshoot the critical mark of the book in hand, giving the impression of an opportunity seized to excoriate a writer long disliked. Hardy has, admittedly, a sharp eye for a poem's faults—several of the poems he particularly dislikes were, advisedly, omitted by Warren from the later collections[21]— but his relish in critical demolition precludes his seeing that even the many blemished poems in this volume have something to commend them. The analogies are too slick in 'Nocturne: Travelling Salesman in Hotel Bedroom' (YEO, pp. 54–55), but the compassion underlying the Audenesque satire is evident in the poet's projecting himself into the lonely salesman's sense of missing out on life:

> Far off, in the predawn drizzle,
>   A car's tires slosh the street mess,
> And you think, in an access of anguish,
>   It bears someone to happiness.

This is not distinguished verse, but it is not 'posturing'. Despite its affinity with the early, excellent 'To a Face in the Crowd', 'Lullaby: Exercise in Human Charity and Self-Knowledge' (YEO, pp. 5–6) is cloyingly sweet; in this poem, as in 'Man in the Street' (SP, pp. 195–96) and in much of 'Ballad: Between the Boxcars' (YEO, pp. 46–50; abridged in SP, pp. 212–14), one feels that, however, characteristic of Warren the themes may be, the poet has been deflected from the intricacies of his subject into the problem of filling out his rhyme scheme. There is a self-conscious cuteness about the 'Nursery Rhymes' (YEO, pp. 64–70) and the nine 'Short Thoughts for Long Night' (YEO, pp. 71–99), but 'Clearly About You', which Hardy condemns, provides an effectively button-holing introduction not only to 'Garland for You' but to the whole book, sharply exemplifying the kind of truth one may prefer not to know about one's origins and the modern methods by which evasion of the deeper self may be attempted.

The book's best poems are those which strike the reader as 'coming from the event' (Appendix, p. 245), whether the event be real as in the first, third and fifth poems of the 'Mortmain' group and in 'In the Moonlight, Somewhere, They are Singing' (SP, p. 210), or imagined as in 'Two Studies in Idealism.' These poems, focusing on the poet's father, on his son, on his 'young aunt and her young husband' and on two representative figures from the Civil War, founding fathers of a kind, would have had a more sustaining context in the Gabriel sequence of *Promises*.

The long title of the first part of 'Mortmain' (SP, p. 202) is part of the poem itself: 'After Night Flight Son Reaches Bedside of Already Unconscious Father, Whose Right Hand Lifts in a Spasmodic Gesture, as though Trying to Make Contact: 1955'. The stanzas that follow expose the inadequacy of such a bald summary, the first of them veering from the reductive factualness of the title to the grandiose alliterations of 'Time's concatenations and / Carnal conventicle' and 'Ruck of bedclothes ritualistically / Reordered'. But this is wrong too: 'Christ, start again!' The first stanza dramatises the poet's difficulty in describing his experience. His emotions are turbulent and he shouts to be heard above the clangour of his feelings; only a grand style will measure up to such a moment. Then, realising that the gesticulant manner was ill chosen, he begins again with the simple facts that he is 'travel-shaken' and that he is powerfully affected both physically and morally ('gut- or conscience-gnaw') by the portentous spasm of his dying father's hand. Warren manages his shifts of tone here with a skill similar to that employed in 'The Return: An Elegy', but with greater economy as he juxtaposes the father's attempt to make contact and remembered snatches of the language whereby contact existed between his father and himself as a child:

> . . . *oh, oop-si-daisy*, churns
> The sad heart, *oh, atta-boy, daddio's got*
> *One more shot in the locker, peas-porridge hot.*

There is no suggestion here of the factitious harshness that Morton D. Zabel saw endangering the success of Warren's method for the last stanza expands precisely out of these echoes of the past into a lament for the loss of self which the father's death involves.

The mysterious relation between father and son is pondered

further in 'Fox-Fire: 1956' and in 'A Vision: *Circa* 1880.' The
success of these poems depends largely on Warren's being
content, despite his longing to understand, merely to convey
the quality of his feelings—what he calls 'the trick of the heart'
—without diminishing their intensity by any of the imposed
philosophising that spoils 'In the Turpitude of Time: N.D.'
(SP, pp. 205–6). 'Fox-Fire: 1956' (SP, pp. 204–5) simply
offers the poignant image of the poet's holding his father's old
grammar book while hearing his 'small son laugh from a
farther room'. The mystery of the relation of father to son and
to the son's son burns on as 'that poor book burns / Like fox-fire
in the black swamp of the world's error'. Again, in 'A Vision:
Circa 1880' (SP, pp. 206–7) Warren allows his fantasy to speak
for itself as he imagines seeing his father as a boy and longing
to speak to him, to warn him, to change the course of history.
As the dying Willie Stark says to Jack Burden: 'It might have
been all different' (AKM, p. 425). This is an effective and
moving poem not merely because it further develops the theme
of the human need for contact which is central to the
'Mortmain' group—'A Dead Language: *Circa* 1885' (SP, pp.
206–7) is more particularly about the failure of idealism and
seems out of place—but because, while specific to the point of
locating the vision in the 'cedar-dark', purling limewater and
parched pastures of Trigg County, Kentucky, it hits a universal
nerve. We would all like to speak to our fathers in their
boyhoods, to tell them how their futures and our inheritances
could be 'all different', better.

Beginning with *Promises* and continuing through *You,
Emperors, and Others* there is a growing preoccupation in
Warren's poetry with the interdependence that exists not only
between members of a family and between past and present,
but between man and nature and between apparently un-
connected people and events as exemplified by the excellent
'Fall Comes in Back Country Vermont' (SP, pp. 52–56). This
concern with interdependence is reflected in Warren's increasing
tendency 'to conceive of his poems in terms of sequences in
which the poems are not autonomous or self-sufficient but
depend for part of their meaning on the context of surrounding
poems, on their place in the sequence and in the volume.'[22]

It is further reflected in the kind of interdependence he implies within the whole body of his poetry by beginning his two later volumes of selections with the latest work, arranging his poems in reverse chronological order. The reader will begin with the newest poems, but will discover that progress through the book equates movement forward with a movement back into poems which reveal origins of the poet's present sensibility. The continuing process of his poetic vision is also illustrated by the use of poems from 'Notes on a Life to be Lived'. This sequence begins 'Tale of Time: New Poems, 1960–1966', the collection, not previously published in book form, included in *Selected Poems: New and Old, 1923–1966* for which Warren was awarded the Bollingen Prize in Poetry in 1967. In the foreword to *Or Else—Poem/Poems 1968–1974* Warren says that the poems in 'Notes on a Life to be Lived' were composed as parts of a projected long poem, similar to *Or Else*, which he found 'disintegrating into a miscellany' (OE, p. xiii). Abandoning the project, he published the poems as they appear at the beginning of *Selected Poems: New and Old*, but later found that seven of them, as well as 'The True Nature of Time' from *Incarnations*, had a place in the thematic structure of *Or Else*.

Without the poems of 'Notes on a Life to be Lived', the 'Tale of Time' collection includes little work on a level with Warren's best, although one must respect the variety of the poems: writing them undoubtedly helped Warren towards the greater openness and flexibility of style found in succeeding volumes. 'Holy Writ' (SP, pp. 174–82) is a failed exercise in historical imagination written in an unpersuasive *mélange* of tones, contrived biblical cadences and stabbing, irregular rhythms. Comparison with 'Two Studies in Idealism' points the superiority of the earlier, more narrowly focused performance in bringing the dead to life and giving them credible voices. The title sequence of the collection (SP, pp. 141–48), dealing with the death of the poet's mother almost forty years before, is perilously close to a wallow, fundamentally repetitious in its enumeration of the pains of deep bereavement and self-consciously portentous in its references to Time, Truth and History. The long-windedness of 'The Day Dr Knox Did It'

(SP, pp. 167–73) is somewhat redeemed in its last part by a compelling account of how the speaker, fleeing from the implications of his neighbour's suicide, discovers that the mysterious fact of death pursues him everywhere:

> My small daughter's dog has been killed on the road.
> It is night. In the next room she weeps.

The speaker's daughter, too, is being instructed in the central rôle of death in the world of experience.

'Delight' (SP, pp. 183–88) is a disappointing sequence, its first poem flat, its last arch. 'Love: Two Vignettes' works beautifully, the sportive gaiety of language precisely mirroring a state of sheer happiness that modulates into a concluding moment of uncertainty rendered with impeccable restraint; but the humour offered by the rhymes of 'Something is Going to Happen' is laboured, and the finicking definitions of 'Two Poems about Suddenly and a Rose' are irritating. Humour does contribute effectively to 'Homage to Emerson, on Night Flight to New York' (SP, pp. 153–58). Warren confesses to 'a pathological flinch' from the oversimplifications of Emersonianism: 'when it comes down to Hawthorne and Emerson meeting on the woodpaths of Concord, I'm strictly for Hawthorne' (Appendix, p. 248). In the context of so many poems about death it is not surprising that the brooding effort to re-experience, to explain and to endure such losses should lead the poet to test again the comforting transcendentalism of the philosopher who 'had forgiven God everything'. The poet can concede that 'At 38,000 feet Emerson / Is dead right', but while the luxuriously vague belief that 'significance shines through everything' seems to cover the case at such a remove from earth, it is also true that 'At 38,000 feet you had better / Try to remember something specific, if / You yourself want to be something specific'. Life on earth demands that you be 'something specific', and the Sage of Concord has less to say about the realities of living than an old coloured man's comically superstitious mockery of the wart the poet had on his finger when a boy. At least the old coloured man recognised that, despite abstract notions of race, 'You is human-kind'. Just as Robert Frost declares that 'Earth's the right place for love', the poet elects to descend from Emersonian altitudes, to the earth where he has friends whose 'lives have strange shapes'—which Emerson would not have understood—and whom he thinks he loves:

> Now let us cross that black cement which so resembles the arctic ice of
> Our recollections. There is the city, the sky
> Glows, glows above it, there must be
> A way by which the process of living can become Truth.
> Let us move toward the city. Do you think you could tell me
> What constitutes the human bond?
>
> (SP, p. 158)

It is this 'human bond', as well as how 'the process of living can become Truth', which Warren is concerned to know and to celebrate.

Chapter Six — Notes

[1] Dickey, James, 'In the Presence of Anthologies', *Sewanee Review*, **66** (1958), 307.

[2] Strandberg, p. 208.

[3] Stewart, John L., misses the point entirely, dismissing 'the irrelevant anguish of air' as an inflated way of saying 'small gusts'. (Stewart, p. 529).

[4] Strandberg, p. 181.

[5] The poet expresses a similar impulse in the second last stanza of 'The Dogwood', Part Two of 'Dark Woods'. Here the sudden whiteness of the dogwood bloom is felt as an affront in a world in which there is so much darkness:

> . . . then you felt a strange wrath burn
> To strike it, and strike, had a stick been handy in the dark there.
>
> (SP, p. 235)

[6] Strandberg, p. 188.

[7] The 'Ballad of a Sweet Dream of Peace' fails partly because Warren's fantastic allegory arbitrarily substitutes a *paysage moralizé* for the real world.

[8] Auden, W. H., *Collected Longer Poems* (London: Faber and Faber, 1968), p. 111.

[9] In a lively and perceptive early essay on Warren's poetry, W. P.

Southard refers to the verse of 'End of Season' (SP, p. 297) and concludes: 'That loose line is his favourite, and his best. His tight metrics mostly don't come off, they're too tight, a strain . . . He gets an easy effect, of a voice admirably accenting its various speeches, and I have a hunch he writes it that way: just talks it out, to see how the diction hits the ear'. (W. P. Southard, 'The Religious Poetry of Robert Penn Warren', *Kenyon Review*, **7** (Autumn, 1945), 653.)

[10] Bohner, p. 138.

[11] Bohner, p. 141.

[12] Brooks, Cleanth, *A Shaping Joy: Studies in the Writer's Craft* (London: Methuen, 1971), p. 228.

[13] Strandberg, p. 234.

[14] Stewart, p. 525.

[15] Stewart, p. 520.

[16] Brooks, *A Shaping Joy*, p. 224.

[17] Longley, p. 228.

[18] Fitts, Dudley, 'Exercise in Metrical High Jinks', *New York Times Book Review*, Oct, 23, (1960) p. 32.

[19] Hardy, John Edward, *Poetry*, **99** (Oct, 1961), 60.

[20] Hardy, p. 62.

[21] In a recent interview Peter Stitt asks Warren about his method of selecting poems for reprinting. Warren tells Stitt: '. . . when I was preparing my *Selected Poems* of 1966, I consulted with Allen Tate, William Meredith and Cleanth Brooks. If two of them were strongly negative about a poem, I would take it out, unless I had my own strong reasons for leaving it in. And my editor, Albert Erskine, is very helpful'. (Peter Stitt, An Interview with Robert Penn Warren, *Sewanee Review*, **85** (1977), 473.)

[22] Spears, Monroe K., 'The Latest Poetry of Robert Penn Warren', *Sewanee Review*, **78** (1970), 349.

The Flesh and the Imagination

In 'Treasure Hunt' (SP, pp. 108–9) one of the simplest poems of *Incarnations: Poems, 1966–1968*, Warren urges the reader to hunt for whatever meaning may be found in the world: 'The terror is, all promises are kept. / Even happiness'. The implication that other promises are more likely to be kept, but that happiness may deflect us from the quest for meaning, gathers force from a context which stresses suffering and death. Although *Incarnations* is a less integrated collection than *Or Else*, most of its poems are about the meaning of flesh—living and dead, human, animal and vegetable.

Paul Valéry, confronting 'the furious energies of nature' (SP, pp. 107–8) expressed in the turbulence of the sea-wind that commands white sail, white surf and white gull, is absorbed into the extinguishing whiteness by his white Panama hat, his mind turned 'like a leaf'. The first poem in the book warns us: 'Do not / Look too long at the sea, for / That brightness will rinse out your eyeballs. / They will go gray as dead moons' (SP, p. 103). The 'glorious, golden, glad sun', which for Melville was eternally 'the only true lamp', has turned killer, although it is still agent of truth, in the grim iconography of 'Island of Summer':

. . . the sun has
Burned all white, for the sun, it would

Burn our bones to chalk—yes, keep
Them covered, oh flesh, oh sweet
Integument, oh frail, depart not
And leave me thus exposed, like Truth.

(SP, p. 113)

What is man's truth when his flesh is burned away? The
contemplation of eternity brings no answer:

In the momentary silence of the cicada,
I can hear the appalling speed,
In space beyond stars, of
Light. It is
A sound like wind.

(SP, p. 118)

Warren is too honest to let the problem rest on the shelf of
rhetoric. In the last poem of the book the speaker is surrounded by a blinding white fog that has risen from the snow
at his feet. Finding himself 'contextless' and disinhabited from
the security of his own flesh, he is totally exposed in the
anguished cry which ends the poem:

The body's brags are put
To sleep—all, all. What
Is the locus of the soul?
What, in such absoluteness,
Can be prayed for? Oh, crow,
Come back. I would hear your voice:
That much, at least, in this whiteness.

(SP, p. 138)

The poems of *Incarnations* are uneven in quality. Sometimes,
as Victor H. Strandberg observes, Warren's 'gambles do not
pay off':[1] 'Wet Hair: If Now His Mother Should Come' (SP,
pp. 121–22) is embarrassingly sentimental; the speaker's
asking the cabbie in 'Driver, Driver' if he knows 'what flesh
is, and if it is, as some people say, really sacred' (SP, p. 135)
is not saved by its context from being prosaic and banal; 'The
Leaf' contains the flat, unmetrical statement that 'Destiny is
what you experience, that / Is its name and definition, and is
your name' (SP, p. 117). We regret such lapses, but forgive them
in our appreciation of Warren's commitment to his theme and

his refusal to lay any flattering unction to the reader's or his own uncertainly located soul. Deep in his 'intolerable wrestle with words and meanings' T. S. Eliot says: 'The poetry does not matter' ('East Coker', Part II). It does, of course, matter a great deal, as Eliot well knows, and he can say this meaningfully only because he is in the act of producing poetry of the highest quality; but the statement tells the reader to attend to 'Four Quartets' as a process by which the poet, taking risks, experimenting with ways 'of putting it', hopes, eventually, to get it right. Warren's book, with its failures and successes, is also a process that moves towards the conclusion of 'Fog', in which the speaker stands at last in a moment of 'nada' confessing his helplessness and his need in direct, spare, perfectly judged poetry. The implication of these lines is clearly intended to express a contrast to the orthodox Christian meaning of incarnation: 'If there is a promise of salvation, of resurrection in this book, it obviously can come only through this world of ours.'[2] We are left with paradox: 'The world means only itself' (SP, p. 107) but 'We must try / To love so well the world that we may believe, in the end, in God' (SP, p. 116). The poet's appeal to the crow to come back returns us to the world of the flesh to hunt again for the incarnate treasure of its meaning.

In 'Night is Personal' (SP, pp. 125–26) the Warden is adjured to 'keep the morphine moving' for the doomed convict because 'we are all / One flesh'. Penetrating to the heart of the physical world in 'Island of Summer', the poet discovers that 'the human bond', whose meaning he sought in 'Homage to Emerson', is part of a larger network of connections joining man to the rest of the natural world. Warren seems to feel again the authority of the naturalism which drew him in 'Kentucky Mountain Farm' and which eventually prompted him to distinguish man as separate from the natural world in terms of his need to live by an idea. The distinction seems less certain now: the world of nature and the world of man are equally subject to remorseless laws:

. . . for history,
Like nature, may have mercy,

Though only by accident. Neither
Has tears.

(SP, p. 105)

But this is not capitulation to the indifference of the early
naturalism or backsliding towards communion in Jeremiah
Beaumont's 'blank cup of nature' (WEAT, p. 506) for, if
Warren is preoccupied with man's enclosure in his frail integument of flesh, he denies the blankness of nature by projecting human qualities into the biological world even to the
point of endowing his ivy—and the wall which it assaults—
with the capacity to dream (SP, p. 112). The fig experiences
'bliss' and 'languor' in 'Where the Slow Fig's Purple Sloth'
(SP, p. 104) and the red mullet 'sees and does not / Forgive'
(SP, p. 113). Illumination in this sequence comes especially
from non-human flesh:

> When you
> Split the fig, you will see
> Lifting from the coarse and purple seed, its
> Flesh like flame, purer
> Than blood.
>   It fills
> The darkening room with light.

(SP, p. 104)

The fleshly flame of the mullet 'Burns in the shadow of the black
shoal' (SP, p. 114). The peach's flesh in 'Riddle in the Garden'
(SP, pp. 106–7) provides more specific illumination, becoming,
as it falls, increasingly human:

> . . . its *pudeur*
> has departed like peach-fuzz wiped off, and
> We now know how the hot sweet-
> ness of flesh and the juice-dark hug
> the rough peach-pit, we know its most
> suicidal yearnings, it wants
> to suffer extremely, it
> Loves God . . .

Monroe K. Spears notes that Warren's images of the natural
world—and especially of its fruit—in 'Island of Summer' are

L

'anti-Marvellian: concerned, that is, not with the contrast between the innocence of animals and plants and the guilt of human beings, but with the community between them, both moral and physical.'[3] The most obvious expression of this community is the continuous cycle according to which man eats the fig and then dies, whereby 'the root / Of the laurel has profited, the leaf / Of the live-oak achieves a new lustre' (SP, p. 105). This is why, in 'Riddle in the Garden', the poet warns the reader: '. . . do not / touch that plum, it will burn you . . . for you / are part of the world' (SP, p. 107). The fundamental idea of the cycle of life is unexceptional but the intensity of Warren's expression of it makes it new: we are all, it seems, incarnate in everything that lives. Warren's position is less secure when he postulates a system of relations that stretches actively backwards in time as well as infinitely forward. This is the central point made in the oversyncopated argument of 'The Leaf' (SP, pp. 116–18), which presents the reader with a large collection of images that fail to cohere. The last two sections assert the poet's belief in human continuity:

> . . . The world
> Is fruitful, and I, too,
> In that I am the father
> Of my father's father's father. I
> Of my father, have set the teeth on edge. But
> By what grape? I have cried out in the night.
> From a further garden, from the shade of another tree,
> My father's voice, in the moment when the cicada
>   ceases, has called to me.
> The voice blesses me for the only
> Gift I have given: *teeth set on edge.*

Warren does not adequately prepare us for his principle of retroactive fatherhood. We recognise the same imagination that gives Jack Burden his paradigm of human connectedness: 'I eat a persimmon and the teeth of a tinker in Tibet are put on edge' (AKM, p. 234), but Jack prepares us for this dramatic formulation by his spider's web theory of life as universal involvement. Warren is too arbitrary in 'The Leaf': atypically, his vision seems merely whimsical, unearned.

The longest poem in 'Island of Summer' is 'Myth on Mediterranean Beach: Aphrodite as Logos' (SP, pp. 109–12) which describes a hunchbacked old woman in a bikini who parodies Venus rising from the sea and exposes the illusions of life lived in terms of the flesh. The poet's appraisal of the woman—'A contraption of angles and bulges, an old / Robot with pince-nez and hair dyed gold'—is brilliantly ambiguous. This grotesque figure must attract derision, yet there is nothing satirical in the description of her entry into the water:

> She foots the first frail lace of foam
> That is the threshold of her lost home,
> And moved by memory in the blood,
> Enters that vast indifferency
> Of perfection that we call the sea.

Her re-emergence from the sea is a 'Botticellian parody' which has a paralysing effect on the lovers she passes on the beach; but although she 'draws their dreams away', she has, in heroic refutation of her own grotesqueness, realised her own dream. 'And glory attends her as she goes'. Perhaps the human capacity to dream remains supreme after all, in spite of competition from ivy, fig and mullet.

In the two sequences given under the general title, 'Internal Injuries', Warren seeks to effect our incarnation in the flesh of two suffering figures by way of the sympathy he evokes in us. In 'Penological Study: Southern Exposure' the flesh is that of a convict painfully dying of cancer, and in the sequence specifically entitled 'Internal Injuries' it belongs to a sixty-eight year old black woman, victim of a New York traffic accident. Both sequences immediately involve the reader by their violence and the swift pace of their narratives as well as by the intrinsically arresting human cases they present. They do not wear as well as 'Island of Summer', or the two beautiful and haunting poems, 'Skiers' and 'Fog', that comprise 'In the Mountains', the short sequence with which Warren ends his choice of poems from *Incarnations* in *Selected Poems, 1923–1975*. The most successful part of 'Penological Study' (SP, pp. 119–27) is the first poem with its refrain, 'Where the cans, they have no doors' providing an ironically mundane climax of humiliation which draws the reader into identification with the doomed man in his agony and his determination to 'tough it through'; but the poet's attempts to philosophise outward from the convict's predicament are heavy-handed.

'Internal Injuries' (SP, 127–35) is better controlled, both sociologically and psychologically incisive. Warren keeps sentimentality at bay: the woman's loneliness is offset by the fact that she is guilty of stealing from her Jewish employer, although:

> ... there wasn't no way
> To know it was you that opened that there durn
> Purse, just picking on you on account of
> Your complexion ...

(SP, p. 128)

Sympathy must be resolute to remain engaged with a victim of racial prejudice, a component of whose humiliation is the fact that the Cadillac which knocks her down is just a 1957 model, driven not by a white man but by 'a spic, and him / From New Jersey'. The poet defines with unnerving accuracy the way in which the woman is dehumanised, reduced to a metronomic scream and a hat lodged under the wheel of a truck, accidentally preserved for the moment because 'traffic can't yet move'. The poet's thought that the prowling jet 'must be hunting for something' rises out of his belief that everything must now focus on the victim as he himself does from his taxi. 'Defect of attention / Is defect of character', he thinks, bitterly formulating the city's judgement of the screaming woman from whom all the people in the scene are as remote as the jet, though they may stare with 'insensitiveness' or look at her 'like a technical problem'. It is the sense of total disjunction as well as his own helplessness, that induces in the poet a panicking need to escape from these crimes against the human bond and to 'go somewhere where / Nothing is real'. His frustration and panic are, of course, indications of his sensitivity to that bond as an object of fact which, however it may be abused, can never be destroyed. Nothingness for Warren is no more viable an escape than Emersonianism from the pains and limitations of the flesh. In both *Audubon* and *Or Else* he turns again to the world and discovers how the faculty of imagination may help us to live in it.

II

When Warren was preparing *World Enough and Time* he immersed himself in Americana of the early nineteenth century, including the writings of Audubon. An early attempt to write a poem about him came to nothing but later, in the sixties, Warren did the section on Audubon for a history of American literature on which he collaborated with Cleanth Brooks and R. W. B. Lewis. The impact Audubon made on Warren's imagination is clear from the introductory note to his selections from the ornithologist's works:

> Audubon came very near to fulfilling his 'astonishing desire to see much of the world'—at least that world that was his dream. His dream was not unique. For two hundred years, men had been dreaming of the Eden beauty of the great forests, the majestically uncoiling rivers, and the endless plains of the inner America. For some that dream had been of a land to be possessed and exploited for the use of civilisation, but for others it was of a land in which man could joyfully enter nature . . . Audubon knew that it was too late for his dream of man's sinking into nature, and he could even praise, though in somewhat ambiguous inflections, the course of history that had rendered that dream anachronistic. Now he could only hope for a faithful record, and a fitting monument, to render 'immortal' the world that had once provoked that dream.[4]

In Part Five of *Audubon: A Vision* Warren writes that the hero of his poem 'dreamed of hunting with Boone, from imagination painted his portrait' (SP, p. 96). The poet, in his turn, seeks to paint from an imagination stimulated by Audubon's writings, a portrait of the great American ornithologist. The poem begins by discarding the most preposterous of the legends about Audubon's identity—that he was the lost Dauphin—and penetrates to the heart of the man by imaginatively subjecting his consciousness to the world in which he walked. The resulting poem is one of Warren's most compelling treatments of the

theme of selfhood and of the problem of achieving happiness
in a world both beautiful and brutal. It belongs to a group of
poems in which Warren is particularly concerned with the
imagination. *Audubon* is not only *about* the imagination, it also
exemplifies the way in which the poet's own imagination works
on historical materials to produce a vision grounded in fact.

The central incident of Warren's poem occurred early in
Audubon's compiling of his record. It is the spring of 1812 and
Audubon is alone on the prairie, somewhere between Ste
Genevieve (Missouri) and Henderson (Kentucky). In Part Two,
'The Dream He Never Knew the End Of', Warren imagines his
coming on a cabin presided over by a tall, ugly woman, being
put up for the night in company with a one-eyed Indian, and
barely escaping the sudden violence of the frontier. The woman
and her two sons would murder Audubon for his watch and he
escapes only because of the timely entrance of three travellers.
Next morning the woman and her sons are hanged.

Warren's source for this incident is 'The Prairie', the third
of the 'Delineations of American Scenery and Manners' with
which Audubon intersperses his descriptions of birds in the
five-volume *Ornithological Biography*. At three points Warren's
recreation of the incident differs significantly from Audubon's
narrative. When the woman in 'The Prairie' is 'all ecstasy'
over his watch, Audubon is preoccupied with feeding his dog
and himself: 'Thoughtless, and, as I fancied myself in so retired
a spot, secure, I paid little attention to her talk or her movements.'[5] Warren's hero is all attention from the moment the
woman hangs the watch round her neck:

> . . . near it the great hands hover delicately
> As though it might fall, they quiver like moth wings, her eyes
> Are fixed downward, as though in shyness, on that gleam,
>   and her face
> Is sweet in an outrage of sweetness, so that
> His gut twists cold. He cannot bear what he sees.
>
> (SP, p. 88)

The poem's second important departure from its source occurs
at the moment of crisis. After a silent warning from the one-
eyed Indian, the real Audubon observes the woman whetting

her carving-knife; he confesses that 'the sweat covered every part of my body', but fear does not paralyse him: 'I turned, cocked my gun-locks silently, touched my faithful companion, and lay ready to start up and shoot the first who might attempt my life.'[6] Warren's hero experiences a sense of having entered a nightmare, 'knows it / Is the dream he had in childhood but never / Knew the end of,' and, although he knows what he must do to defend himself, sinks into a 'lassitude' which 'Sweetens his limbs'. Unable to act, he 'cannot think what guilt unmans him, or / Why he should find the punishment so precious' (SP, p. 90). The third notable discrepancy between the two narratives is in their descriptions of Audubon's state of mind after frontier justice had been visited on the woman and her sons. In 'The Prairie' Audubon does not even refer to the hanging, expressing himself 'well pleased' with the way things have turned out and closing his account of the incident with the patriotic observation that during twenty-five years of wandering 'this was the only time at which life was in danger from my fellow creatures.'[7]

Some readers have found the vision of the poem hard to accept not on philosophical or artisitic grounds but because of the liberties they think Warren has taken with the facts of a historical figure's life. Thomas Lask objects to the 'hidden sexuality' Warren imparts to the relationship between Audubon and the woman and concludes that although 'it can be argued that the poet has the right to re-create the man as he sees fit . . . there ought to be a cautionary warning to indicate the fissure between the original and the image.'[8] For Allen Shepherd, 'Warren's attempt . . . to provide a moral dimension beyond the psychological is both crucial and suspect since neither unmanning guilt nor precious punishment seems to have adequate referent within the context of the incident.'[9] It is surprising that Shepherd lets the matter rest there, for he understands the essential difference between Audubon's story in 'The Prairie' and Warren's poem: 'Although Audubon may have rounded out a good story, his primary purpose was to record, not to interpret. Warren is at least as much concerned to interpret, to render dramatically an issue in this *exemplum*-like sequence, as he is to transcribe a narrative.'[10]

There is, moreover, something suspect about Audubon's narrative. Although he claims to have paid 'little attention' to the woman's admiration of his watch, he records it with succinct thoroughness: 'She was all ecstasy, spoke of its beauty, asked me its value and, put the chain round her brawny neck, saying how happy the possession of such a watch should make her.'[11] That the woman made a strong impression on Audubon is clear from his precise references to her gruff voice, negligent attire and ugly mouth, his calling her an 'incarnate fiend' and 'infernal hag', and his according her the only direct speech in the narrative. Given the amount of detail he does provide, his failure to say exactly what was done to the woman and her sons must strike the reader as evasion:

> We marched them into the woods off the road, and having used them as Regulators were wont to use such delinquents, we set fire to the cabin, gave all the skins and implements to the young Indian warrior, and proceeded, well pleased, toward the settlements.[12]

In the fourth of his 'Delineations' Audubon describes the improvisations of frontier law as it was upheld by Regulators. Their punishments ranged from simple banishment, through lashing with hickory twigs or nettles, to burning down a miscreant's cabin and execution by shooting. On occasion the heads of delinquents 'have been stuck on poles, to deter others from following their example.' Audubon gives a detailed account of the fate of one, Mason, a notorious horse-thief and river pirate, at the hands of Regulators but he mentions no instance of hanging.[13] Telling the reader that the woman and her sons in 'The Prairie' were 'used as Regulators were wont to use such delinquents' leaves their fate open to speculation. Audubon is particular about other matters; why not about this?

Such inconsistency and evasion must have suggested to Warren that the incident described in 'The Prairie' deeply affected Audubon, but that he repressed his perplexingly strong feelings towards the woman. Out of his total sense of Audubon's life and character Warren does 'interpret' the incident, but he does so within the known scope of Audubon the man and the peculiarities implicit in the story. The poet does not cook the books.

The whole poem develops out of its first part. In [A] Warren gives us his Audubon watching one of America's most splendid birds:

> Moccasins set in hoar frost, eyes fixed on the bird,
> Thought: 'On that sky it is black.'
> Thought: 'In my mind it is white.'
> Thinking: '*Ardea occidentalis*, heron, the great one.'
> Dawn: his heart shook in the tension of the world.
> Dawn: and what is your passion?
>
> (SP, p. 85)

Of course Audubon's heart shakes 'in the tension of the world': he lives in that tension by a defining passion for the beauty of the birds of America which involves him in killing them. Within a page's length of the *Ornithological Biography* he says appreciatively of the great white heron that 'They walk majestically, with firmness and great elegance', and then, matter-of-factly. 'It is difficult to kill them except with buckshot, which we found ourselves obliged to use'.[14] The birds themselves live 'in the tension of the world': Plate 281 of *The Birds of America* depicts the elegant and majestic heron with a fish in its mouth, and while the white-headed eagle referred to in Part Five of the poem draws praise from Audubon for its 'strength, daring and cool courage' and its ability to glide through the air 'like a falling star', the savagery of its attack on a swan leads him to deplore 'the cruel spirit of this dreaded enemy of the feathered race' and to repine, with Benjamin Franklin, that this of all birds 'should have been chosen as the emblem of my country.'[15]

Warren has caught in his poem Audubon's responsiveness to the individual characteristics of different species: each bird— heron, crow, buzzard, eagle, goose—'selves' in the way of Gerard Manley Hopkins' kingfishers and dragonflies. The bear, too in I [B] is completely involved in its own specific creaturehood:

> The bear feels his own fat
> Sweeten, like a drowse, deep to the bone.
>
> (SP, p. 86)

Watching the bear, Audubon thinks: 'How thin is the membrane between himself and the world.' The bear could not define itself as the above lines do, any more than the great white heron could call itself by a Latin name or the whooping crane liken the air it cleaves to 'fluent crystal' or 'transparent iron' (SP, p. 99). These precisions come from the human imagination, the 'membrane' that distinguishes man from other creatures of the natural world.

When, in Part Two, Audubon sees the woman, she is a strong physical presence, a creature, albeit a less prepossessing one than the bear, peering out from her lair:

> The face, in the air, hangs. Large,
> Raw-hewn, strong-beaked, the haired mole
> Near the nose, to the left, and the left side by firelight
> Glazed red, the right in shadow, and under the tumble and tangle
> Of dark hair on that head, and under the coarse eyebrows,
> The eyes, dark, glint as from the unspecifiable
> Darkness of a cave. It is a woman.
>
> (SP, p. 87)

Audubon's watch immediately becomes the defining passion by which the woman is transformed: 'Her body sways like a willow in spring wind. Like a girl'. The change is shocking, her face is 'sweet in an outrage of sweetness', so that Audubon's 'gut twists cold. He cannot bear what he sees' (SP, p. 88). Here is the extreme feeling which the real Audubon represses in 'The Prairie' but which is betrayed by the inconsistency and evasion we have noticed.

In this scene Warren prepares the ground for Audubon's reaction to the prospect of death. Within the general context of human sin and guilt imaged by the dream of Part Two [F], Audubon is specifically unmanned by the kinship that can now be seen to exist between the woman and herself. Part Five of the poem begins: 'He walked in the world. Knew the lust of the eye,' and the lust of the woman's eye is essentially the same as his. Elsewhere Warren says: 'Audubon was the greatest slayer of birds that ever lived: he destroyed beauty in order to create beauty. Love is knowledge.'[16] The woman's readiness to kill in order to know and fulfil herself through beauty is the moral counterpart of Audubon's ambition 'to acquire a true knowledge of the Birds of North America' (SP, p. 96). It is no mere sexual masochism that 'sweetens his limbs' with 'lassitude'; his 'punishment' will be 'precious' because it is to be inflicted by a fellow criminal.

When the woman is hanged Audubon suddenly sees that her face is 'beautiful as stone, and / So becomes aware that he is in the manly state' (SP, 91–92). His sexual response expresses Warren's equation of love and knowledge, for Audubon, recognising his moral kinship with the woman, has come to know her in the intense moment of his own impending death. The woman is self-fulfilled in death and, therefore, beautiful. Her laughter, provoked by the suggestion that she might wish to pray, expresses much more than contempt for the God who may have created both her executioners and herself. In the second 'Interjection' of *Or Else* the poet warns the reader that intense concentration on a single object, even a fragment of crushed rock, may afford an unnerving experience:

. . . Not all witnesses
of the phenomenon survive unchanged
the moment when, at last, the object screams
in an ecstasy of
being.

(SP, p. 26)

The woman's laughter is her scream of ecstasy in the fulfilment of being, achieved through her commitment to the trans- figuring beauty of Audubon's watch which her imagination reveals to her. Audubon does not 'survive unchanged'. The woman's fulfilment, in spite of her failure to take possession of the 'magic' of the watch, asserts the power of imagination and challenges his own sense of identity: 'He tries to remember his childhood. / He tries to remember his wife. / He can re- member nothing' (SP, p. 92). He can only 'continue to walk in the world', driven by his dream, his defining passion for the birds whose self-sufficiency echoes the woman's completeness of being. As he comes to know the woman's beauty by be- coming the agent of her death, so with the birds in Part Six:

He slew them, at surprising distances, with his gun.

Over a body held in his hand, his head was bowed low,
But not in grief.

                                                  (SP, p. 99)

The image of Audubon reverently bent over the bird he has just
killed recalls the picture of his standing alone in guilt and awe
before the mysteriously beautiful, rigid corpse of the hanged
woman and yearning 'to be able to frame a definition of joy'
(SP, p. 92).

The poem itself seeks to express such a definition and to be a
'story of deep delight' such as the poet asks for in Part Seven.
The vision offered is of a world of tension in which 'human
filth' is complemented by 'human hope', bestiality by beauty,
the anguish of self-uncertainty by the triumph of self-realisation, all through the redeeming power of the imagination by
which love is knowledge and time itself may be transcended in
'the dream / Of a season past all seasons' (SP, p. 98). This
celebration of the imagination is Warren's answer to 'this century, and moment, of mania' (SP, p. 100). In *Audubon*, as in
Brother to Dragons, Warren has both performed an exercise
in creative biography and taken from history a story which,
in his hands, becomes a 'little myth' that may help us to live
better.

                              III

If *Audubon* teaches us that there is a vital rôle for the syn-
thesising power of imagination even in these maniacal, modern
times, *Or Else—Poem/Poems 1968–1974* reveals a poet, acutely
aware of his own vulnerability to time, using his imagination
to understand a world which is at once continuous and frag-
mented. 'Necessarily,' says the poet in the second 'Interjection'
(SP, pp. 25–26), 'we must think of the world as continuous',
for without a sense of continuity, 'you wouldn't know / you
are in the world, or even that the / world exists at all'. But
discontinuity is necessary too:

     . . . only, oh, on-

ly, in discontinuity, do we
know that we exist, or that, in the deepest sense, the existence of anything
signifies more than the fact that it is
continuous with the world.

The poem's mixture of continuity and discontinuity in its
awkwardly syllabic verse is, no doubt, intended to exemplify
the principle it asserts, just as all the poems of *Or Else* may be
viewed as discrete units or as parts of a larger whole. Warren
says of the book:

> . . . it can be considered a long poem, or it can be considered a
> group of short poems. Some of the poems were written with my
> being unaware of their place in the sequence. It wasn't undertaken
> as a planned sequence; the true sequence grew. This kind of
> structure is related to how you feel your experience—I couldn't
> tell you exactly how, but it is related.[17]

The collection is readily enough felt as a sequence whose
themes, elaborated by a now ageing man, re-define the world in
terms Warren has made familiar. The poet's concerns are still
with time and the relationship of the present to the past—
especially his own—and with the human need to live by an idea
in a world where innocence is inevitably lost like 'the evidence'
in 'Blow, West Wind' (SP, pp. 24–25) or the boy's shoe in
'Little Boy and Lost Shoe' (SP, p. 62). 'Rattlesnake Country'
(SP, pp. 45–50) associates an arid landscape with ruined lives
and in the climax of the poem the white flame that spells the
rattler's death is joined to the 'hot whiteness' of an alien sky,
signalling time's eventual execution of us all.

There is love, too, in this mingled world: love which is,
perhaps, fundamental to 'the human scheme of values' in
'Vision Under the October Mountain' (SP, pp. 59–60); a tender
passion for the beloved from whom the poet has been separated
in 'The Faring' (SP, pp. 57–58); the sexual yet protective love
which seizes the man at the end of 'Birth of Love' (SP, pp. 78–
80) and even the possibility of God's love in the sixth
'Interjection' (SP, p. 61). In the beautiful 'Sunset Walk in
Thaw-Time in Vermont' (SP, pp. 76–78) the poet's joy in the
woods and waters suggests to him that he may initiate a chain
of immortality by blessing his son with the hope that he will

one day stand thus in the midst of nature and bless, in turn, his own son:

> For what blessing may a man hope for but
> An immortality in
> The loving vigilance of death.

'All I can do is to offer my testimony' (SP, p. 50), says the poet, aware that he is in a position to do so only because the clock which is 'getting ready to strike forever o'clock' is still 'taking time to make up its mind and that is why I have time / To think of some things that are not important but simply are' (SP, p. 43). This is disingenuous: the things Warren thinks of in these poems are all felt as important intimations of meaning, although the stance taken in a particular poem may be one of uncertainty. Whether about something important or unimportant, however, a bad poem is not made intrinsically better—although it may, warts and all, be more interesting— merely because its author thinks it has a place in a sequence. The variety of Warren's art and the process of his mind in this volume will, of course, engage the reader who has already come to love his work and believe in his vision. As *Incarnations* may be read as a process that moves towards the climactic lines at the end of 'Fog', so *Or Else* works through the hopes and austerities of the Warren world to culminate in the affirmation of 'A Problem of Spatial Composition'. The poetry 'matters' more in *Or Else*, however, because the failure of so many of the individual poems endangers interest in the process. Like *You, Emperors, and Others*, the book contains a good deal of the worst of Warren, as well as some of the best.

The key both to Warren's method and his aim in *Or Else* is given at the end of 'I Am Dreaming of a White Christmas: The Natural History of a Vision' (SP, pp. 26–34):

> All things listed above belong in the world
> In which all things are continuous,
> And are parts of the original dream which
> I am now trying to discover the logic of. This
> Is the process whereby pain of the past in its pastness
> May be converted into the future tense
> Of joy.

This frankness is very appealing: we warm to the poet in his enterprise and wish him well. After all, if he does find the 'logic of his dream', thus converting the 'pain of the past', we shall all be in his debt. But our faith in the likelihood of the poet's success is undermined by the very poem in which he states his purpose. 'I Am Dreaming of a White Christmas' is a ponderous, self-indulgent excursion into the speaker's not especially interesting past in order to contemplate the enigma of his belonging to an inimical present which is, inexplicably, both distinct from and continuous with that past. Here, despite the free form of the poem, Warren seems trapped in his own mannerisms: there are too many imperatives, too many rhetorical questions, too many histrionic spaces, and over-insistent descriptions in lines packed too tight to breathe:

> . . . Times Square, the season
> Late summer and the hour sunset, with fumes
> In throat and smog-glitter at sky-height, where
> A jet, silver and ectoplasmic, spooks through
> The sustaining light, which
> Is yellow as acid. Sweat,
> Cold in arm-pit, slides down flesh.
> The flesh is mine.
>
> (SP, p. 32)

Similar excesses spoil 'Chain Saw in Vermont in Time of Drouth' (SP, pp. 39–41)—although the symbolic use of the saw is effective—'Flaubert in Egypt' (SP, pp. 55–6), 'Reading Late at Night, Thermometer Falling' (SP, pp. 67–72) and 'Folly on Royal Street Before the Raw Face of God' (SP, pp. 73–5) as well as 'Homage to Theodore Dreiser' (SP, pp. 51–4) in which the crude sexual imagery seems gratuitous in spite of Warren's insight into this indelicate, tormented man. 'News Photo' (OE, pp. 67–73) is an only partially successful evocation of the tawdry idealism which leads a Southern bigot to shoot a pro-Negro Episcopalian minister. The poem is too long for its content and goes suprisingly lame when, in the last section, the man, acquitted but un-appreciated, imagines Robert E. Lee raising his hat to him and laughing. The poet knows that if Lee were alive and among the crowd craning 'their heads to horn in / on the act and get in the papers', his laughter would imply recognition of the perversion of his own ideals in actions like that of the bigot whose veneration of him is an irony that would have reduced the great General to tears. A similarly perverted idealism appears in the 'Ballad of Mister Dutcher and the Last Lynching in Gupton' (SP, pp. 35–9), but this is Warren at his anecdotal best. The irony of Mr Dutcher's one bid to realise his ideal is that, although a flair with the lynch-rope is his 'one talent kept, against the / advice of Jesus, wrapped in a / napkin, and death to hide', the lynching is botched.

Under the title, 'Can I See Arcturus from Where I Stand', the latest poems Warren offers in *Selected Poems: 1923–1975* seem awkward, with the exception of 'Midnight Outcry' (SP, p. 9), a precise and tender portrayal of 'the terrible distance in love'. This should not give rise to thoughts of failing powers. Between the achievements of *Promises* and *Incarnations* came the uneven, often experimental poems of *You, Emperors, and Others* and 'Tale of Time'. It seems reasonable to predict that the more direct and open qualities of the most recent poems are symptoms of a continuing evolution in poetic style and that Warren will surprise us with further verse to rank with his best. The thrust, vividness and economy of 'Heat Lightning' augur well (TLS, 5 May 1978). In *Audubon*, in much of *Incarnations* and in the best of *Or Else* there is undoubtedly a deepening of vision and an assurance of utterance marked by the absence of those often violent refractions of theme by which, in earlier poems, he seeks to convince himself and the reader that he apprehends the full complexity of the subject in hand. Authority of voice and vision is especially evident in 'Time as Hypnosis', 'Composition in Gold and Red-Gold' and 'A Problem in Spatial Composition', all of which display what Warren calls in his essay on Coleridge 'a high degree of expressive integration' (SE, p. 262) and, like *Audubon*, are concerned with the imagination.

The life-declaring power of recollected images substantiates the neo-Wordsworthian 'unsleeping principle of delight' in the eighth 'Interjection' of *Or Else* (SP, p. 75). This neat poem is really a salute to the imagination. A weightier testimony to human dependence on imagination is expressed in 'Time as

Hypnosis' (SP, pp. 23–4), aptly dedicated to I. A. Richards. The snow-covered landscape is an image of annihilation, reproducing on earth the eternal emptiness of the sky to which it imparts its dizzying light:

> All day in a landscape that had been
> Brown fields and black woods but was now
> White emptiness and arches,
> I wandered. The white light
> Filled all the vertiginous sky, and even
> My head until it
> Spread bright and wide like another sky under which I
> Wandered.

The boy's mind is absorbed into the annihilating whiteness: like the poet in the 'absoluteness' of 'Fog', he becomes 'contextless' (SP, p. 137). The general death, symbolised by the snow, is particularised by the field mouse's epitaph, 'the single / Bright frozen, red bead of a blood-drop' at the end of its delicate tracks. Looking back at his own tracks and ahead at 'the blankness of white . . . Then the sky', the boy is set parallel to the field mouse. Death comes physically to the mouse—a creature purely of nature—in the owl and metaphysically to the boy in the blankness of the snowscape and the emptiness of the sky:

> All day, I had wandered in the glittering metaphor
> For which I could find no referent.

The hypnotic power of snow and sky has paralysed the boy's imagination, transforming it, in Wallace Stevens' phrase, into 'a mind of winter':

> All night, that night, asleep, I would wander, lost in a dream
> That was only what the snow dreamed.

Obscuring the natural detail by which the boy customarily takes his bearings, the snow also represents the power of nature and eternity to deprive man of the faculty by which he maintains his hold on the world and on his own identity. 'Looking into the heart of light', like Eliot's Tiresias in the hyacinth garden of 'The Waste Land', the boy is 'neither / Living nor dead'. Without imagination man's mind is, indeed, a blank, his life a desolation.

M

The obligation laid upon the imagination to achieve the completeness of vision defined by *Audubon* is the theme of 'Composition in Gold and Red-Gold' (SP, pp. 62–4). Autumn suffuses this scene with gold, binding sun-light, apples, chipmunk, girl and brook in one ideal texture. The cat adds the finishing touch:

> The tail of the cat, half-Persian, weaves from side to side,
> In infinite luxury, gold plume
> Of sea-weed in that tide of light.
> That is a motion that puts
> The world to sleep.

It is, obviously, another case of hypnosis. Mesmerised by the movement of the cat's tail, the poet is lulled by the rich perfection around him until sudden violence 'unstitches the afternoon', adding the 'flame-gold' at the base of the chipmunk's skull to the colours of the scene. Warren's concern is now clearly with the relationship between the imagination and reality.[18] Scenery, like poetry, wants to be pure, but, in the real world, scenes are not, and the poet is not allowed to rest content until the climactic colour of 'flame-gold' brings the impure fact of death into the centre of his scene. Good aesthetics are concerned not just with form and colour but with the completeness of truth. The 'flame-gold' of the dead chipmunk is the most vividly beautiful as well as the most forbidding colour in the scene. The poet's imagination, now fully awake, perceives that this death 'completes the composition' by making it a true image of the world, and moves beyond the scene to find in the unseen trout's determination and the vanished eagle's flight, affirming images of continuing life.

Warren returns to the theme of the imagination in 'A Problem in Spatial Composition', the concluding poem of *Or Else* (SP, pp. 80–81). The 'problem' involves us again in the relationship between art and truth. Looking westward across a forest toward the setting sun, the poet's eye orders what it sees in terms of the rectangle of a high window that gives on the scene. References to 'lower right foreground', 'upper left frame' and the 'perspective' from which the scene is viewed stress the poet's awareness of his own act of composition. The question is whether the poet's subjective ordering of the scene to his aesthetic satisfaction results in a true picture of the world, whether truth of coherence is also truth of correspondence. The poet knows exactly how his own imagination works. The 'tall scarp of stone' is a fact and continues to be one 'in knowledge'. The imagination turns the scarp into a 'mass of blue cumulus' according to 'truth of perception', but does not deny its factual existence as a scarp: the simile expands the object without undermining its original state. Fact and idea co-exist perfectly. Similarly, the poet realises that his 'perspec tive' is responsible for the image of the branch that 'Stabs, black, at the infinite saffron of sky'. Perspective closes the gap between tree and sky, but the poet is aware that the gap is still there. "All is ready,'' then, because the poet has made it so, but, as in his picture of Audubon, without distortion of the facts.

The hawk brings the poem's only awkward moment as it glides down 'In the pellucid ease of thought'—a strained phrase bespeaking an unassimilated idea. The hawk's element, the sky, has already been established as a legitimate symbol of 'forever' and when the bird settles on 'the topmost, indica- tive tip of / The bough's sharp black and skinny jag skyward', it brings the eternity of the sky into contact with the temporal earth. We may or may not agree with Peter Stitt that 'The hawk's instantaneous disappearance from the scene is akin to man's disappearance from life at death. . . . The hawk in the poem is analogous to the spirit of man, as birds so often are in English and American poetry generally.' But it is clear that 'When he resumes his flight, the bird returns to the eternal realm of sky, having rested for but a moment on the time- bound earth.'[19] More important than any equation between the bird and the human spirit is the fact that the bird's perching on the tree is something that happens outwith the poet's control. The bird—an object of fact—enters the composition—a matter of art—'at the upper left frame', and the poet's imagina- tion accepts the event into his picture. He knows that it is his 'perspective' which yields the image of contact between the earth and sky in the branch that 'jags upward . . . higher / Than even . . . / The Mountain'; the actual arrival of the hawk to effect the same contact endorses the earlier image and rewards the imagination for its scrupulousness by confirming its vision. 'The Imagination', as Keats says, 'may be compared to Adam's dream—he awoke and found it Truth.' The moment both completes the poet's account of the relation between the imagination and the world, and expresses the possibility that we may, at times, catch glimpses of the eternal on earth. If 'A Problem in Spatial Composition', like the Ancient Mariner's blessing of the water snakes, is 'a little fable of the creative process' (SE, p. 258), it is also a compact and eloquent fable of 'the tension of the world', intimating how, through the imagination, that tension may be resolved.

Wallace Stevens, one feels, would have liked this poem. In his discusssion of the imagination as value in the modern age, Stevens writes:

> The world may, certainly, be lost to the poet but it is not lost to the imagination. I speak of the poet because we think of him as the orator of the imagination. And I say that the world is lost to him, certainly, because, for one thing, the great poems of heaven and hell have been written and the great poem of the earth remains to be written.[20]

Whatever may be lost to Warren, it is not the world. A long, vigorous career has produced a body of poetry that includes many fine poems of the earth. How many of them are great must be, of course, a 'tale of time'.

Chapter Seven—Notes

[1] Strandberg, Victor, 'The Incarnations of Robert Penn Warren', *Shenandoah*, **20** (Summer, 1969), 95.

[2] Stitt, Peter, 'Robert Penn Warren, The Poet', *Southern Review*, **12** (April, 1976), 267.

[3] Spears, 'The Later Poetry of Robert Penn Warren'. pp. 351–2.

[4] Brooks, Cleanth, Lewis, R. W. B., and Warren, Robert Penn, *American Literature: The Makers and the Making*, **I**, (New York: St Martin's Press, 1973), 1062–63.

[5] Audubon, John James, *Ornithological Biography; or, An Account of the Habits of the Birds of the United States of America; accompanied*

by descriptions of the Objects represented in 'The Birds of America', and
Intersperesed with Delineations of American Scenery and Manners,
I, 16 (Edinburgh: Adam Black; Adam and Charles Black, 1831–1839).

6 Audubon, **I,** 83.

7 Audubon, **I,** 84.

8 Lask, Thomas, 'On the Frontier', *New York Times*, 13 Dec, 1969,
p. 37.

9 Shepherd, Allen, Warren's *Audubon:* 'Issues in Purer Form' and 'The
Ground Rules of Fact', *Mississippi Quarterly*, **24** (1971), 50.

10 Shepherd, p. 51.

11 Audubon, **I,** 82.

12 Audubon, **I,** 84.

13 Audubon, **I,** 105–7.

14 Audubon, **III,** 547–48.

15 Audubon, **I,** 161, 168.

16 Stitt, Peter, 'An Interview with Robert Penn Warren', *Sewanee
Review*, **85** (1977), 475.

17 Stitt, 'Interview', p. 476.

18 Sister M. Bernetta Quinn prefers to interpret the poem as myth:
'The mountain in the background, deserted by its solitary eagle after
the crime, may possibly be a symbol of Calvary at the end of Good
Friday; the fish leaning hidden against an icy current in the alder-
shaded stream, a reminder of Christ. Here, the Promised Land ironically
wears a garment of flooding gold, just as the earth in Rilke's 'Evening'
wraps itself in a vesture of darkness.' The poem can, no doubt, carry
such a reading, but hardly insists on it. (See Sister M. Bernetta Quinn,
O.S.F., Robert Penn Warren's Promised Land, *Southern Review*, **8** (1972),
336.)

19 Stitt, Peter, *Robert Penn Warren, The Poet*, p. 275.

20 Stevens, Wallace, *The Necessary Angel* (New York: Random House
Vintage Books, 1965), p. 142.

8

Uses of Pastoral

Four novels—*The Cave, Wilderness, Flood* and *Meet Me in the Green Glen*—focus and develop Warren's interests in a significantly rural setting. With the exception of *Wilderness* these novels are rich in vivid, well-defined characters, yet it may be said of Warren as he says of Conrad:

> He is no Dickens or Shakespeare, with relish for the mere variety and richness of personality. Rather, for him a character lives in terms of its typical involvement with situation and theme: the fable, the fable as symbol for exfoliating theme, is his central fact.
>
> (SE, p. 39)

Wilderness fails because its under-nourished characters and skeletal fable prevent the theme from exfoliating realistically. In the three novels to be discussed in this chapter Warren goes to the country for the heart of his fable: a cave of Platonic implication which expresses the attractions and terrors of naturalism and whose darkness brings illumination; an impending flood by which the Tennessee Valley Authority conveys a man-made apocalypse to the small town of Fiddlersburg; and a green glen of love, lost and found. In each novel realistic characters live in terms of their involvement with a fable of which the expressive centre is both a fact and an idea. Warren thus demonstrates in his art the kind of balance which his books urge us to strive for in our lives.

At times, in *The Cave*, the balance is precarious. Leslie Fiedler feels that Warren 'insists, insists!'[1] but while the characters all clearly develop the theme of the entrapped self, they remain individuals, neither subservient to the idea, like Adam Rosenzweig, nor swamped by detail like Amantha Starr. Warren's insistence on the common problem is acceptable precisely because it *is* remarkable that characters so diverse should share so much. This is the point of the book. To find the resolution of the various conflicts artificial—as Charles H. Bohner does[2]—is not merely to find fault with Warren's technique but to disallow his vision.

People in Tennessee and Kentucky still remember the tragedy of Floyd Collins who died in Sandy Cave, Kentucky in January, 1925. Collins was exploring in search of a potential underground tourist attraction when a dislodged boulder trapped his foot. The facts of this story gave Warren his opportunistic reporter— a newspaperman from Louisville actually went underground to interview Collins—his crowd of barely controllable spectators, the exploiting media and the hillside funeral service.[3] By making his cave-crawler, Jasper Harrick, the centre of so many people's lives, Warren turns the Collins story into a modern variation of Plato's allegory of the cave. Like Jasper in his literal cave, each character is trapped within the figurative cave of his or her own nature, mistaking shadows for reality.

Images of darkness and emptiness associate the various metaphysical caves with Jasper's physical one. Monty Harrick's need of Jo-Lea Bingham makes him vulnerable, but the discomforts of love are preferable to the annihilating inner darkness in which Jo-Lea 'would suddenly become faceless, and the world . . . ashes' (C, p. 8). Jack Harrick, virtuoso of the roistering, unexamined life, is forced to take stock of himself when he hears that the now Tillie Sumpter has prematurely delivered his child stillborn. He finds a void within himself, 'a big black hole' (C, p. 139), like the cave that becomes his son's tomb. Definition of the self in terms of guilt may be burned away by hectic living, but love is more arresting. Holding Celia Hornby's hand in the dark, Jack is 'caught in the vertigo of his own non-being' (C, p. 387). He is attracted to Celia's apparent 'self-sureness' (C, p. 145), but his momentary intimation of immortality is quickly succeeded by a desolate sense of the blankness of his life: 'he had been hit like a field-mouse by a hoot owl and snatched into the dark sky' (C, p. 144).[4] Celia, in her turn, needs to fill her inner space with someone as positive as Jack seems to be. Jack eventually realises that he has been too preoccupied with his own needs to see 'what emptiness she had to fill to be herself' (C, p. 387). An 'empty ache' is 'the realest thing about Dorothy Cutlick' (C, p. 40) and Nick Papadoupalous' conviction that he is doomed to be a loser is lodged 'in the deep, dark, angry, tear-sodden secret centre of his being' (C, p. 41). Although MacCarland Sumpter knows his wife never truly admitted him, he had so lived by the relationship that her death overcomes him with 'an agony of emptiness, into which the blackness flowed' (C, p. 83).

There is hope for all these characters in that they long to escape from their dark inner caves of emptiness; but there is no such hope for Isaac Sumpter. For a time he supplies Rachel Goldstein with an illusion of the definition she needs, 'I want you because you are you' (C, p. 113). Rachel tells Isaac, unaware that his nihilism—'There was no God and there was no self' (C, p. 101)—issues from an incurable emptiness which is later expressed by his empathy for the body trapped in the cave:

> Whether it was his own body, or Jasper Harrick's, he couldn't tell. No, it was not Jasper's, it had to be his own, for you couldn't see anything, you could still feel things, and if he knew that the body was there, it would have to be because he himself was the body in that water, and he himself was that knowledge in that absolute darkness.
>
> (C, p. 193)

Empathy later becomes envy for Jasper Harrick, not just because 'he had had that little Jo-Lea Bingham, who was juicy as a peach', but 'because he lay in the cool, cool dark, and did not suffer' (C, p. 324). Isaac is the one character in the novel who remains essentially empty, despite his assertions that '*Nobody is pulling the string on me . . . I am myself*' (C, p. 279). The picture of him, 'wholly himself', in New York is heavily ironic: he is lost as totally as Slim Sarrett in the last chapter of

At Heaven's Gate. Disconnected from the human bond, he lacks both God and self, immersing himself in the big-city equivalents of the naturalistic void the country had taught him to crave.

Warren explains Willie Stark's rise to power in terms of the politician's 'faculty of fulfilling vicariously the secret needs of others' (AKM, p. vii). Jack Harrick attains his popular notoriety for the same reason. 'That is Jack Harrick', Miss Abernathy tells Celia, 'the hero of all the hillbillies! The tales they tell about him—just so they themselves can feel big' (C, p. 161). Jasper, a 'chip off the old block', as the overshadowed Monty realises, also provides vicarious fulfilment to the people of Johntown:

> He had that trick of being himself so completely, it looked like he wore the whole world over his shoulders like a coat and it fit. That was why everybody reached out and tried to lay a hand on him, get a word off him, have something rub off him, hold him back a minute, before he moved on toward wherever he was going.
>
> (C, p. 19)

Ironically, all the principal characters in the novel do 'get a word off him', for Jasper's entrapment in the cave supplies the imagery that defines their various states of emptiness. A further irony is that his 'trick of being himself so completely' is, like his father's similar gift, an illusion. He gives himself away:

> It's a nice temperature down there . . . It is not summer and it is not winter. There aren't any seasons to bother about down there . . . Blizzard or hot spell . . . a lot of things don't matter down there . . . in the ground at least a fellow has a chance of knowing who he is.
>
> (C, pp. 240–41)

As much in need of identity as all the others, Jasper goes underground in search of himself. The irony of his fate is that what begins literally and figuratively as a self-seeking act ends in the death of the character who seemed complete, but promotes the completion of others. Jasper does, after all, rub off on them all.

The *Times Literary Supplement's* anonymous reviewer complains that 'the power that moves all these people is sex',[5] but the successful characters in *The Cave* achieve their sense of identity through the discovery of love, which replaces the naturalistic mode of sex with the ideal mode of caring for others. There is, certainly, plenty of sexual activity. K. W. Gransden is withering: 'I do not deny that the sexy bits achieve a certain functional success: they make the book more readable.'[6] Charles Samuels is overcome: 'In *The Cave* the characters suffer not from thwarted desires for purity and coherence but from sexual deprivation. They possess not the agonised and subtle minds of Warren's typical creations but merely partake of a panting universal *Id*.'[7] This suggests that the sex in the novel does not refer beyond itself and that the suffering characters are essentially caricatures. Such a view is belied, for example, by the character of Nick Papadoupalous, whose mind may not be subtle, but whose agonised desire for purity and coherence does make him a typical creature of Warren's imagination. Nick's 'sexual deprivation' is the context for a thoroughly Warrenesque drama of the ideal and the real. His ideal seems unattainable until he finds in Giselle Fontaine a replica of Jean Harlow, the 'platinum-blond, swivel-built movie queen' (C, p. 42) who lies inaccessibly at rest in Forest Lawn Cemetery, but Nick cannot be faithful simultaneously to the ideal Miss Harlow and the real Giselle. When the night-club Venus reverts to the tubercular Sarah Pumfret, Nick, deprived of both the ideal and the real, turns for solace to Dorothy Cutlick. But Dorothy's passive embraces are meaningless: squinching her eyes, she gets on with her Latin (C, pp. 60–61) parodying the fantasy Nick has acted out with Giselle. Celia Harrick provides Nick with the 'bone-shaking happiness' of looking, for the first time, 'into a human face . . . Just for the humanness' (C, p. 309). This first communion with another human being brings him a sense of his own human identity—pointed by Celia's valiant pronunciation of his name—and sends him back, in love, to the reality of his wife.

If Warren, like Conrad, 'is no Dickens', he does, nevertheless, display a Dickensian flair for caricature in such characters, as Bill Christian, Duckfoot Blake, Sugar Boy, Percival Scrogg and, most of all, Nick Papadoupalous. None of these characters, however, is pure caricature, reducible to the sum of his oddities.

Duckfoot Blake comes close, but as the plot of *At Heaven's Gate* thickens around him, it becomes clear that there is more to Duckfoot than his cynical wit, financial wizardry and bad feet. His escape from the power of Bogan Murdock is also an escape from the caricature version of himself. In *The Cave* two characters in particular, Nick Papadoupalous and Timothy Bingham, change in the same way. Nick is, of course, an extravagant creation and he generates much of the novel's comedy, but the discovery of 'humanness' frees him from the obsession by which he is caricaturised. The man who sits by his dying wife's bed, telling her she will recover and wondering what she looked like when a little girl (C, pp. 364–5) is a three-dimensional, human being shown, at last, in the act of loving the woman whom he had married and betrayed for purely sexual reasons. To judge this sentimental is not merely to reject Warren's admittedly bold method but to deny the redemptive opportunities of life.

The opening paragraph of Chapter 2 enumerates the limitations of Timothy Bingham:

> Mr Timothy Bingham, chief stockholder, president, and cashier of the People's Security Bank of Johntown, Tennessee, wore pince-nez glasses rather than plain steel rims, which he would have preferred, because his wife, between whose legs he had not managed to get in five years, thought pince-nez more refined and suited to his position, and hers.
>
> (C, p. 36)

The TLS reviewer finds ineptitude in the fact that the single clue we are given to the life of Mr Bingham is a sexual one; but, with Mrs Bingham's imposition of pince-nez, the sexual point is absorbed into the larger, comic horror of the whole marital relation. Mrs Bingham's refinement is at least as selfish as the naturalistic satisfaction she withholds from her husband. The turning-point in the Bingham story is the moment when the .38 goes off in the banker's hand and Slim Cutlick collapses screaming, damaged only by the broken whiskey bottle in his pocket:

> 'Tell him if he comes back I won't be responsible,' Mr Bingham

said, for the wine was heady, and he felt his finger closing on the
trigger, and his eyes narrowing dangerously.

'Yes, sir,' the sheriff had said, and had said it with respect.

(C, p. 66)

If the ultimatum is parodic, it gets a straight-faced response
from the sheriff and the comedy of this scene is later enclosed
in the seriousness of Dorothy Cutlick's solicitude for Bingham
at the end of the book (C, p. 399).[8] By his rehabilitation of
Dorothy in giving her someone to care about, by his routing of
Mrs Bingham, the banker, like Nick Papadoupalous, earns his
way out of caricature. The reader, like the sheriff, must learn
to respect Mr Bingham.

Warren does not deal in mutually exclusive categories of
characters, real people and what George Orwell calls 'gargoyles'.
Orwell observes that Dickens "was constantly setting into
action characters who ought to have been purely static.
Squeers, Micawber, Miss Mowcher, Wegg, Skimpole, Pecksniff
and many others are finally involved in 'plots' where they are
out of place and where they behave quite incredibly."[9] There
is a deliberate element of caricature in the figure of Leontine
Purtle in *Flood* and Jed Tewksbury's mother in *A Place to
Come To* is a bit of a gargoyle; but these characters also function
as human agents in the action of their novels, they are not
merely side-shows. In *The Cave* Warren deliberately uses the
reader's expectations about character and falsifies them to make
his point. The monstrosities in Dickens' books, Orwell says,
'are still remembered as monstrosities, in spite of getting mixed
up in would-be probable melodramas. Their first impact is
so vivid that nothing that comes afterwards effaces it.'[10]
Nothing in *The Cave* effaces the memory of Nick in his squinch-
eyed grapplings or Timothy Bingham in his hen-pecked
diffidence; but the lingering vividness of the first impact these
characters make on us serves to emphasise the change they
undergo as they cross over from the realm of caricature to the
realm of the real. The translation in each case dramatises the
character's growth of self and his grasp of reality.

In a final meeting, Jack Harrick and MacCarland Sumpter
finish the lifelong debate they have conducted against each
other:

'Folks need to believe you are a good man. They got to believe
somebody is. So they will pick on you and believe you.'
   'But the truth—' MacCarland Sumpter cried out.
   'It changes,' Jack Harrick said. 'Truth changes. A man changes
and I reckon truth changes.'
   'God doesn't change,' MacCarland Sumpter affirmed, and again
shivered.
   'Well, maybe He ought to,' Jack Harrick said.
   'That is blasphemy,' MacCarland Sumpter said.

(C, p. 384)

It is Harrick, the man of fact and flesh who realises that the
general need for ideals matters more than Sumpter's individual
guilt. His reward, perhaps, is the neat resolution with which
Sumpter catches himself blaspheming as he formulates man's
purpose: 'To help God change the way He wants' (C, p. 385).
Rejecting the ideal condemns man, like Isaac Sumpter, Sue
Murdock or Percy Munn, to the trivialities of a continuous
present. But the ideal must earn its livelihood in the world of
time and change. Giselle Fontaine's act had given Nick
Papadoupalous a vision of perfection: 'Being out of Time, she
had no past, glimmering like a dream, too beautiful to be real'
(C, p. 176). A shadow on the wall of his personal cave, the
ideal image of Giselle must yield to the still absolute but living
ideal which Nick finds in Celia Harrick. The same continuing
human ideal at last empowers Jack Harrick, literally and
figuratively, to harmonise his own death with his buried son's,
and to consign his 'box' to Monty.

II

'The pastoral ideal', Leo Marx reminds us, 'has been used to
define the meaning of America ever since the age of discovery,
and it has not yet lost its hold upon the native imagination.'[11]
Washington Irving defined the most familiar archetype:

> I mention this peaceful spot with all possible laud; for it is in
> such little retired Dutch villages . . . that population, manners
> and customs, remain fixed; while the great torrent of migration and

improvement, which is making such incessant change in other parts of this restless country, sweeps by them unobserved. They are little nooks of still water which border a rapid stream.[12]

In *Flood* Warren takes us to Fiddlersburg, a Southern Sleepy Hollow, which awaits the Tennessee Valley Authority's 'great torrent of improvement'. Fiddlersburg, however, has not exactly been a 'little nook of still water', even if Calvin Fiddler's killing of Alfred O. Tuttle is the result of a marriage that might never have happened but for the citified Lettice Poindexter's influence on Maggie Tolliver. Frog-Eye, the swamp-rat companion of Brad Tolliver's youth, may be a shrewd judge of people and a crack shot, but he is a depraved character who would be at home in the diseased naturalistic kingdom of La Grand' Bosse in *World Enough and Time*. Brad's vindictive, book-burning father is, for all his solitary weeping, closer to Huck Finn's Pap than any model of rustic virtue. The apparently virginal blind girl, Leontine Purtle, for whom relocation will supposedly be especially difficult, turns out to be the town's semi-professional, thoroughly knowing her way around; and up in the state penitentiary there is Pretty Boy Rountree who, 'with a claw hammer of the value of six dollars ... did with malice aforethought and against the peace and good order of the State of Tennessee, beat the pore bleeding be-Jesus out of the head of pore old Mrs Milt Spiffort' (F, pp. 294–95). These are the 'cracks in Fiddlersburg' whereby Blanding Cottshill recognises the naiveté of his pastoral ideal:

> A farm up-river, an office on the square, in Fiddlersburg in my case, folks squatting on their heels under the maples, swapping talk with you, the hunting and the fishing, training a bird dog, breaking a colt, maybe fooling with politics, watching the seasons change and your kids grow up and get ready to do what you were doing. I reckon a man figured it was a way of feeling all of a piece, in himself and with things around him.
>
> (F, p. 345)

John L. Longley Jr. writes of 'the ease and flow of the pastoral mode' which may disguise the 'metaphysical dimension' of *Flood* from the common reader,[13] but Warren has not regressed to simple agrarianism. He uses the pastoral mode, but questions it too. In the words of Senator Norris of Nebraska: 'Every locality in the United States has an interest in this unseen force [of electricity], which has become a necessity of life, which goes into every modern home and from the home on up to the largest factory, and which turns the mightiest wheels of commerce.'[14] A more demotic version of the Senator's vision is expressed by Warren's young engineer:

> The dam was going to be great, the young engineer said. Going to be near a hundred square miles under water, going to back up the water for twenty-five miles, he had said, gesturing south, up-river. Most of the land not much but swamp or second-growth. And what good land there was—hell, they didn't know how to farm it anyway. But with power and cheap transportation it would all be different. A real skyline on the river, plant after plant. Getting shoes on the swamp rats too, teaching 'em to read and write and punch a time clock, and pull a switch. It was going to be a big industrial complex, he said. He liked the phrase, industrial complex.
> He had said it again.

(F, p. 113)

If the last sentence of this passage ironises the facility of the young engineer's idealism, it is, nevertheless true that the dam will bring benefits. As a sample of modernism 'The Seven Dwarfs Motel' is appalling, but this is not a simple case of pastoralism versus modernism, the industrial machine laying waste the unspoiled garden. Warren's novel exposes the cliché of such crude polarising. This is part of the 'metaphysical dimension' of a work whose business is with the fake and the real. Yet it is the little town of Fiddlersburg which affords Warren's richly varied *dramatis personae* the apocalypse that his title leads the reader to expect.

Early critics of *Flood* disliked it. At best it is 'a clever piece of engineering',[15] and at worst 'a stew of clichés'.[16] The *Times Literary Supplement's* anonymous reviewer numbers *Night Rider, All the King's Men* and *World Enough and Time* 'among the most memorable novels of our time' and calls them 'powerful fables'. After these achievements *Flood* is a 'saddening book' by a writer 'with nothing to say'. What is saddening, however, is that an adverse review based on a total failure to understand

Warren's novel should, by appearing in so influential a journal, effectively decimate the book's chances of a wide readership. Indeed, *Flood* must be one of the most promptly remaindered novels ever published in Britain. The conclusion of the TLS review gives the book no quarter:

> The characters are conceived in the terms of best-seller fiction, their problems are synthetic . . . This is particularly true of the central character, Brad, who is a comically super-typical model of the Thirties failed writer (one good book, marriage, Spanish Civil War, disillusion, retreat to the South, sex, Hollywood). Near the end of the book Brad has a discussion with Calvin Fiddler in which he says gravely: 'I know this is not a story conference. I know that this is the real thing. It is L–i–f–e.' And the reply? ' "The only one we've got,' Cal answered, very softly." In this exchange, and the many similar conversations in the book there is, alas, no trace of irony.[17]

The reviewer's message is clear: Warren has broken his own rules: his novel offers an unearned vision, a flood of clichés. Thus, despite the warning implicit in Warren's repudiation of a stereotyped contrast between pastoralism and modernism, the reviewer has failed to see that the book deliberately uses clichés in order to expose them.

Although Warren defines Original Sin as 'a contamination implicit in the human condition . . . the sin of use, exploitation, violation' (SE, p. 69), the individual born into this condition is still to be held responsible for his actions. From Coleridge's *Aids to Reflection* Warren derives the view that 'Original Sin is not hereditary Sin; it is original with the sinner and is of his will' (SE, p. 227). As Jeremiah Beaumont says, 'it is the crime of self, the crime of life. The crime is I' (WEAT, p. 505). Brad Tolliver is a pathological user. His original sin is that he exploits his much praised book of stories, *I'm Telling You Now*, as a vehicle of escape. On its success he rides out of town, and out of the past which contains his identity. In New York he feels hollow and insecure, 'like a man bleeding to death from some inner wound'. Because he has left whatever 'inner self' he had in Fiddlersburg, he is a man 'with no story', one of those described in the poem, 'Terror':

. . . whose passionate emptiness and tidal
Lust swayed toward the debris of Madrid,
And left New York to loll in their fierce idyll
Among the olives, where the snipers hid.

(SP, p. 285)

Of course Brad's problem is, as the reviewer says, 'synthetic':
he has made it himself. His participation in the Spanish Civil
War is intended to be judged spurious. He fights not for an
ideal but out of 'his fear of having no story' and the War
provides a ready-made opportunity to mix himself in defining
action. Without commitment to the cause, his enlistment can
only disguise his essential emptiness in the clichéd figure of the
romantic hero: 'He did not yet know that the true shame is in
yearning for the false, not the true story' (F, p. 68).

Even after the dramatically clarifying events of the first four
books of the novel, Brad is held by a false story of himself.
There is no irony in Calvin Fiddler, but Brad's ironic tone and
clipped, side-of-the-mouth style of speech are consistent with
the voice with which we have become familiar. Taken out of
context his remark to Calvin about 'L–i–f–e' looks soft. In
context it is quite different. Brad progresses through a series
of clichés which he surrounds with protective irony. In his
last meeting with Calvin he is still jumping from one cliché
to another:

> '. . . This scene—between you and yours truly—is, as we say in
> my shop, mandatory. It is a must. The necessary confrontation.
> Symmetry calls for it. An inner logic demands it. Let us, poor
> human puppets that we are, surrender to the symmetry, to the
> inner logic, and words will spring unbidden to our lips. Meaning
> will evolve from—'
> He stopped, abruptly.
> 'Christ,' he said. Then: 'I know that this is not a story con-
> ference. I know that this is the real thing. It is L–i–f–e.'

(F, p. 406)

Brad begins by believing that his last meeting with Calvin is
the necessarily symmetrical way of ending their common
story: each will acknowledge the state of enlightenment reached
by the other. His own habitual irony, evident here in the self-

N

mockery of his inflated rhetoric, suddenly reveals to him that
he is corrupting the reality of the moment into a treatment as
falsifying as those he had offered Yasha Jones for their
'beautiful motion picture'. For a second he is thrown, but re-
gains his balance and reasserts his command of the situation,
again protecting himself by the irony of spelling out
'L–i–f–e'. He still thinks he has the 'inner logic', all the knowledge required for a final assessment, but life now lifts him in
two stages out of his improvised certainties. First, he is shamed
into a sense of his own failure to achieve true self-hood by
Calvin's genuine discovery of himself and the beauty of life;
second, although Brother Pinckney sabotages Brother Potts'
plan to pray with the coloured folks, the sick man's winning
through to his last service demonstrates the triumph of the
heart's will over even the logic of cancer. Both symmetry and
irony yield to 'the secret and irrational life of man' (F, p. 439).

Warren recognises the genuineness of Brad's difficulties. How
can the intellectual live in terms of 'the secret and irrational
life of man'? Will not the possession of an analysing intellect
inevitably exclude a man from the unifying country of the
heart, where the self lives in harmony with what Coleridge
calls 'the one Life within us and abroad'? Brad works, 'but
nothing connects' (F, p. 243); he is 'overwhelmed by the moving
multiplicity of the world', and, therefore, guilty of what Yasha
Jones calls 'the sin of the corruption of consciousness' (F,
p. 127). It is easy enough for the uncomplicated man of religion
to 'pray to know that the lives we lived are blessed' (F, p. 81),
but the intellectual Brad rejects Maggie's suggestion that he
should make Brother Potts the centre of his picture (F, p. 243).
He cannot see that the great-hearted minister struggling with
his declining body, his brave, faltering little poem and his
unavoidably tense relationship with Brother Pinckney is the
key to what Yasha Jones calls 'the depth and shimmer' (F,
p. 181) and thus to a unified image of life in Fiddlersburg.

Brad's flight from the heart begins with his youthful recoil
from his father's weeping. Returning alone to Fiddlersburg,
Brad finds himself weeping in the room in which his father had
died, but his tears bring no catharsis because he 'tried to
appropriate the process. He tried to profit from it. He even felt,

momentarily, a pride that he, Bradwell Tolliver, could stand here in the dark house and weep. He waited for the reward, the sweetness, the relief that should come. Nothing came . . . He had been tricked' (F, p. 197). Here Brad's attempt to exploit his brief, spontaneous overflow of powerful feeling is on a level with his use of the Spanish Civil War to create a synthetic image of himself. In both cases, as in the several treatments he considers for the movie, Brad 'wheels and deals' (F, p. 339), substituting expertise for that 'flow of feeling' (F, p. 127) without which his scenarios are merely 'plotty' and his own life a succession of disconnected episodes that fail to form a story. This, eventually, is what he realises at the end as he tears up the telegram from Mort Seebaum—thereby repudiating the fakery of 'the Tolliver Touch'—and thinks, 'I cannot find the connection between what I was and what I am. I have not found the human necessity' (F, p. 439). He knows what he has to do: there is hope, after all, for Brad.

World Enough and Time is subtitled, 'A Romantic Novel', which, Everett Carter reasonably suggests, tells us to expect an attempt to fuse the realm of the ideal with the world of social appearance.[18] *Flood* is 'A Romance of Our Time', which arouses similar expectations. 'There is no use', advises Arthur Mizener, 'looking in *Flood* for the virtue of the Marquand novel—the vivid, detailed, representative image of the everyday world; *Flood* has its own kind of vividness and relevance, but it is not the realistic novel's.'[19] Mizener is one critic who holds *Flood* in high esteem as a novel of ideas:

> Nearly every important American way-station of the spirit is here with all its self-deception—complacent or suffering—and all its human pathos: our nostaliga for the imagined past; our earnest dreams of a sensible, school-lunch future; our longings for the nirvanas of manly lust and pastoral love and romantic disillusion; our delight in gadgetry and mere skillfulness; our desire for the release of war's respectable violence or of political dogma's solemn irresponsibility.[20]

This makes a refreshing change from the shallow opprobria generally levelled at the book, but Mizener underestimates its realism which is often 'vivid', 'detailed' and 'representative'.

The Seven Dwarfs Motel, with its cement frogs, dwarfs and monstrously vulgar billboards, is a realistic, detailed image of innumerable American hostelries of the kind. It is also thematically functional. Brad is disturbed by the sight of a cement dwarf fishing in a stream which looks real: 'Bradwell Tolliver wished that the water did not look real. What always worried you was to find something real in the middle of all the faking. It worried you, because if everything is fake then nothing matters' (F, p. 4). This is the doubleness of life referred to by Blanding Cottshill: Brad's irony makes him aware of it but, lacking heart, he does not know how to cope with it. A similar relation between surface realism and theme is in the description of Fiddlersburg, from the 'You'll Never Regret It Café', the ruined steamboat landing and the river 'heavy-bellied with silt' to the Confederate soldier, still apprehensively 'staring northward'. Brad's basement room on MacDougal Street the old Fiddler house, and the microcosmic life of the penitentiary are all presented in sufficient detail to make them imaginably real in themselves as well as contributions to the texture of meanings.

There is character realism too. Yasha Jones has been dismissed as an impossible philosopher king or 'quasi-saint'.[21] His outward reserve, courtliness of manner and exotic background make him, certainly, a more striking figure in Fiddlersburg than in New York or Hollywood, but the account we are given of his happy marriage, the tragic loss of his wife and the discipline by which he achieves his 'pure and difficult joy' (F, p. 100) offers no special challenge to the suspension of disbelief. If he is at once foil and surrogate father to Brad, he is no saint as he reflects on the rhythm of his natural desires and the techniques by which they are customarily satisfied (F, p.104). Lettice Poindexter of the 'silky hair' and 'preposterous name' is one of Warren's most vivid questers. All her 'one-answer' attempts at self-definition—the Spanish Loyalist cause, psycho-analysis, body culture—predictably, fail. The consistency in these, of course, is the basic idealism, her sheer, resilient whole-heartedness, and it is in terms of this consistency that her final answer, life as a lay worker in a Catholic old people's home, is credible. Her 'blasphemous' description of herself as 'goosed to God' (F, p. 436) makes her just unregenerate enough to be real in her charity. Comparatively minor characters like Blanding Cottshill and Mr Budd are given their own histories and speak in appropriate accents. Even the characters in Brad's file on Fiddlersburg—a much more vital effort than his scenarios—come to life in his summaries. Yasha Jones would approve his creator's effort: Warren's chief concern is with 'the vision', 'the flow of feeling', but his picture is more than adequately documented.

Flood is, however, most obviously a 'Romance of Our Time' in that it examines varieties of love in the modern world. The deepest need of all Warren's principal characters, John L. Stewart observes, 'is for the love of other adults, but they cannot inspire it because they cannot face the responsibilities it entails.'[22] Brad does inspire love in Lettice Poindexter but compulsively destroys his marriage because he cannot respond to her need for love that at once includes and transcends sexuality. Ironically, this becomes his need too, and to supply it he makes a Lady of Shallott out of Leontine Purtle. His romantic illusion about Leontine becomes so necessary to him as a vehicle of redemption and self-fulfilment—another Spanish Civil War—that he is not even checked by the absurdity of lusting for the Lady of Shalott: "When he calls her that, Yasha Jones says, 'What does that make you? Lancelot?' and Brad says, 'It was the Queen he was getting it off.' But though he says it, he does not see it."[23] As the Spanish cause takes its revenge on Brad's self-aggrandising use of the War by sending Dr Echegaray to seduce Lettice, so Mortimer Sparlin is revenged for Brad's liberal condescensions when the Lady of Shalott turns into the whore of Candy Cottage.

If sex without love is, predictably, futile and degrading in Warren's world, love without sex is a perversion of a different kind. Maggie Tolliver's surreptitious readings of the marriage manual and *Fanny Hill* imply a sexual nature unfulfilled in her marriage to Calvin. Yasha Jones has been celibate long enough. Their marriage will, presumably, echo the true love of Cyrus and Matilda Highbridge (F, p. 91). Both have known the pain of isolation and the enhanced awareness that tragedy can bring; both are ready to return to 'a communion with man and nature' in accordance with Warren's prospectus for fulfilment in 'Knowledge and the Image of Man'.

The basic themes of *Flood* are all familiar by now, but, as Warren says in his essay on Hemingway, "The history of literature seems to show that good artists may have very few basic ideas . . . And the ideas of the artist are grand simply because they are intensely felt, intensely realised—not because they are, by objective standards, by public, statistical standards, 'important' " (SE, pp. 116–17). Warren's ideas in *Flood* are grand on both counts: they are 'intensely felt, intensely realised', and "by objective standards . . . 'important.' " His splendidly fugal treatment of them makes *Flood* much more than 'a clever bit of engineering'. It is 'A Romance of Our Time', a vision which, with every reading, reveals more 'depth and shimmer'. Arthur Mizener foresees the possibility that Warren disheartened by the book's initial reception, might use up 'a great deal of creative energy both in his life and in his work, hiding from people in elaborately mannered ways', as Henry James did after 'the very big tempest in a very small teapot' stirred up by his *Hawthorne*.[24] Mizener need not have worried. Not only did Warren's poetry become, in the sixties and seventies, more open and personal, as we have seen, but he went on to write *A Place to Come To*, the most nearly autobiographical of all his novels. Before that, however, he demonstrated his ability to stand firm under critical fire by staying close to Fiddlersburg, both geographically and thematically, in *Meet Me in the Green Glen*, another romantic fable about love in the country. If not to Parkerton it is to the antediluvian Fiddlersburg that Cy Grinder takes young Cassie Killigrew for a movie and an ice cream soda (GG, p. 76). It is from the state penitentiary at Fiddlersburg that Angelo Passetto comes fatefully walking down the road in the rain, and it is to the same penitentiary that he is unjustly committed to die in the electric chair for the crime of loving neither wisely nor quite well enough and for the inadvertent, tragic folly of making Murray Guilfort realise too clearly his own incapacity to love at all.

III

Meet Me in the Green Glen fared no better than *Flood* in the unforgiving, anonymous columns of the *Times Literary Supplement*.[25] The review's heading—'Old Kentucky Style'—is inexact as well as belittling. The novel is thoroughly of Tennessee as the opening section of Chapter 12 makes plain by taking the reader from the inner truths of individual lives to the external facts of population and income statistics for the state, for Nashville and for the valley[26] in which the book is principally set. The easy tag is an insult to Warren's scrupulous regard for the particulars of his region. The whole TLS review is marred by this sort of facility. The reviewer properly expects irony in the novel's title, taken from John Clare:

> Love, meet me in the green glen,
>   Beside the tall elm tree,

but concludes that 'nothing is ironic', whereas the entire book is a demonstration of the irony that the need for love characterises us all—rich man, poor man, lawyer man, Sicilian—but that our failure to recognise this need in ourselves and in others can lead to elaborate cruelties, delusions and tragically misdirected energies. The reviewer ignores all this, preferring to make much of an obvious parallel between Warren's book and 'The Virgin and the Gipsy' (What sort of monopoly does Lawrence hold?), misleadingly comparing the novel to *The Sound and the Fury* and finally dismissing it as 'a commingling of sexual thriller with whodunit'.

Faulkner's great novel is also distinctly regional, even more so in that his purpose is to explore the meaning of the decay of an 'aristocratic' Mississippi family while Warren's subject is love in the kind of context described by Brad Tolliver as he contemplates the fate of his sister:

> The South—it is full of women like that. Or used to be. Women stuck with something—the paralysed old father, the batty mother, the sister's orphan kid, the uncle with paresis, the booze-bit

brother. Stuck with that—and lonesomeness. Hell, I've seen 'em. Lots of 'em built for something very, very different. Sitting it out. Lonesome in the long hot summer afternoons or fall nights, sort of storing up lonesomeness like honey, storing it up for someday, somebody. You know what I mean. That devotion, that absoluteness, just stored up for somebody. But . . . nobody comes.

(F, p. 168)

In *Meet Me in the Green Glen* it is the husband who is paralysed, his illegitimate, all but orphaned kid who confuses the issue of love, and Cassie Killigrew Spottwood who, in her lonesomeness, stores up absolute devotion for, as it happens, Angelo Passetto. Warren's book uses a region that is rich in certain primary colours and extreme human situations[27] to discuss universal matters. The sad consequence may be that readers who know nothing of the region may think it unreal. As Warren says of Southern writing in general: 'intensities of inside effects sometimes look queer to those who are not inside (Appendix, p. 257). Faulkner protected the world he made by his stylistic habit of inflating character and action to unimpeachably mythic proportions. Warren is a much more realistic writer, and, therefore, more vulnerable; but it is depressing to find his evocation of life in that Tennessee world—a mixture of nostalgia, loneliness, tremendous private heroisms, and sheer climate—so easily dismissed. After all, George Wallace's political success there as recently as the early seventies makes the point that the region is hectic, complex and that all manner of old atmospheres still prevail. Racial feelings still persist, to be manipulated by the Murray Guilforts of this world; 'a clean and energetic' black still shows 'what one of them could do, if they put their mind to it' (GG, p. 347); and the gentler sects still quail before 'the booming onslaught of the Church of Christ' (GG, p. 271).

In a persuasive review of *A Place to Come To*, R. Z. Sheppard pays tribute to Robert Penn Warren as 'one of the few distinguished literary men who can aim a novel at the gut and not offend the head.[28] This is precisely the gift which Denis Donoghue finds lacking in *Meet Me in the Green Glen*: 'Often in Mr Warren's longer fictions and especially in his big novels I find the relation between episode and feeling insecure, and generally the feeling is exorbitant. Feeling and interpretation flow in, but their abundance is often gross if we think of what occasioned them.'[29] Presumably Donoghue does not object to the proposition that the betrayal of love, sexual abuse, murder and the deliberate miscarriage of justice may reasonably generate powerful feelings. His particular quarrel with *Meet Me in the Green Glen* is that its characters 'are so empty' that Warren 'must himself produce the fullness of the world and give it to the narrator, the narrative voice.' In other words, the novel is a failure because one cannot believe that such empty characters could, in any circumstances, experience the feelings attributed to them by the narrator. Angelo especially offends: 'Poor Angelo . . . is a clod, capable of nothing . . . he cannot think in any language, his mind is as rudimentary as his English . . . but the narrator out of his own fullness gives him lavish gifts of meditation.' Donoghue offers the following passage from Chapter 5 as an example of the book's vitiating narrative exorbitance:

> Was this the way things always were in the end? If all you had out of living was the memories you couldn't remember the feelings of, did that mean that your living itself, even now while you lived it, was like that too, and everything you did, even in the instant of doing, was nothing more than the blank motions the shadow of your body made in those memories which now, without meaning, were all you had out of the living and working you had done before?
>
> (GG, pp. 123–124)

It is, in the first place, perverse and misleading to say that Angelo cannot think. 'The man was trying not to think of anything' (GG, p. 6), we are told when he makes his entrance, but he thinks and dreams, repeatedly, of the moment in the courtroom when Guido Altocchi called him *Traditore* (GG, p. 61); he thinks of his mother and father back in Savoca (GG, p. 124); he thinks of the girl he had been crazy about long before the perfume he gives Cassie proves to be the same as used by that very girl and thus betrays him back into the failures of his past (GG, p. 185). Absolute realism would demand a flow of internal monologue in a language compounded of immigrant Sicilian

and broken American, but Warren's concern is with the profounder realism of the feelings that underlie whatever linguistic
forms might inhabit the mind of such a character. The demands
of the more superficial realism are met by Angelo's associative
response—'Sandy Claws!' (GG, p. 7)—to the stag shot by Cy
Grinder, by the halting mixture of languages he uses with Cassie,
by his calculated use of Italian in the seduction of Charlene, and
by the incongruity between depth of feeling and awkwardness of
expression in his farewell letter to Cassie from prison.

In the second place, it is unfair of Professor Donoghue to
isolate for ridicule the above passage extracted from Chapter 5.
Without its sustaining context it appears to support his argument; in context (GG, pp. 122–23) it is appropriate and logical.
Burying himself in the unreality of the Spottwood house as a
refuge from Sicilian vengeance and his own guilt, Angelo discovers that his whole life has become a dream. He tries to
remember what it would be like to be, as he once was, in a world
where the music of his radio comes from, even to remember the
feel of 'something—anything—that had once happened to
him'; but although 'shapes, gestures, sounds would come into
the darkened theatre of his head . . . colours, they never came'.
Gradually Angelo becomes aware that he has not only lost his
sense of past feelings, but that 'he did not know what feelings
he had now'. The passage quoted by Donoghue then follows, a
legitimate, psychologically credible outcome of this sequence of
thought.

If this seems scarcely a 'lavish gift of meditation' in terms of
Angelo's established character, a comparison with Faulkner will
further demonstrate Warren's restraint. On two occasions
Warren describes Angelo's reaction to the power of the earth on
which he lies. The first occasion occurs on the day of the hog-
killing. The dismembering of the hog presents Angelo with a
spectacle of annihilation into which he feels himself drawn by
Cassie's nihilistic gaze of recognition that becomes 'in a flash,
non-recognition.' The unreality within which he has sought to
hide becomes too much for him and he runs from the scene. He
lies on a mat of dead cedar needles on the ground, feeling the
hardness of the stone that comes up through the needles, numbing his flesh:

With that awareness, he stretched out his arms and pressed his body hard against the earth. The hardness of the secret stone seemed to reach the very bone of his body. He thought of nothing being left of his own body but bone, bone against stone. He lay there for a long time. His breastbone now ached from what pressed up against him out of the earth. There was nothing to do but get up, and go down the hill.

(GG, pp. 48–49)

Earlier in the novel we are told of Cassie's 'intuited understanding of the vengeful alienation from himself' implicit in Cy Grinder's marriage to Gladys Peegrum (GG, p. 81). In the above account of Angelo's response to the earth beneath him, Warren makes available Angelo's 'intuited understanding' of what he feels. It is peaceful lying on the ground, but he cannot stay there, because the earth that seems 'to reach the very bone of his body' will absorb him even more completely than the unreality of the Spottwood house and its shadowy woman. At this stage Angelo craves reality almost as much as concealment and he seeks it both in Charlene, who, as she moves up the path, 'flamed into reality' (GG, p. 53), and in his obsessional pursuit of tasks—his 'flight into occupation' (GG, p. 49)—on the farm.

The second occasion on which Angelo is shown in significant contact with the earth occurs after Charlene's rebuff and the institution of the depersonalising morning couplings with Cassie which induce in him such a mixture of 'anger . . . desolation powerlessness and yearning' (GG, p. 115) that his flight into work becomes a fury and the prospect of engulfment in the earth more appealing. Here the earth offers Angelo an escape from the tensions of life like Jack Burden's Great Sleep or Jeremiah Beaumont's 'blank cup of nature' (WEAT, p. 506):

. . . lying on his back with the light out, breathing the dry, cool dustiness of that secret earth, not drowsing, wide awake in that darkness, he felt a lassitude creep over him, rising from the earth beneath him, like water rising, and then, as the deliberate flood seemed to close over him in the dark, he knew that it was peace, a nothingness that was, strangely, a kind of sweetness. It would be sweet to lie here forever.

(GG, p. 116)

Absorption into the nothingness of nature seems momentarily preferable to the annihilating darkness of Cassie's non-recognition, but when, having dozed off, Angelo jerks awake to find himself in real darkness with the 'mass and weight of the house . . . over him . . . coming slowly down on him', he realises that he is not ready for extinction: " '*I fix pipe*,' he said to himself. '*Me, I fix*' " (GG, p. 117). The principle of selfhood is more tenacious than he had realised.

Faulkner's Mink Snopes is cunning enough to kill Jack Houston in *The Hamlet* and Flem Snopes in *The Mansion* but not enough to resist Montgomery Ward Snopes' encouragement to make the attempted escape from Parchman Penitentiary which earns him a further twenty years in prison. He has what Denis Donoghue would be obliged to call 'a rudimentary mind', even if it functions in redneck English and is displayed to the reader over a longer period of time than Angelo's. At the end of *The Mansion* Mink lies at ease on the ground which 'never let a man forget it was there waiting, pulling gently and without no hurry at him between every step, saying, Come on, lay down; I ain't going to hurt you. Jest lay down.'[30] Thus far Faulkner realistically conveys the flow of Mink's thought: diction and rhythm are appropriate to the mind of his character. A little later Mink's contemplation of the earth becomes ambitiously philosophical, though diction is still realistic: '. . . a man had to spend not just all his life but all the life of Man too guarding against it.'[31] But when Mink, his struggles over, yields to the pull of the earth, Faulkner's language changes, leaving realism behind. As sleep comes on him, Mink feels himself seeping into the ground which is already full of people free at last from the troubles of their lives:

> . . . all mixed and jumbled up comfortable and easy so wouldn't nobody even know or care who was which any more, himself among them, equal to any, good as any, brave as any, being inextricable from, anonymous with all of them: the beautiful, the splendid, the proud and shining phantoms and dreams which are the milestones of the long human recording—Helen and the bishops, the kings and the unhomed angels, the scornful and graceless seraphim.[32]

It is, to say the least, improbable that 'inextricable' and 'anonymous' were ever in Mink's vocabulary, but the words do not
jar because they define the feelings that have grown in Mink in
the course of the two preceding paragraphs. Equally, Warren's
Angelo can hardly know the word 'lassitude', or be capable of
formulations like 'the deliberate flood' and 'a nothingness that
was, strangely, a kind of sweetness'; but these expressions do
give credible shape to thoughts and sensations that are consistent
with Angelo's character since the moment it arrived in the rain
to be subjected to the process of the novel. This is hardly
narrative exorbitance. Faulkner ends his passage, as Cleanth
Brooks puts it, 'with a final flourish of rhetoric in which he
flashes names that Mink could never have heard of . . . But if
Faulkner is putting words into Mink's dying mouth, it is easy to
forgive him . . . He is simply embellishing with literary terms
an experience which is substantially Mink's own.'[33] Warren
does not go anything like so far. His business in this poetic
novel, as in *Brother to Dragons* and *Audubon,* is as much to
interpret the inner lives of his characters as to show them doing
things. The skill—and restraint—with which he expresses the
almost inarticulate feelings that form the basis for action make
Meet Me in the Green Glen as technically impressive as it is
thematically commanding.

In his essay on 'The Genius of Nathaniel Hawthorne',[34]
Anthony Trollope makes a perennially valid observation: 'The
creations of American Literature generally are no doubt more
given to the speculative,—less given to the realistic,—than are
those of English literature. On our side of the water we deal
more with beef and ale, and less with dreams.' Sufficient unto
Meet Me in the Green Glen is the realism thereof; the book deals
principally with dreams. Each of the main characters is as
trapped in his or her dream as Angelo in his prison or Sunderland
Spottwood in his paralysed body. By the end of the story Cy
Grinder, Cassie, Angelo and Leroy Lancaster have all, in their
different ways, succeeded in bridging the gap between dream
and world, thereby demonstrating that the green glen of love is,
despite Marvell, not 'begotten by Despair / Upon Impossibility,'
but simply where you find it.

On parole from the state penitentiary at Fiddlersburg,

Angelo Passetto, a figure reminiscent of the tramp in 'Blackberry Winter', is 'going nowhere' (GG, p. 6). Seeking refuge from a past that defines him in terms of guilt, unhappiness in youth and disappointment in love, he enters the 'dark hollowness' of the house of Spottwood to build his immunity to life in the deliberate cultivation of 'blankness of being' (GG, p. 51). Like the speaker in 'Internal Injuries' who hastens away from the travestying of the human bond in the scene of the accident, Angelo 'Must go somewhere where / Nothing is real, for only Nothingness is real' (SP, p. 133). The fundamentally alien element of unreality becomes oppressive to him, however, and after his flight from the horror of the butchered hog, he senses within his inner darkness the self he would suppress: 'Something had stirred in the depth of black water, for an instant glimmering white like the belly of a fish as it turns. Something had breathed in the dark' (GG, p. 49). Although he knows that he is living in a dream as the price of not dreaming about the past, existence as 'the shape with no name', which he is to Cassie (GG, p. 109), even when they have technically become lovers, eventually fills him with frustration and despair.

Cassie's abandonment by Cy Grinder, her overbearing mother and brutally dominant husband have forced her to retreat into herself to such an extent that she can hardly distinguish between subjective impression and external reality. At the beginning of the novel she wonders 'if there were people who always knew, right off, what was inside and what outside their head' (GG, p. 4). Angelo becomes real to her only when he has been defined 'outside her head' by Murray Guilfort's warning. Now she can identify with a real man whose captivity in prison echoes her own entrapment. Calling him by his name she offers him freedom and her hand (GG pp. 148–50). True sexual love now supplants the 'blank act'. Both Angelo and Cassie had denied the need of love in a world which seemed to offer none. Now, for a spell, both find self-fulfilment in an ideal rhythm of giving and taking.

The disintegration of this harmony is almost unbearably painful and brilliantly conveyed. Angelo's attentions to Cassie's appearance begin as expressions of love. Dressing her hair, making up her lips and liberating her 'leetle feet' from the ungainly brogans, Angelo's celebration of the woman in Cassie is also an assertion of himself in terms of his love for another. 'But nobody ever did this—not ever—,' Cassie says, and Angelo replies, 'But Angelo—yes! . . . Yes! And me Angelo' (GG, p. 165). This is in contrast to Murray Guilfort who attempts to assert himself in terms of his hatred for Sunderland Spottwood. But this is the crisis point for Angelo. The emergence of the self even by way of love entails acknowledgement of the past. As he feels Cassie's cool hand on his forehead he sees again the contorted face of Guido Altocchi and it is not enough that the voice of Cassie tells him he is innocent. Cassie takes Angelo to look upon her husband because she knows that, if she is to be loved for herself, her past must be known and faced. Angelo cannot face his past and, therefore, cannot sustain the reality of love. Instead he turns Cassie into a scarlet woman, another dream which he fuels with his presents from Parkerton and keeps intact by a scrupulous separation of day from night (GG, pp. 170–71). The gap widens between the world of reality—his daily tasks around the house and farm—and the new dream. He almost closes it when he comes on Cassie in the day-time reality of her old brown sweater, untidy hair and practical brogans and calls her, for the first time, by her name; but the lingering perfume brings the intolerable past into the glare of the present. As the dream he has built round Cassie withers in the light of day, he goes to Charlene for a relationship which, involving no reference to the past, can only be a return to the void.

Angelo's defeat is matched by Cassie's. She had given love and, she thought, freedom: rejection is too much to be absorbed into a recultivated nothingness. Her act of vengeance ironically fulfils the wishes of the late Guido Altocchi, makes her a truer woman than the sneering Arlita, and restores the lovers to each other. Her confession and Angelo's '*Piccola mia—piccola mia!*' bring the green glen of true love into daylight at last, triumphant above the people who, Leroy Lancaster realises in his own pang of jealousy, 'would kill Angelo Passetto because he had stood there in the full shining of that woman's face' (GG, p. 275). Although Angelo's letter to Cassie repeats that 'it no work rite', the movement of his heart is given in the progression from 'I want to love you' and 'I try' to 'I love you' (GG, p. 365). Thus Cassie is justified in her final illusion, that Angelo took the freedom she gave, and has gone 'Somewhere far away, and he is happy. And I'm happy too, because I made him happy, for oh, I loved him' (GG, p. 359). As Murray Guilfort realises too late: 'The dream is a lie, but the dreaming is truth' (GG, p. 370).

Not all dreaming is truth. Cy Grinder and Leroy Lancaster thwart themselves by adhering so intransigently to their ideas of life that they are disabled when reality does not conform to their conceptions of what it should be. The young Cy Grinder lives in terms of his idea of himself as 'an untarnished Adam walking the new earth with the breath of the Worldwide Correspondence School blown into him' (GG, p. 77). Until he possesses the certificate that will proclaim him recast in the mould of his ideal he will not consummate his love for Cassie, irrespective of her feelings for him. Mrs Killigrew's intervention forces him back upon the squalid reality of his family and into the sweating body which was 'he deeply felt, his real self' (GG, p. 76). Abandoned, Cassie rightly concludes: 'He loves something else better than me' (GG, p. 79). If Cy cannot have his ideal, he will have nothing and his crowning act of nihilism is marriage to the physically repulsive Gladys Peegrum, whereby he finally plunges away from his shattered ideal into a life of mortified flesh. The passion he displays in killing the stag expresses his hatred of the nature in which he has immersed himself instead of in 'the destructive element' of his dream.

Cassie jerks Cy out of himself twice in the present action of the novel: firstly, when she denies him the stag; secondly, when she commands him in the name of the past to drive her to Nashville to see the Governor, thus implicating him in the complex of events which would not have happened but for his desertion of her. On the way back from their abortive effort to save Angelo, Cy tells Cassie how she may bear the fact that Angelo is to die, and how Angelo may face death: 'If you just don't remember nothing. Just don't wait for nothing. Just keep *now* in your head. A man can stand anything if it is only just that second. If a man just keeps *now* in his head, there ain't nothing else' (GG, p. 321). Cy's method of living differs from his technique for dying only in its admission of the future.

Despite Cassie's eruption back into his life, he continues to resist the past and is pleased by the plan to flood the valley (GG, p. 341). But the life of each day includes joy in his daughter, thoughts of whose future project him beyond mere '*now*' and fill him with a happiness deeper than 'cold contentment'. Cy's use of his wife as a vehicle of self-mortification is part of his Original Sin as defined by Warren in his early essay on Faulkner. Loving his daughter, Cy realises that the face of Gladys Peegrum Grinder is 'like the face of the little girl' and he finds himself, for the first time, contemplating the mysterious otherness of the woman who 'now slept in his bed and had slept there every night for now so many years' (GG, p. 376). The anguish Cy feels as the novel ends is the sign that his 'redemption through love' (SE, p. 69) has begun.

Of the two lawyers among Warren's principal characters, one is redeemed, the other damned. Leroy Lancaster leads a life of respectable ineffectuality until the trial forces him to acknowledge that he 'had wanted Angelo to die' (GG, p. 277) for having known the kind of passionate love that had eluded him. This access of self-knowledge stirs Lancaster to action, and although he loses the case he achieves a forceful identity in the real world, winning the office of prosecutor and the grudging respect of Murray Guilfort, and fathering, somewhat incredibly, a boy on the tender Corinne. Warren should have resisted the temptation to reward him with an emblematic son: the emphatic pointing of his fulfilment draws the reader's attention to the sketchiness of a character hastily assembled in the last act of the drama further to exfoliate its theme.

Trapped inside 'the darkness of his own head' (GG, p. 29), Murray Guilfort seeks to escape from himself into a surrogate marriage that includes the romantic ideal of sex embodied first in Sophie, then in Mildred who leaves him bereft and ailing in a dream gone dead when she disappears into reality by marrying a retired dentist. If Willie Stark's political success is owing to his gift for 'fulfilling vicariously the secret needs of others' (AKM, p. vii), Murray Guilfort is an inverted version of Warren's demagogue: he depends on others for vicarious fulfilment. His identification with Alfred Milbank is so strong that when Milbank dies in the middle of an assignation, Guilfort

o

falls ill. Although he wants Spottwood to die, he needs the sight of the once invincible, now stricken man as a justification of his own 'blankness of being': he may be empty, frustrated, sexually dissatisfied, but at least he is not physically paralysed from the neck down. But his need of Spottwood goes deeper than this. In a last bitter savouring of his own hollowness he thinks:

> He had always been there inside himself, and he had always been trying to get out. To be Sunderland galloping up the lane on a gray stallion, great hoofs flinging red clay like blood. To be Alfred Milbank, with his bulging eyes, leaning over the bar table in Chicago, hotly breathing out the fumes of whiskey, saying: 'And as for me, I solemnly affirm that, within the hour, I shall lay out one hundred dollars for a big juicy chunk of illusion.' To be a judge on the Supreme Court, so people would respect him. To be—even—Angelo Passetto, in a dark house.
>
> (GG, p. 366)

Guilfort's supplies of money to Cassie, his carefully preserved receipts, his assertions of power over Angelo's destiny and his stage-managing of the trial are ways of arrogating to himself the living done by others which he is too empty to do. At the end there is nothing left for him but to sink into the 'black inward abyss of himself' (SE, p. 55).

There is in *Meet Me in the Green Glen*, as in 'The Ancient Mariner', a 'relatively high degree of expressive integration' (SE, p. 262). As Denis Donoghue reminds us in his review of the novel, Warren's essay, 'A Poem of Pure Imagination: an Experiment in Reading', refers to Coleridge's view "that when 'the imagination is conceived as recognising the inherent interdependence of subject and object (or complementary aspects of a single reality), its dignity is immeasurably raised.' " (SE, p. 207). If 'Blackberry Winter' is to be approved—as it is by Donoghue—because it demonstrates such interdependence of subject and object in comparatively small compass, surely *Meet Me in the Green Glen* must be praised for achieving a similar interdependence over a much wider area of time and human experience.

As in *The Cave* the thematic relatedness of Warren's charac-

ters in *Meet Me in the Green Glen* is underscored by a system of
imagery which establishes the interdependence Denis Donoghue
values, ensuring that the book gives, in his phrase, 'an impression of being single, that is to say, single minded'. The 'one
splotchy, sliding-down grayness' (GG, p. 3) of the landscape in
the opening scene functions, like the fog in *Bleak House*, as an
objective image of blank formlessness. It is complemented subjectively by the various inner blanknesses of the characters:
Angelo's 'blankness of being' (GG, p. 51) and the unreality of a
life without definition in 'the dark hollowness of the house' (GG,
p. 109); Murray Guilfort's 'dark cellar' (GG, p. 21) and the
'movement of shadows' (GG, p. 143) in his featureless youth;
the meaningless existence cultivated by Cy Grinder; the nothingness of Cassie's life prior to Angelo; Leroy Lancaster's 'blankness' (GG, p. 271). Interdependence is also achieved in terms of
light. Guilfort's interior darkness is lit by 'a single point of
acute light' (GG, p. 28); Angelo sees himself in a mirror by
flickering candle-light (GG, p. 108); and Cassie feels a light at
'the very centre of herself, and of the whole world that fled away
from that glowing centre' (GG, p. 74). Guilfort never achieves a
broader light than this, but when, briefly, love frees both
Cassie and Angelo from their isolation, the light at Cassie's
centre expands outward: 'Everything simply was, and was
shining' (GG, p. 152). The grayness of the opening scene and
Angelo's furtive, ill-lit image of himself give way to a brightness
of air in which he feels real and 'all the objects of the world
seemed to stand clear and separate' (GG, p. 158). On the last
page of the novel the stirrings of love bring Cy Grinder out of his
'inner darkness' to stand beneath 'the moon, with the sky, and
the whole world in its light' (GG, p. 376). By such interdependence of subject and object Warren unifies the elements of this
intense, eloquent fable of love.

Chapter Eight—Notes

[1] Fiedler, Leslie A., *No! In Thunder: Essays on Myth and Literature*
(Boston: Beacon Press, 1960), p. 129.
[2] Bohner, p. 153.

[3] In 1951 the Collins story was made into the film, 'Ace in the Hole' (or 'The Big Carnival'). The film was directed by Billy Wilder from a script by himself and Charles Brackett, the producer.

[4] The simile anticipates the images of the field-mouse and owl in 'Time as Hypnosis' (SP. p. 24). The actual death of the field mouse in the poem prompts the boy to a sense of the metaphysical blankness which is imaged in the snow and which invades his own mind. See above, p. 179.

[5] 'Fables for Our Time', *Times Literary Supplement*, Nov, 27, 1959, p. 692.

[6] Grandsen, K. W., *Encounter*, **14** (May, 1960), 78.

[7] Samuels, Charles, 'In the Wilderness', *Critique*, **5** (Fall, 1962), 50.

[8] Dorothy's caring for Bingham marks her release from the isolation in which she has lived, and refutes the objection that 'Dorothy Cutlick who lays herself down for the friendly Greek Papadoupalous comes to nothing after a long build-up'. See John Coleman, 'Property Values', *Spectator*, **4** Dec, 1959, p. 836.

[9] Orwell, George, 'Charles Dickens', in *The Collected Essays, Journalism and Letters of George Orwell*, **I**, 'An Age Like This', ed. Sonia Orwell and Ian Angus (Harmondsworth: Penguin Books, 1970), p. 498.

[10] Orwell, p. 499.

[11] Marx, Leo, *The Machine in the Garden: Technology and the Pastoral Ideal in America* (New York: Oxford University Press, Galaxy Books, 1967), p. 3.

[12] Irving, Washington, 'The Legend of Sleepy Hollow' quoted from rpt. in James Cochrane, ed., *The Penguin Book of American Short Stories* (Harmondsworth: Penguin Books, 1969,) p. 13.

[13] Longley, pp. 169–70.

[14] Huxley, Julian, *TVA: Adventure in Planning* (London: The Scientific Book Club, 1945), p. 5.

[15] Barrett, William, 'Readers' Choice', *Atlantic Monthly*, **213** (June, 1964), 134.

[16] Mordecai Richler, 'The Big Southern Novel Show', *Spectator*, 30 Oct, 1964, p. 581.

[17] *Times Literary Supplement*, 5 Nov, 1964, p. 993.

[18] Carter, Everett, 'The 'Little Myth' of Robert Penn Warren', *Modern Fiction Studies*, **6** (Spring, 1960), 5.

[19] Mizener, Arthur, 'The Uncorrupted Consciousness', *Sewanee Review*, **72** (Autumn, 1964), 691.

[20] Mizener, p. 698.

[21] Stewart, p. 501.

[22] Stewart, p. 517.

[23] Mizener, p. 696.

[24] Mizener, p. 691.

[25] 'Old Kentucky Style', *Times Literary Supplement*, 21 April, 1972, p. 439.

[26] For the valley that gave Warren the 'germ' of *Meet Me in the Green Glen*, see below, Appendix, p. 256.

[27] An interesting sidelight on the kind of violence often found in Warren's writing occurs in an observation he made in 1968: 'I remember a murder map of the United States, in 1926 or 1927, when I first began to look at things like that. One murder map of the United States, if you take it in terms of status homicide—honour, homicide for status or for bad nerves, made Tennessee look awful black. Detroit was lily white. Chicago was lily white. New York lily white.' Theodore Solotaroff *et al.*, 'Symposium: Violence in Literature', *The American Scholar*, **37** (Summer, 1968), 493–94.

[28] Sheppard, R. Z., 'Sacred and Profane Grit', *Time*, 14 March, 1977, p. 58.

[29] Donoghue, Denis, 'Life Sentence', *New York Review of Books*, **17** (2 Dec, 1971), 28.

[30] Faulkner, William, *The Mansion* (New York: Random House, 1959), p. 434.

[31] Faulkner, *The Mansion*, p. 435.

[32] Faulkner, *The Mansion*, pp. 435–36.

[33] Brooks, Cleanth, Faulkner, William: *The Yoknapatawpha Country* (New Haven and London: Yale University Press, 1963), p. 243.

[34] Trollope, Anthony, 'The Genius of Nathaniel Hawthorne', *North American Review*, **129** (Sept, 1879), 203–22.

9

Country Hick

W. H. Auden neatly defines one aspect of our interest in a new book by a writer who has held our attention in the past. However enthralled we may be by the objectivist insistences of the modern tradition,

> . . . our judgement of an established author is never simply an aesthetic judgement. In addition to any literary merit it may have, a new book by him has a historical interest for us as the act of a person in whom we have long been interested. He is not only a poet or a novelist; he is also a character in our biographies.[1]

Readers whose interest in Robert Penn Warren's work has made him a character in their biographies will notice at once the similarities between the career of Jed Tewksbury in *A Place to Come To* and that of his maker. Dugton, Alabama is a small town not unlike Guthrie, Kentucky, which may have been a 'hellhole' indeed to the brilliant young Vanderbilt undergraduate, especially during university vacations in the long, hot Tennessee summers. The tall, awkward youth who made such an impact on Allen Tate is echoed in an early description Jed gives of himself: 'There stands the youth, well over six feet, unbarbered and with unruly dark hair, arms looking gangly because of length and the bigness of the hands hanging down (one clutching a book that in that hand seems trivial), wearing a soiled white shirt with collar open . . . long legs in blue jeans . . . feet in

216

brogans' (PCT, p. 34). Like Jerry Calhoun, Willie Stark, Brad Tolliver and Warren himself, Jed is, in Rozelle Hardcastle's phrase, 'a country hick come to town' (PCT, p. 301). H. L. Mencken's indictment of the South as 'The Sahara of the Bozart' is reflected in the pretentious mediocrity of the sculpture produced by Lawford Carrington—'Mr Nashville and Leonardo da Vinci in one package' (PCT, p. 155)—but Jed's goings home remind us that Warren's imaginative loyalty to his region in book after book is as profound as Faulkner's commitment to his Yoknapatawpha or the expatriate Joyce's allegiance to his dear, dirty Dublin. Both Jed and Warren succeed professionally, both are academics and marry twice. The redeeming gush of love Jed feels for his son, Ephraim, recalls the loving father of *Promises* and 'Sunset Walk in Thaw-Time in Vermont'. Jed's disenchantment with his 'vast number of cards that measured three by five inches' (PCT, p. 399), coincides with Warren's statement that he 'will never write another line of criticism of any kind.'[2]

The *Bildungsroman*, then, is close to the life and doubtless provides long-time Nashvillians with a *roman à clef* by which they may extend their own biographies. It is also a *Künstler-roman*. In much of his more recent poetry, from *Audubon* to 'A Problem in Spatial Composition', Warren's theme is the imagination. In *A Place to Come To* he orchestrates his basic ideas into a discussion of the relationship between art and life. Jed Tewksbury is an intellectual user. His 'Original Sin' involves the substitution of art for life as he turns the death of his father into a tall tale that buys him social success. Like the unregenerate Brad Tolliver, Jed prefers expertise to truth: when the death of Dr Stahlmann and the moral chaos of the second World War wreck his belief in the ideal of humanist culture, he abandons the *imperium intellectūs* and makes a 'parlour trick' of his dissertation (PCT, p. 100). Unable to love the living Agnes Andresen he converts the fact of her dying into the idea of 'Dante and the Metaphysics of Death', polarising his life into 'laboratory findings' at Agnes's bedside and his 'studies in the theory of death' (PCT, p. 106). This unblessèd rage for order involves him in a perversion of the right relation that should, T. S. Eliot tells us, exist between 'the man who suffers and the mind which creates'. Jed's suffering becomes a concern not for the dying girl but for the quality of his own response:

> As I sat by the bed, I yearned for purity of feeling, for a sense of meaning in my experience, but when feeling gushed up in my heart, I caught myself asking if the yearning itself might not be the mother of self-deceit. Or, even, asking if the awareness of the clinical eye might provoke the enactment desired.
>
> (PCT, p. 107)

Like Jed, Lawford Carrington would, no doubt, prefer to be able to love his wife; instead he casts her face in orgasm into a sculpture of about as much artistic worth as a painting by Tretchikoff. Jed, in his way, is a better artist than this. His academic work earns him international acclaim, but it is still, essentially, as fake as Carrington's. 'Hell', Jed tells Cud Cudworth, 'I'm not a thinker, I'm a college professor' (PCT, p. 175), thus conceding his propensity for intellectual constructs and systematised reality. Arnaut Daniel helps him towards 'some tenderness . . . some intuition' of Rozelle's 'being' (PCT, p. 257), but he is basically too enclosed in his own self-consciousness to respond to the otherness of any of his women, or even to profit from the 'living and suffering fact of Clairbelle Spaethe' (PCT, p. 138) which underlies the girl on the make on the train to Nashville, with her vulgar, strident letter and cheesecake pose.

The redoubtable Mrs Jones-Talbot's 'faculty of appreciation' (PCT, p. 282) brings art and life together as they are meant to be in her study of Dante. She appreciates the beauty and wisdom of Dante and the meaning of her life with Sergio in terms of each other, without falsifying either, reaching a deeper understanding of both. Jed has not found the secret of such balance, such true relation between the aesthetic and the human. Incapable of love, he has retreated into the scholar's surrogate, a course in 'Love in the Middle Ages: Sacred and Profane' and without understanding either love or time has toyed with the idea of doing 'a study, in the Provençal and Italian poets before Dante, of the relation of the concept of Love to that of Time' (PCT, p. 256), a project he is as unqualified to undertake as the young Jack Burden is incapable of understanding Cass Mastern. The swami's smile which seems to indicate to Jed 'that if I didn't mess with his racket, he wouldn't mess with mine' (PCT, p. 254), implies the judgement Jed deserves. Both men are fakes: it takes one to know one. Instead of knowing the world, Jed uses his brand of art to interpret it—as Brad Tolliver uses his scenarios—heedless of Susan Sontag's warning that to interpret "is to impoverish, to deplete the world—in order to set up a shadow world of 'meanings'."[3] Jed's problem is the typically modern one defined by Saul Bellow's *Herzog*. Man must idealise, must think in order to be Cartesianly human: 'But can thought wake you from the dream of existence? Not if it becomes a second realm of confusion, another more complicated dream, the dream of intellect, the delusion of total explanations.'[4]

Jed's friend, Stephan Mostoski, uses his art of physics to explain the world as 'infinite motion in infinite solitude', giving another turn of the screw to the naturalism that has always both attracted and repelled Warren. But Mostoski's explanation proves less than total when the resemblance between his wife and a bayoneted Russian prompts him to wipe his own spit from the boy's face. If this gives Mostoski but 'a momentary pang', his dream of intellect cannot, by his own confession, deplete the world of his love for Ephraim (PCT, p. 382). The heart, like Miss Sontag, is 'against interpretation'. As Warren says of McLuhan's criticism, none of the arts—Lawford Carrington's, Jed's or Mostoski's—'covers the case' (Appendix, p. 258). Life, like literature, demands the immediate, *ad hoc* response to the particular thing, the individual person. 'Away with all duplicates of the world', cries Miss Sontag, 'until we again experience more immediately what we have.'[5]

Paul Theroux, who likes *A Place to Come To*, finds the university parts least satisfactory: 'The best moments in the book are those which have little to do with university life—memories of his southern town, Dugton, and his hatred for his father; episodes of sexual conquest and scenes from the war.'[6] Bernard Bergonzi is harder on the book as a portrait of academe: 'the novel projects a quite unconvincing—and possibly unconvinced—view of the scholarly life.'[7] This is precisely Warren's intention.

The point of view in the novel is Jed's. Academic life loses its reality for him and, therefore, for the reader. His recollections of discovering the magic of language and of the desperate measures by which he gains access to the enchantment of the Castle of Otranto are among the book's most vivid passages, but after Stahlmann's suicide Jed never recovers his scholarly illusions. For all his honours, Jed is finally so unconvinced that he tells Rozelle: 'the main function of work is to kill time' (PCT, p. 361).

Whatever losses Jed sustains, he holds to his expertise until his last visit to Dugton exposes its inadequacy. As a 'good technician' he coldly and capably arranges Rozelle's flight from her husband on the basis of his thesis that her life with Carrington or with himself on her money will match the fate of the two Gauls entombed below the *Forum Boarium*. He and Rozelle ransack each others bodies for a shared oblivion in place of their mutual Dugton past, but Jed cannot love well enough to allay his fear of the future and Rozelle does not love him enough to risk Carrington's wrath and a life without luxury (PCT pp. 310–12). Still the technician, Jed systematically attempts to 'feel the joy of being part of the human project' (PCT, p. 335) by marrying the long-lost Dauphine and under-taking civic obligations, like Flannery O'Connor's Sheppard who, in 'The Lame Shall Enter First', 'stuffed his own emptiness with good works like a glutton.'[8] The ineffectuality of this calculated attempt to return from isolation to life in community carries a warning about facile applications of the programme given in 'Knowledge and the Image of Man'. The marriage fails, the do-gooding fades, and Jed is left alone with his technique, his amiable, nihilistic Polish friend and the contingent fact of his son. Loving Ephraim has nothing to do with technique and is beyond the scope of any thesis. The experience points Jed towards the past in which, perhaps, Young Buck looked down at him as he slept (PCT, p. 340), and which contains the place he must come to in order to escape from his own disastrous expertise. Return to Dugton proves the end of technique as the heart, at last, supervenes.

When Jed begins to tell us his story he has been dispossessed of his crippling flair for thesis by the events he describes. Confessional, gingerly questing, he feels his way along the

tangled lines of his life in search of meaning, not imposing it.
He knows poker better than the boys of Jonquil Street with
their tattered cards and Coca-Cola bottle tops, but confesses,
'I do not know the rules or the values of cards in the game that
I am now playing' (PCT, p. 170). His tentativeness is dramatised
by his self-consciousness about language. Speculating about the
sudden change in his view of the past, Jed draws a distinction
between *'fact inert'* and *'fact operative'* only to dismiss his own
pedantry as 'stultifying lingo' (PCT, p. 19). A little later he
supposes that the use of third person narrative reflects his
shame at exploiting the circumstances of his father's death. He
refers to the magic of language (PCT, p. 62), to his own choice
of metaphor (PCT, p. 93) and of tone (PCT, pp. 9, 344), fully
aware of his own probing for definitions and of the strengths,
weaknesses, colourations and general provisionality of the
language in which this improvisatory process goes forward.
Thus Warren achieves through language the purpose Conrad
Aiken finds in Faulkner's style, which is a way of keeping 'the
form—and the idea—fluid and unfinished, still in motion, as it
were, and unknown, until the dropping into place of the very
last syllable.'[9]

Puzzled by the speed with which he has written the opening
account of his father's death and the haunting scene under the
chinaberry tree, Jed remarks that he is 'inclined to be painfully
slow and careful' in his formulations (PCT, p. 9). That this
part of his story has come 'rushing out' underlines its importance,
but Julian Symons says in his TLS review that his 'heart sinks'
at the language of the opening paragraph: 'a particularly
American verbal coarseness has been encouraged by the
Revolution of the Sexual Word[10].' This is uncharacteristically
imperceptive of Mr Symons: perhaps he is put off by the 'man
talking to men' side of American fiction which, Cyril Connolly
once pointed out, we have most reason to envy. In any case,
apart from its two demoticisms, the first sentence of the opening
paragraph, with its measured rhythm and parenthetical phrases,
is positively stately, and the second sentence sparely registers
a marvel. The whole paragraph rolls with the 'perfect precision'
of the wagon referred to:

I was the only boy, or girl either, in the public school of the town of Dugton, Claxford County, Alabama, whose father had ever got killed in the middle of the night standing up in the front of his wagon to piss on the hindquarters of one of a span of mules and, being drunk, pitching forward on his head, still hanging on to his dong, and hitting the pike in such a position and condition that both the left front and the left rear wheels of the wagon rolled, with perfect precision, over his unconscious neck, his having passed out being, no doubt, the reason he took the fatal plunge in the first place. Throughout, he was still holding on to his dong.

(PCT, p. 3)

If this came in a rush, Jed still contrived to be careful. Not only does he convey, by his scrupulous description of what happened, his own sustained wonder that it could have happened at all, but his expression accommodates the crudities of the men gathered under the chinaberry tree in order to underline the inability of academic inclination to obfuscate the affrontingly earthy truth of the matter. Jed's professional success has carried him away from Dugton into the world of the elaborate period, of 'in such a position and condition that . . . ' and 'his having passed out being . . .,' but he will not achieve identity or happiness until he can come to terms with Dugton, with 'piss' and 'dong' and the despair of the father who, born out of phase, could not understand why the definition of man should be himself 'Setten in a wagon in the middle of the night with a bottle in his hand and looken at a mule's ass' (PCT, p. 14).

When Mr Tutwayler and his forthright associates under the chinaberry tree discuss Buck Tewksbury's spectacular demise in the vocabulary that so offends Julian Symons, they suddenly become aware of Jed's eyes on them and then of his tears. 'Look,' whispers Mr Tutwayler, 'look—the pore little chap, and him a cryen for his daddy that's dead' (PCT, p. 7). It is not for his dead daddy that the boy cries but for the thumb cocked discreetly towards him, the wall-eyed knowingness, the whole 'absurd parody of secrecy' which now has him pinned and wriggling in a dawning sense of 'what the world might be'. Ridicule in the schoolyard expands this sense into outrage at the contempt visited upon him and at the father who has caused it. He proceeds to build his defences by developing the aggressive party piece whereby he attempts to repudiate his father and join the world. His technique is good, his performance applauded, but his repudiation is only partly successful. Vaguely identifying with Gervaise's representation of Coupeau's last alcoholic pains in *L'Assommoir*, he feels 'mysteriously sad and blank' (PCT, p. 22), and at the next request that he put on the celebrated performance, repudiation of the father yields to defiance of the world: 'You know, I jest wonders why ain't none of you folks ever told me how any of yore fucken fathers died.'

Jed runs from the house on Jonquil Street when he returns unexpectedly to find his father's place taken, and Dr Stahlmann's rôle as father is as short-lived as Jed's sojourn in the *imperium intellectūs*. At the Carringtons' New Year's Eve party Jed's identity is threatened by Rozelle's passionate response to her husband when he unveils the sculptured head of Butler, and by the assumptions made about his relationship with Maria McInnis. This time the story 'Bout Pap, how he got kilt' functions so successfully as self-assertion that it inspires Maria to embark on a programme of becoming which will involve acceptance of her past to the end that she may live as solidly herself in the present as she thinks Jed does. 'The only thing we have to work on, or with, is our past', Jed says, 'This can be a question of life and death' (PCT, p. 19). Living, his mother keeps him from his past by banning him from Dugton; dead, she brings him back by way of the simple love of Perk Simms which transcends all repudiations, contempts and ambitions. Like Leopold Bloom, Jed is weary, he has travelled. Like Odysseus he must return to his rocky isle in Dugton, Alabama, where, in Yeats' phrase, 'all the ladders start' and where the fiery Elvira lies beside the father life teaches him to understand. Dugton is the beginning of his *terra*.

All Jed's other places fail him. He suffers what Stephan Mostoski calls 'the death of the self which has become placeless' (PCT, p. 348). Dr Stahlmann rescues him from the 'placelessness' of Chicago, but the Castle of Otranto falls by the great man's suicide and is ground into the ignominy of apartments by modern commercialism. The *imperium intellectūs* itself is discredited by Stahlmann's use of it as a moral bolt-hole in which he hides from the evil of his homeland (PCT, p. 71). Time exiles a man from 'the country of the young' and there is no place for the ageing Jed in 'self-contained, self-fulfilling' Ripley City, S.D. Although Jed finds a temporary *patria* among the Italian partisans, it is of the most rudimentary kind, held in formation not by an ideal nor by the human bond, but by a mere determination to survive. Sex, for a spell, affords a place for both Jed and Rozelle to come to, in which 'each is the other's hermitage' (PCT, p. 207), but proves no more of a 'one-answer system' for them than it was for Jed's father. Jed's single afternoon with Mrs Jones-Talbot is a genuine relation between two individuals, as open and dignified as the clean, ritual mating of horse and mare that precedes it. The issue is mutual understanding and abiding affection. By contrast, Jed's furtive couplings with Rozelle are a desperate plunge into a timeless non-place in which he can

> . . . abolish the self that had once stood under the chinaberry tree in Claxford County, Alabama, had sat late at night with an open book and had not known why, had yearned for something and had not known what, had buried a wife on a prairie where snow now lay, and had fled in guilt, and, seeing the smiling face of Maria in the Cudworth candlelight, had had, briefly, the dream that he might enter the dream in which these people around him, in Nashville, Tennessee, seemed to live.
>
> (PCT, p. 209)

There is more to be learned from the Cudworth candlelight than from the artificial glitter of the Carringtons' million-dollar barn. It is not the arty crowd but the friendly ex-lawyer who possesses an intuitive grasp of the importance of place and its relation to time and love:

> . . . I was born here, in this old house, and I look out the window and know what I'm seeing, and I know some people I like to be with, and I like what I do all day long, and maybe that's all that realness is, anyway, and when Sally pops that little squawking blob of protoplasm out, I'll be feeling so real I'll yell.
>
> (PCT, p. 174)

This is just the kind of passage unsympathetic reviewers extract for display in proof of what they regard as Warren's sentimentality. In context it is entirely appropriate to the character who speaks it when exhilarated by his wife's pregnancy and lit by generous intakes of bourbon. It is also thematically functional. The dream in which Jed thinks the people of Nashville live is an illusion; Cudworth is just what he seems to be and although Jed is embarrassed by his candour, he must be chastened too. This man's dream is real: he has found *sua terra*.

In its involvement with the discrepancy between the ideal and the real, Jed's life is typically Warrenesque. Although the womenfolk gathered in sympathy for the widowed Mrs Tewksbury know, perhaps biblically, the reality of the deceased, they attribute the widow's dryness of eye to shock. 'With the wisdom of years' that have brought him awareness of the split between appearance and reality, Jed realises that the condoling ladies would have preferred his mother's emotions to be less determined by the truth about her husband and more by the idealising conventions of bereavement. She should have played the game 'according to the rules that everybody accepted' (PCT, p. 4). Idea triumphs over reality when the preacher concentrates on God's infinite mercy rather than on the individual life now ended, but later in the novel reality takes its revenge when the dying Agnes bravely rejects her God (PCT, p. 109) and again when her father, overcome by the fact of her death, cannot pray (PCT, p. 113). The magic of the Latin language promises an ideal world 'that was real and different', a 'mystic peephole . . . on a bright reality beyond' (PCT, pp. 26, 28), but Dauphine's expensive bohemianism and Dr Stahlmann's culture are casualties of the war in which Jed decides to participate because he would 'rather be a boulder than a rabbit (PCT, p. 77).

Dr Stahlmann's ideal paradigm of historical cause and effect does not work for Jed in the real world. 'The boulder', he discovers, 'has no concern whatsoever with the principles of geology or the law of gravity' (PCT, p. 85), that is, with its own nature and limitations. Preoccupied with his, Jed is both part of the landslide of twentieth-century history—from the legacy of the South's lost cause and the horror of modern war to the exaltation of the intellect and the worship of sex—and a rabbit, determined by that history, looking for a place to jump to. The idea of war is the German lieutenant's belief in the Geneva Convention; the facts of war are Gianluigi's mutilated cheek and hand and a bullet in the back of the head. The ideal of love is Agnes's 'tender striving', or the mirrored image of Jed and Maria McInnis dressed for a Christmas party (PCT, p. 177), or Dauphine as 'an allegorical figure of Flesh Yearning for the Beyond of Flesh' (PCT, p. 337). Reality is the 'devouring negativity' Jed and Rozelle find in orgasms which are, at best, "like the 'black hole' of the physicists" (PCT, p. 220), and at worst 'necrophilic' (PCT, p. 313).

The pathos of imperfect reality carries Jed into his relation with Mrs Jones-Talbot. As he moves towards the stairs that lead to her bedroom he thinks that 'nothing—mysteriously nothing—would have happened if I had not seen that smudge of dirt on the tan left ankle that thrust so firmly down into the beat-up old sneaker' (PCT, p. 280). A similar imperfection had converted his 'passionless', 'blank enactment' of sex with Roselle into the frantic 'clutch, struggle and spasm' of their stolen afternoons out of time: 'The skin of the heel must have had some small, dry scaliness and it was that imperfection that, when the heel made, in its pressure, the slightest rubbing, demanding movement against my flesh, brought actuality, in that instant, to focus' (PCT, p. 198). The smudge on Mrs Jones-Talbot's ankle connects Jed with her resolution of past and present, the idea of Sergio and the fact of the excellent Mr McInnis. Rozelle's heel tips him into the actuality of sex out of which he forms his ideal 'vacuum of time' until her repeated departures from him make the real world to which she returns something he can no longer ignore. He runs from time-lessness into time itself, 'for when I escaped Nashville, it was an escape into time, into its routines and nags, which make life possible after all' (PCT, p. 317). But life in an ever-extending present is unfulfilling too, as Warren demonstrates in the lives of Sue Murdock, Isaac Sumpter and Cy Grinder. Completeness is possible only by a marriage of the timeless ideal and temporal reality. If Jed is to have a self and a future he must look to the past for his 'Truth', touch base again like Antaeus, and stand, like the poet, 'in that cold blaze of Platonic light' (SP, p. 255).

Jed's redemptive journey into the past has three main

stops: Italy, Chicago and Dugton. In Italy he discovers that no
viable idealism has developed out of the old partisan associations.
His comrades of the war have all become cynical materialists
except for Gianluigi, locked in his pure, self-excoriating fantasy.
There is nothing here for Jed to live by. Rozelle's assurance that
'You are real and not a charade' may be her truth but it is not
yet his. Her account of life with the ex-swami from Jackson,
Mississippi—an example of Dr Stahlmann's 'perfect existentialist man' (PCT, p. 76)—suggests an exotic but genuine relationship in which two people face the past so honestly together that
they can still belong to the South, both savouring and transcend-
ing its clichés. *En route* for his South, Jed finds in Chicago not
the *imperium intellectūs* and the Castle of Otranto but the
human bond that results from his attempt to rescue the old
Italian lady. In a brilliant passage Warren deprives Jed of moral
self-satisfaction in his act through having him respond to the
beauty of the young mugger who moves 'like Ephraim, like a
hawk in sunset flight' (PCT, p. 387). The point here is that Jed
responds positively and spontaneously—outwith any thesis of
feeling—both to the old lady's predicament and to the boy's
beauty of movement. His feelings are not curbed by the moral
system represented by the police. He does the right thing in
terms of this system, but his heart expands beyond it. He
finds himself, after all, bound to an Italian, and, as the old
woman's *figlio*, ironically enacts the rôle of *tesoro del cuore* more
immediately than he had ever done for the mother who swore
she would break his neck if he ever returned to Dugton but, with
maternal inconsistency, always kept his bed made up.

Dugton closes the gap between the ideal and the real. 'Living
with a woman like yore ma', Perk tells Jed, 'is like you was
living in a—a dream—and time ain't gone by, the way she
could make you feel that everything kept on being the truth'
(PCT, p. 394). The truth of Mr and Mrs Perk Simms has not been
half-empty whiskey bottles and smeared lipstick, as the young
Jed had anticipated when he ran from the house, but the dream
of love made real in daily living. A marriage, we may assume,
like that of Willie and Adelle Proudfit in *Night Rider*, or the
Highbridges in *Flood*, and like the marriage that, with certain
unimportant social differences, might have joined Agnes

P

Andresen or Rozelle Hardcastle or Dauphine Phillips, née
Finkel, to Jed Tewksbury. The husband and wife of Dugton
have succeeded where all Jed's arts have failed. He has lost his
citizenship of the *imperium intellectūs* and his *simplicitas* is no
longer *sancta*; but he does know the blessedness of finding the
key to that *terra* which consists of 'the things that made you
what you are and that must be lived by you because you are
you' (PCT, p. 232). Jed's *terra* begins with the scene under the
chinaberry tree and the weeping child with whom, at the
beginning of the novel, he feels he has 'no connection' (PCT,
p. 8). Connection is made when Jed, disposed to weep again,
eventually understands his father—and the symbolism of the
fifty-cent sabre—better than his mother did, although her
recollections of Buck in letters and her wish to be buried by him
suggest that she felt more than she allowed herself—or was
able—to express. Like Cy Grinder's self-mortifications, Old
Buck's rampaging sexuality and blazing drunks were negative
expressions of the dream he was born too late to make real:

> If he had been born in 1840, he would have been just ripe for
> sergeant in a troop of Alabama cavalry. You could see him; high
> in stirrups, black mustaches parted to expose white teeth and emit
> the great yell, the sabre, light as a toy in his big hand, flashing like
> flame. Buck leading the charge, Buck breveted rank by rank, Buck
> the darling of his tattered wolfish crew, Buck in some last action
> under Forrest—say, in the last breakthrough into Tennessee—
> meeting lead as the sabre flashes and the yell fades from his
> throat.
>   Poor Buck, I thought.
>   Then I said out loud: 'Poor Buck.'
>
> (PCT, p. 400)

Jed's pity is an acknowledgement of his kinship with the father
who also failed to fulfil himself in terms of the idea. Instead of
weeping, as in his youth, for the contempt of the world, he
experiences compassion for the father who begat him and in
doing so finds the 'human necessity' simply defined by Brad
Tolliver as 'the connection between what I was and what I am'
(F, p. 439). Claxford County is, after all, the country hick's
point of origin, Dugton his place to come to. It is there that he
finds the unacademic 'country of the heart' (F, p. 440) from

which, now back in Chicago, he sends his humble, honest and dignified letter to Dauphine and looks out towards the possibility of a future with her and their son.

Chapter Nine—Notes

[1] Auden, W. H., *The Dyer's Hand* (London: Faber and Faber, 1963), p. 4.

[2] Stitt, Peter, 'An Interview with Robert Penn Warren', *Sewanee Review*, **85** (Summer, 1977), 477.

[3] Sontag, Susan, *Against Interpretation* (New York: Farrar, Straus and Giroux, 1966), p. 7.

[4] Bellow, Saul, *Herzog* (London: Weidenfeld and Nicolson, 1965), p. 166.

[5] Sontag, p. 7.

[6] Theroux, Paul, 'A Lifetime of Writing', *The Times*, 2 May, 1977, p. 11.

[7] Bergonzi, Bernard, 'Tales from the South', *The Observer*, 1 May, 1977, p. 24.

[8] O'Connor, Flannery, *Everything that Rises Must Converge* (New York: New American Library, 1967), p. 164.

[9] Aiken, Conrad, *A Reviewer's ABC* (London: W. H. Allen, 1961), p. 197.

[10] Symons, Julian, 'In the Southern Style', *Times Literary Supplement*, 29 April, 1977, p. 507.

Conclusion

To read Warren entire is to become aware, as may be with any writer, of an *oeuvre* with its own family of consiliences and reverberations. It is also to experience, in the curving of one man's mind and art, literature as process rather than product. Reading Warren one has the sense, as Bernard Bergonzi remarks of the later poetry, 'of being given successive insights into the unfolding of a poet's mind rather than of being shown a series of icons.'[1] *A Place to Come To* is not as immediately impressive as *All the King's Men*; it lacks the endlessly fascinating central figure provided in Willie Stark, as well as the astonishingly powerful blending of moral values with realistic characterisation achieved in the earlier novel. Jed Tewkesbury is, however, Warren's most vital and appealing narrative voice after Jack Burden and his story presents the familiar 'basic themes' more richly mixed and more panoramically displayed than in any of the other novels. *A Place to Come To* is a major event in the unfolding of the most experienced, substantial and rewarding literary mind at work in America today.

In Jed's last conversation with Rozelle he tells her: 'I have never had the slightest notion of what happiness is . . . what I had thought of all my life as happiness was only excitement' (PCT, p. 361). Jed's story is, certainly, full of excitement and this points to the difficulties a Warren novel faces when it lands on the reviewer's desk. Most of the novelists currently in fashion with the intellectual establishment appear to be of E. M. Forster's party. One can imagine Barth, Bellow, Cheever, Hawkes, Heller, Roth or Updike repining, more or less in chorus, 'Yes—oh dear yes—the novel tells a story.'[2] This is an aspect of the novel that Warren accepts and enjoys. The reviewer, however, is not prepared for this: a novel of intellectual pretension should offer not story but myth, or an extreme quality of language, or deep anxieties about being a novel at all, or an intricate symbolic order just this side of opacity, or, at least, the special refinements of ethnic sensibility. Warren's novels—as well as poems like 'The Ballad of Billie Potts', *Brother to Dragons* and *Audubon*—are concerned with myth, with language, with the imagination and with the problems of the modern world. They also, blatantly and without excuses, tell stories. There even are, in the novels which employ *exempla*, stories within stories. The reason for this atavism seems to be that 'even in the age of the Uncertainty Principle and culture fracture, Warren has not lost his sense of life as a sustained drama.[3] The foreground of the sustained drama presented in a Warren novel typically offers excitements—regional, political, sexual, homicidal—which the facile eye may associate with the bids for best-sellerdom in writings by the later John O'Hara, James Jones, Herman Wouk, or Irwin Shaw, thereby missing the profounder activities that occur beneath the surface glitter. 'What is love?' the poet asks in *Audubon*, and answers, 'One name for it is knowledge' (SP, p. 99). Warren does not make Jed's mistake: his books are about human happiness and how it may be achieved by discovering love through knowledge.

Long before the American Adam found himself beyond the ruined garden with his lost innocence the Jews had become habituated to the ways of the travelling ghetto. 'Nobody lived in Eden any more', says Bernard Malamud's Fixer, Yakov Bok. He reflects:

> Once you leave [the *shtetl*] you're out in the open; it rains and it snows. It snows history, which means what happens to somebody starts in a web of events outside the personal. It starts of course before he gets there. We're all in history, that's sure, but some are more than others, Jews more than some. If it snows not everybody is out in it getting wet.[4]

Many of us today are likely to feel wet with the snow of history —as Sandor Himmelstein says in Bellow's *Herzog*, 'We're on the same identical network' as the Jew.[5] We may be tempted to seek refuge from the press of the world in Dostoevsky's underground, there to wrestle with the grammatical fiction of 'I', the 'me miserable' of modern culture, and to see, beyond the semantic phantom of our selfhood, the extent of our faithlessness. We may yet go on in the silence, like Samuel Beckett's Unnamable, but the prospects are bleak. With greater resilience we may light out for 'the territory' with Joseph Heller's Yossarian; or if we feel ourselves to be candidates for John Updike's questionable sainthood we may run, ah, run with his Rabbit. But if burial or flight seem either insufficient or too desperate remedies, we may look to a writer like Warren. His Jasper Harrick knows the underground attractions, his Jack Burden, Jeremiah Beaumont and Angelo Passetto report on the effects of opting out; Jed Tewksbury can tell us what life is like as a rabbit and the fierce, unforgiving Dr Echegaray will advise us that, however wet we may get, our obligation 'is to enter history, not to flinch from history' (F, p. 147).

Pondering the unity of Warren's work, Cleanth Brooks says:

> The poetry, the fiction, and even the critical essays of Robert Penn Warren form a highly unified and consistent body of work; but it would be impossible to reduce it, without distorting simplifications, to some thesis about human life. The work is not tailored to fit a thesis. In the best sense it is inductive: it explores the human situation and tests against the fullness of human experience our various abstract statements about it.[6]

Warren's strength, the authority of his statements about the world, derives from the belief he shares with Kierkegaard that 'abstract thought cannot grasp the meaning of existence and that feeling—passion as he [Kierkegaard] termed it—provides the knowledge that is the key of existence and action.'[7] In a recent poem we are told to 'learn to live in the world' by thrilling to the 'electric tang of joy—or pain' (SP, p. 6). In *Democracy and Poetry* Warren defines poetry as an affirmation of man's ability to come to terms with himself: 'What poetry most significantly celebrates is the capacity of man to face the deep, dark inwardness of his nature and his fate.'[8] It is man's mind, his intellect and his imagination, which gives him this capacity for it is man's mind that enables him to be 'the form-making animal par excellence. By making forms he understands the world, grasps the world, imposes himself upon the world.'[9] Yet in his creation of forms, his imposition of himself on the world, man must never forget that reality has its own independent existence. As the boy in 'Court-Martial' discovers when his dream crumbles, 'The world is real. It is there' (SP, p. 232).

While he believes in feeling as the source of knowledge, Warren is alert to the distorting tendencies of sexual passion. Sex is associated with the corrupting isolationism of Percy Munn and Lucille Christian's unfulfilling relationship and with the evasion of identity implicit in Jeremiah Beaumont and Rachel Jordan's 'divine frenzy and sweet blackness' (WEAT, p. 414). Jed Tewksbury uses Rozelle sexually to achieve abolition of the self (PCT, p. 209). This is not to advance the claims of abstract or spiritual love at the expense of the reality of sex, but to reject the split between mind and body which is as much a legacy of Freud as of Puritanism. There is no reason to suppose that Mr and Mrs Jack Burden will enjoy a marriage only of true minds or that Mr and Mrs Yasha Jones will, together, perpetuate the celibacy they have known during their periods of isolation. Leroy and Corinne Lancaster's son is an emblem of grace. Warren's message is well paraphrased in Susan Sontag's account of Norman O. Brown's critique of Freudian dualism:

> We are not body versus mind . . . this is to deny death, and therefore to deny life. And self-consciousness, divorced from the experiences of the body, is also equated with the life-denying denial of death . . . What is wanted . . . is not Apollonian (or sublimation) consciousness, but Dionysian (or body) consciousness.[10]

If Warren's work 'is not tailored to fit a thesis', it does, Brooks concedes, develop 'characteristic themes'. Warren is 'constantly concerned with the meaning of the past and the need for one to accept the past if he is to live meaningfully in the present.'[11] This theme is succinctly expressed in the rhetorical question that begins the fifth section of 'Rattlesnake Country': 'What was *is* is now *was*. But / Is *was* but a word for wisdom, its price?' (SP, p. 49). This sets Warren in contrast to Wallace Stevens who, while he would have concurred with much in the idea of imagination propounded in the three fine poems discussed in Chapter Seven—'Time as Hypnosis', 'Composition in Gold and Red-Gold', and 'A Problem in Spatial Composition'—believed that the 'integrations' of the past were of no use in the present. In Stevens' view, 'the poet must consign the past to oblivion to live in the only authentic time.'[12] Warren's work in all *genres* presents images of the self in its struggle for fulfilment. The historical background changes but the issues involved are eternal: there is no such thing as oblivion. The setting of *Brother to Dragons* is 'No place' and 'Any time', which, Warren says in the prefatory note, 'is but a whimsical way of saying that the issue that the characters here discuss is, in my view at least, a human constant' (BTD, p. xiii). Man's history itself becomes, as Richard Gray puts it, 'a product of the continuing interchange between the human consciousness and his circumstances, past and present.'[13] The value of Agrarianism was that on the basis of a questionable realism it managed to oppose the rationalist abstractions of twentieth-century scientific idealism, constantly referring to the concrete fact of individual human experience including the fact of apprehended mystery. Warren's scepticism towards abstractions, inhumanly absolute standards, rests not on metaphysical speculation but on our individual experience of imperfection, the pull nature exerts on us, as well as our felt need to idealise our lives. It is our experience so defined that compels us to identify simultaneously with the 'bloody and sentimental maniac', Lilburn Lewis and with the determinedly visionary Thomas Jefferson. Like Audubon, we murder to create.

This emphasis on the self does not mean that Warren is indifferent to social values: " 'Authenticity' is merely one of the two poles of action, and the other pole is a sense of objective standards, just as the individual is one pole of the existence of the self, and the other, society, or more specifically, community."[14] In his short but incisive book, *Segregation: The Inner Conflict in the South*, Warren diagnoses Southern racial problems in terms of the ennobling interchange that should occur between the individual and his society. Under the circumstances prevailing in the mid-fifties it was impossible that the Southern interchange should ennoble anyone: 'I don't think you can live with yourself when you are humiliating the man next to you' (*Segregation*, p. 83). Brutalised by his treatment of blacks, the white Southerner sacrifices his 'moral identity' to a system which perpetuates itself and keeps him brutal. Somehow the individual must break from this circle and make a beginning with himself. As Eliot says, 'Home is where one starts from', and Piers Plowman knew that, before setting off for Truth, man must plough his half-acre. But although the integrity of the self comes first for Warren, his prospectus for self-realisation in 'Knowledge and the Image of Man' advocates separateness only as a necessary prelude to fulfilment through moral action in the world of relations. Jack Burden and Anne Stanton must leave the house at Burden's Landing to enter 'the convulsion of the world' (AKM, p. 464), and Jeremiah Beaumont must return to the human community for his life to achieve its tragic meaning. It is incumbent upon us to sympathise intelligently with a mad young aristocrat on an Italian beach, to feel the agony and emulate the fortitude of a condemned man dying of cancer, because their flesh 'suffers for you and for me' (SP, p. 258).

Warren's effectiveness as a poet and a novelist and as a commentator on socio-historical matters derives from his ability to make us sense directly both our inner selves and our selves in a historical context. In order to effect his shocks of recognition he often resorts to melodrama, a reflection, perhaps, of his belief that we have been taught to evade the inner drama too readily and that we do so, like Lucy Jefferson Lewis and Laetitia Lewis, only at the risk of self-destruction. Melodrama becomes the composite image for an inner life which is typically hectic but all too often suppressed. In *World Enough and Time*, *Band of Angels*, *Brother to Dragons* and *Audubon* the melodrama was there for Warren in the specific historical materials out of which he sought to make his image of man. The melodrama of *Night Rider* and *All the King's Men* and the implicit melodrama of the central situation of *The Cave* were more immediate. Recalling the Louisiana of 1934 and 1935, Warren says:

Melodrama was the breath of life. There had been melodrama in the life I had known in Tennessee, but with a difference: in Tennessee the melodrama seemed to be different from the stuff of life, something superimposed upon life, but in Louisiana people lived melodrama—seemed to live, in fact, for it, for the strange combination of philosophy, humour and violence.[15]

When he says that Tennessean melodrama seemed 'something superimposed' on life, Warren does not mean imposed by the artist but, somehow, by the people of the region. Melodrama is a reality in both Louisiana and Tennessee, and it is a reality in his books, except when the disproportions customarily associated with melodrama in art are revealed by the failure of characters like Amantha Starr and Adam Rosenzweig to develop in the measure of what happens to them.

Shortly after his depression in May, 1924 Warren wrote from his home in Guthrie to Donald Davidson, requesting material about Joseph Conrad: 'I am trying to do Mr Ransom a term paper on Conrad and I am in sad need of reference books for facts and criticism; have you any such?'[16] This marks the beginning of a life-long involvement with Conrad whose vision of man's need to 'surrender to the incorrigible and ironical necessity of the idea' (SE, p. 45) helped to bring Warren out of his crisis and led him to develop a similar, though less austere, interpretation of the human condition. Conrad's view of man consorts well with more local influences. Warren is thoroughly in the American grain of Hawthorne, Melville and, despite his aestheticism, James. Like them he recognises the existence of sin, shows the conflict between good and evil in an ambiguous world and attests the rôle of suffering in the purification of the self by the acquisition of knowledge. Ever since Rip VanWinkle awoke to discover that he had slept through his country's finest hour, American writers have been concerned, often guiltily, with the past. Warren's present is as involved in the past as the blood of Holgrave, the man of today in *The House of the Seven Gables*, is involved in that of the Maules. His teachers and intellectuals from Professors Millen and Dalrymple to Slim Sarrett, Isaac Sumpter and Jed Tewksbury, while not uniformly unpardonable, commit the sin of Ethan Brand, forgetting, as Conrad did not, that the idea must work in the world, not collide with it. His idealists are in varying degrees Ahabian in their wilful superimposition of a limiting, subjectively conceived idea on the world's body, and the conclusions of *At Heaven's Gate, All the King's Men* and *A Place to Come To* prompt us to call their heroes Ishmael (*See also* Appendix, p. 247 ff.).

A Southerner before he was an American, Warren comes from a conservative region in which persists much formal—albeit largely fundamentalist—and still more behavioural Christianity. His view of man accords with the Christian position which regards human freedom as the source not only of good but also of an evil which resists the ingratiations of modern psychology. Like Wolfe and Faulkner, Warren 'has created a kind of fiction out of the materials of his region and its past which can and does counterpoise the despairing view of man that naturalism and realism have taken in our time.'[17] Neither Warren's philosophy nor his voice has ever lost its Southern accent. His poetry can charge off the page like Whitman's or Pound's, and it can sweeten the line with a liturgical cadence like Eliot's. Closer to home, there are ironies and phrasings worthy of the Ransom of 'Dead Boy' or 'Judith of Bethulia' and vatic moments that recall the Tate of 'Ode to the Confederate Dead'. But the 'liquid drive', as Frank Owsley called it, of Warren's most fluent expression both in verse and prose owes most to the rhythms of the Southern *raconteur* who, sitting on the front porch, will tell you either nothing at all over the bourbon and water, or will tell you everything in one measured, passionately monotonous and convoluted sentence. This, spiked with his learning, flavoured by his high intelligence and shaped by his craft, is the basis of style in Warren's work.

With *John Brown, the Making of a Martyr* Warren demonstrated the readiness to 'enter history, not to flinch from history' that has typified his career. The historically based Jeremiah Beaumont, with his tragically simplifying dream and his preoccupation with his own identity, is the novelist's most complete fictional metaphor for the South. In his 1961 meditations on the centennial, *The Legacy of the Civil War*. Warren dismantles both the Southern and Northern dreams to expose their over-simplifications. The War gave the North its Treasury of Virtue, the South its Great Alibi. The Treasury of

Virtue affords the North redemption of all sins and by the Great Alibi the South explains everything:

> By a simple reference to the 'War', any Southern female could, not too long ago, put on the glass slipper and be whisked away to the ball. Any goose could dream herself (or himself) a swan—surrounded, of course, by a good many geese for contrast and devoted hand-service. Even now, any common lyncher becomes a defender of the Southern tradition, and any rabble-rouser the gallant leader of a thin gray line of heroes, his hat on sabrepoint to provide reference by which to hold formation in the charge. By the Great Alibi pellagra, hookworm, and illiteracy are all explained, or explained away, and mortgages are converted into badges of distinction. Laziness becomes the aesthetic sense, blood-lust rising from a matrix of boredom and resentful misery becomes a high sense of honour, and ignorance becomes divine revelation. By the Great Alibi the Southerner makes his Big Medicine.
>
> (*Legacy*, pp. 54–55)

The Great Alibi and the Treasury of Virtue are ways of forgetting that history is history. A moral realist, however, cannot forget history or that, within history, structures change. History brought change to the South in the Depression, the Second World War, the second period of Reconstruction. By the time of *Segregation: The Inner Conflict in the South* (1957) Warren had long departed from his early Agrarian acceptance of the South's separatist bi-racial system and had come unequivocally to favour desegregation. In *Who Speaks for the Negro?* (1965) he goes home again to see what has become of the old structure. The book is yet another investigation into the tangle of idea and world, stereotype thinking and intransigently messy reality.

The structure that remains in the South still includes the split white Southerner whose striking out at change is an act of aggression toward that part of himself which 'has sold out, which is the household traitor, which lusts after the gauds and gewgaws of high-powered Yankeedom' (WSN, p. 426). But if this is a fact of the situation it is one to be acknowledged and put to use: 'the recognition of necessity is the beginning of freedom' (BTD, p. 214). Following Howard Zinn in his excellent book on *The Southern Mystique*[18], Warren observes: 'A man may say that he is a hard-core segregationalist. But how hard is that core? Is it as hard as his love for, or need of money? As his desire to have his children educated? As his simple inclination to stay out of jail? The only real hard-core segregationalist is one whose feelings about Negroes take precedence over all other feelings mobilised in a given situation' (WSN, p. 409). Negro leadership—and one would add white leadership too—is 'committed to playing a most complicated tune on the strings of white desires, and convictions.' (WSN, p. 409). The tune must be complicated if the desired moral order is to be established in the actual with maximum success and minimum pain. Yet 'it would be *realism* to think that pain would be a reasonable price to pay for what we all, selfishly, might get out of it' (WSN, p. 444).

It is still, no doubt, the proper rôle of the Southern intellectual to follow Warren's example and guide his countrymen in the way of that realism. It is Warren's profound and realistic sense of the obligation upon us to earn our dreams by demanding that they work in a world of prose and imperfection that gives his works their fundamental distinction, making them ever more rewardingly a place to come to. He is a writer by whom all our biographies may be immeasurably enriched.

Conclusion—Notes

[1] Bergonzi, Bernard, 'Nature, Mostly American', *Southern Review*, **6** (Winter, 1970), 209.

[2] Forster, E. M., *Aspects of the Novel* (London: Edward Arnold, 1949), p. 27.

[3] Sheppard, R. Z., 'Sacred and Profane Grit', *Time*, 14 March, 1977, p. 58.

[4] Malamud, Bernard, *The Fixer* (Harmondsworth: Penguin Books, 1967), p. 281.

[5] Bellow, *Herzog*, p. 84.

[6] Brooks, Cleanth, *The Hidden God: Studies in Hemingway, Faulkner, Yeats, Eliot and Warren* (New Haven and London: Yale University Press, 1963), p. 98.

[7] Warren, Robert Penn, *Democracy and Poetry* (Cambridge, Mass., and London: Harvard University Press, 1975), p. 48.

[8] *Democracy and Poetry*, p. 31.

[9] *Ibid.*, p. 72.

[10] Sontag, *Against Interpretation*, pp. 260–61.

[11] Brooks, *The Hidden God*, p. 98.

[12] Hillis Miller, J., *Poets of Reality: Six Twentieth Century Writers* (Cambridge, Mass: Harvard University Press, 1965), p. 265.

[13] Gray, Richard, 'The American Novelist and American History: A Revaluation of *All the King's Men*', *Journal of American Studies*, **6** (Dec, 1972), 306.

[14] Warren, Robert Penn, *Democracy and Poetry*, pp. 46–47.

[15] Warren, Robert Penn, *All the King's Men* (London: Secker and Warburg, 1974) p. xiii.

[16] Letter dated 30 Aug, 1924. DDC, File 1.

[17] Holman, C. Hugh, *The Roots of Southern Writing* (Athens, Ga: University of Georgia Press, 1972), p. 95.

[18] Zinn, Howard, *The Southern Mystique* (New York: Alfred A. Knopf, 1964).

Appendix

Robert Penn Warren: An Interview

The conversation which provides the basis of the following text was recorded by the writer on 11 September, 1969 at Mr Warren's home in Fairfield, Connecticut. Extracts from the tapes were printed in *Scottish International*, **9** (February, 1970), 3–9. Between 1969 and 1974 the text of the original interview was expanded in the course of further exchanges between Mr Warren and the writer, and the final text appeared in *Journal of American Studies*, **8** (August, 1974), 229–45. The complete text is given here with added notes.

MW I'd like to begin with a question about the Fugitive group. Would you say that there was any special critical emphasis in these early Fugitive discussions of poetry? You have said before that there's a fallacy in assuming there was a systematic programme behind the Fugitive group.

RPW That would certainly be a fallacy. I think the best way for me to talk about it would be by referring to how the group began. It began some years before my time as a group of young college instructors and men in the City of Nashville with no connection with the University, who found a community of interest in discussing philosophy. They met at each other's houses and talked philosophy till a late hour. Bit by bit, some of the people involved began to write poetry and show their poetry to each other. By the time I came along, writing poetry or discussing it was the main interest. The group was very small, ten or twelve or thirteen people[1] with no formal organisation, simply a matter of friendship. And then they began to publish a little magazine called *The Fugitive*.[2]

MW There was a certain resistance to that magazine, wasn't there, by the authorities at Vanderbilt University?

RPW Well, certainly, the head of the English Department[3] was embarrassed by it, and begged his instructors not to do it.

MW Why should that have been embarrassing to him, do you think? Because it published a *new* kind of poetry?

RPW I think so. But, after all, some business men in town put up the money for it. A comic situation. Maxwell House coffee gave the prize—which, I think, Hart Crane won.[4] That was the first year.

MW There is a notion that the Fugitives were a group of people who went in for *close reading* of one another's poems and whose critical standards were what we would call objectivist. This I take to be a fallacy.

RPW There was no theorising that I can think of around that point. If you are going to criticise individual poems you have to talk about the actual words on the page, this line or that line, this word or that word, but as I remember the discussions, they were very far ranging and all sorts of implications might come in. It was hit or miss. There were many temperaments here, and certainly some of the people were very much concerned with history in the relation of literature to the historical materials, or how one stage of history emphasises one kind of poetry. For instance, some of the people in the group were very deep in balladry which would be anything *but* biased toward formalism. Then there were people like Ransom who was trained in classical philosophy and often led the discussion of a poem off into the world of general aesthetics. Many lines of approach came together in particular applications, in discussing particular poems. But there was no general theorising that I can remember.

The next phase of the group's interest—several years later—moved over to the matter of society and history. So this would, in a way, refute the notion of this being a little group of formalists working out a theory of pure, limited, objectivist poetry: the group became more and more oriented—almost paradoxically—toward history (American history) and at the same time toward aesthetic theorising.

MW Your own orientation was, for a time, distinctly historical wasn't it, with *John Brown, the Making of a Martyr* as your first major publication?

RPW Yes it was. But this was, in a way, a question of homesickness, I guess. As long as I was *living* in Tennessee and Kentucky and knew a great deal about various kinds of life there from the way Negro field hands talked or mountaineers talked, what they did and what they ate, on up to the world of Nashville, Tennessee, I had no romantic notions about it. I was just naturally steeped in it and I knew that world. I also had read a good deal of Southern history and was partly raised by a grandfather who was a great reader of history and talked it all the time. He was a Confederate Veteran, a captain of cavalry with Forrest and full of that and things like *Napoleon and his Marshals*,[5] and military history generally. I had a deep soaking in that as a little boy. But this didn't seem to apply to the other half of my life, in which my whole passion was John Donne, John Ford, Webster's plays, Baudelaire. Then, as soon as I *left* that world of Tennessee and went to California, and then to Yale and Oxford, I began to rethink the meaning, as it were, of the world I had actually been living in without considering it.

MW And this led to your first book, *John Brown, the Making of a Martyr*?

RPW That's right.

MW To an outsider the book also looks like part of a campaign: it seems to fit in with the whole motivation behind *I'll Take My Stand*. Quite apart from a simple matter of interest in this piece of history, is it at all reasonable to see the book as an Agrarian's attempt to demythologise a northern martyr?

RPW I think that's a fair account of it, but it wasn't a conscious motive. It preceded my connection with the whole Agrarian business. As for the immediate provocation, a publisher proposed a contract to me for it, and I grabbed it. I began the book when I

Q

was a graduate student at Yale in '27–'28 and I finished it at Oxford. It overlapped with but began before I had much share in the Agrarian conversations.

MW You were at Oxford when *I'll Take My Stand* came out. So you weren't really in on the Agrarian conversations, were you?

RPW No, only in passing through on a visit to Nashville.

MW So the interest in John Brown was something you developed independently?
RPW That's right. But it was tied in this way. Other friends of mine, by this time, were ferociously restudying American history. I wasn't alone in this: Allen Tate was doing it, you see—

MW And Frank Owsley?[6]

RPW Frank Owsley was a professional American historian so he was doing it. In fact I didn't know Frank at that time except most casually. But this was happening to a number of people. It was part of a turning back, a turning from their interest in poetry to try to see the setting of the kind of poetry that interested them. The notion of Ireland was deep in this too, though it was not specified often—the notion of a somewhat backward society in an outlying place with a different tradition and a rich folk-life, facing the big modern machine. This notion was in the background, talked about not as a model but as a parallel somehow. There were three factors in this: on the one hand there was the new poetry— Pound and Eliot—which was appreciated very early there and read in Nashville when it was not read in New York, and then Yeats and the Irish. Young Tennesseeans who had been off in the First World War, or had studied at Oxford or in Paris, seized on this parallel.

MW So that poetry was very intimately associated with the concept of a small outlying nation with its own history and its own problems?

RPW The folk and the international were the two elements that entered into it.

MW Was Yeats rather specially the poet who embodied all that these people in Nashville were thinking about, i.e. an international poetry but with a national root?

RPW The folk element for some of the Fugitives was very important and in that case, yes, Yeats would have had a special importance; but also Hardy, for instance. Ransom was mad for Hardy. So was I as a boy, and still am.

MW Could one explain that in terms of Hardy's anti-establishment, anti-religious stance, his notion of fate, his liberation from the whole nineteenth-century set?

RPW Well, I think that may be true, though I'd never thought of it. I *would* single out the notion of fate: a fatalism was deeply ingrained in the Southern mind. Things could not be changed— things lay beyond any individual effort to change them. A sense of entrapment. I think you can probably make a case that Hardy touched this nerve. Another thing was Hardy's use of folk materials, his portraits of little ironies of folk life. This touched some of those people very deeply. I'm sure they touched Ransom.

MW There is a Hardyesque quality about Ransom's poetry, isn't there?

RPW Indeed there is. It's very dramatic in the way Hardy's poetry is dramatic.

MW I'm thinking of the deceptive way in which a Hardy poem— 'In the Moonlight', for example—can appear very slight, and yet contain T.N.T. Ransom is very like that, I think.

RPW He's very like that and I think this is not so much a matter of modelling yourself on that, because Ransom's classical training is, I'm sure, as much behind his poetry as anything—perhaps more than any other single thing—but Hardy played right into this. His simplicities and the folk element played into it, plus this bias towards poetry as coming from the *event* in life rather than being a beautiful abstraction.

MW I'd like to turn now to your most famous book, *All the King's Men*. This is not only the most widely read and most highly regarded of your novels but also the story that has occupied you longest—from the original play in 1937 until the published version of the play in 1960; so it's something that you've been involved with for a very long time. Could you explain this at all?

RPW　Let me make a slight comment on that spread of time, which I find almost embarrassing to think of—twenty-three years. The point is that a lot of the involvement with the later phases of it—the play aspect of it—came by a kind of accident. I was drawn back to it by a producer wanting to do it. With this, of course, there was my own dissatisfaction with the original version of the play—a verse play then—that preceded the novel by some eight years. The reason I never tried to produce the first version[7] was that I never felt happy about it and in fact, the novel was written because I wasn't happy about that play. The original version of the play was a tight play about the dictator, the Huey Long figure, and the people around him. Now the theory of that play was that the dictator, the man of power, is powerful only because he fulfils the blanknesses and needs of people around him. His power is an index to the weaknesses of others. In other words his power lies in the defects of others rather than a thing existing in itself, and so he fulfils the needs of people around him. The idea that gradually developed in the course of writing the play was the contrast between the 'hero' as a person and the 'hero' as a reflex of history. In the original version, my politician was not named Stark, but Talos—the name of the 'Iron Groom', the robot, the servant to the Knight of Justice, in Spenser's *Faerie Queene*.[8] This was a sort of private joke, but it indicates the line of thought, and Talos does sound like a 'Southern' name.

But this notion did not work in this little tight play, and the choruses did not quite carry it. It was a tight personal story and I did not feel satisfied with the range of reference to the world outside, to society and to the history outside of it. And, as I say, behind that play and the book there was a sort of soaking in Machiavelli, a little Guicciardini and William James and just a lot of reading of history. Now, I don't mean to suggest that after a certain amount of reading I said to myself, 'I think I'll write a play about all this.' It just happened. And the biggest part of the 'happening' was probably that I lived in Louisiana—that 'banana republic', as I think Carleton Beals[9] called it—at the time when Huey P. Long held it as his fief and when he was gunned down in the grand new sky-scraper Capitol which he had built to his greater glory.

But back to the original play: my dissatisfaction with it led a bit to the novel, to get some sense of the world *around* the man— the man as *seen* rather than the man as presented. The strong man should be seen through the weaknesses of others, or the needs of others rather than taken as an abstract power presented directly. That was, I suppose, the shift of interest that made the novel; but then afterwards, problems became more technical.

MW So that this is one explanation anyway of the long preoccupation. And a technical interest in getting it right as drama.

RPW Part of that, yes. And that process of being interested in the stage for a while, I'm sure, changed my poetry a great deal.

MW Many of the themes and preoccupations, particularly in your fiction, seem characteristically American. Do you think there is any sense in seeing your work in terms of a tradition, a kind of American dialectic that runs, I think, from Hawthorne right down to the present time? To put it very crudely, you have first of all the Puritan dichotomies, then you have Transcendentalism, and for the Transcendentalists life becomes a Blakean affair: all life is holy. Emerson cancels evil out of the human algebra; Hawthorne brings it back; Melville says 'No' in even greater thunder, and points out through Moby-Dick—perhaps the most eloquent of all American symbols—that truth is this *doubleness* of the whale. I would like to suggest that you are concerned with this kind of problem in *All the King's Men*, and elsewhere. Willie Stark himself is a mixed man: Jack calls him 'the man of fact' and Adam Stanton 'the man of idea', but virtue lies in wait for Willie just as virtue lies in wait in those lines in *Brother to Dragons*, 'More dogged than Pinkerton, more scientific than the F.B.I.'[10] This seems to explain Willie's inability to stay remorseless: Willie as human simply *cannot* continue to be monovalent.

RPW No he can't: he says so himself at the end, 'It could have been different'.[11] This is his acknowledgement of that fact.

MW Now isn't this an acknowledgement of the truth of fusion, of the oneness of opposing categories of value and the way they inevitably cohabit? You *can't* split one off from the other. Ahab's great sin—his tragedy too—is that he tries to split the moral atom and blows himself up in the process. Now I think this notion of doubleness enters the American spiritual blood-stream. It's there in Faulkner too: Joe Christmas is really a kind of Moby-Dick. As Ahab forces the whale to become *all* evil, imposing the demonism he sees in the world on the essentially ambiguous hump of the whale, so the community of Jefferson forces Joe Christmas to become all Negro, all black, and thus forces him into the abyss. So they split the moral atom too. In *All the King's Men* Willie Stark realises—he feels it on the pulse and he feels it in the bullet— that he *has* to be a mixed man.

RPW I think what you're saying is perfectly true about the American system. Or not *system*, but the central *tension* in American literature, I think, is pretty well described by what you are saying. Not pretty well: it's extremely accurate, and beautifully put. When it comes down to *me* in this little footnote on that grand picture, I wouldn't say that anything as grand as that was in my mind. I *can* say that a certain kind of *issue*, both a moral and psychological issue that's implied by that *was* in my mind— an approach to it. I was not thinking of anything I was trying to do as 'belonging *to*' anything, you see. By the way, when it comes down to Hawthorne and Emerson meeting on the wood-paths of Concord, I'm strictly for Hawthorne. I really have something that's almost a pathological flinch from Emersonianism, from Thoreauism, from these oversimplifications, as I think of them, of the grinding problems of life and of personality. So I'm all for the Hawthorne in the picture.

MW Your early book on John Brown certainly deals with a grinding problem of personality.

RPW I have puzzled a great deal about this—the man had some kind of constant obsessive interest for me. On the one hand he's so heroic, on the other hand he's so vile, pathologically vile. Some fifteen years ago, when Edmund Wilson was working on *Patriotic Gore*,[12] we'd meet at parties and he would say, 'Red, let's go and sit in the corner and talk about the Civil War', and we always did. And the subject of Brown once or twice came up, and he once said, 'But he's trivial, he's merely a homicidal maniac—forget him!' Now this is *half* of Brown. In a strange way the homicidal maniac lives in terms of grand gestures and heroic stances, and is a carrier of high values, but *is* a homicidal maniac! This is a strange situation; and the split of feeling around Brown makes the split of feeling in a thing like my character Stark almost trivial. Brown lives in the dramatic stance of his life, rather than in the psychological content of it; he lives in noble stances and noble utterances, and at the psychological and often the *factual* level of conduct was—it's incredible—brutal. Perfect self-deception—yet 'noble'. Now on this point, I suppose, the people I have chosen to write about—or rather who have chosen me to write about *them*—are trying to find out some way to make these things work together, come together: somehow they are trying to get out of this box. This would be true of a man like the hero of *World Enough and Time*, who *must* find a *cause*, an ideal cause in order to justify some of his most secret and destructive motives—no, that's not accurate—needs.

MW I think in *At Heaven's Gate* the most interesting character is Slim Sarrett. His ruthlessness—albeit a tormented ruthlessness—and his efforts to *create* himself, make him appear as a kind of criticism of Sartre's existentialist ideas about the nature of the self. Is this a possible influence, direct or indirect, or is it just coincidence?

RPW It's pure coincidence. I didn't know anything about Sartre at that time. Except a review of Faulkner's *The Sound and the Fury*[13]—or some other odds and ends, maybe. As a matter of fact that character was almost a portrait of a person I knew, the closest portrait I've ever done in a piece of fiction; but I felt that he was in a way peripheral to what the book is really about. All the novels I've tried to write—published novels, anyway—are concerned, I discovered later, with some *mirror* thing—the mirror of the psychology of the people over against the society they are living in, so the story of the society is reflected in the *personal* stories, the moral and psychological stories of the individual characters, and the other way around too: society then enacts these private dramas. This book in its scheme—not in the inception of the scheme but as it developed—was much influenced by my long immersion in Dante, as I think may be obvious. There are the usurer and the homosexual—the crimes against nature: here is a society where nature is being violated one way or another, and all the characters are somehow *denying* nature. The relation of the father and son in the Jerry character and his father—Jerry is committing a crime against nature: he's impious.

MW He denies his father—and takes a phoney father.

RPW He takes a phoney father. He's not following the Dante scheme: it developed bit by bit—these various crimes against nature. But the usurer, the great banker, and Sarrett, the homosexual, are straight out of the Circle.[14] But it wasn't *conceived* this way: it *developed* this way. If I didn't think of Dante for quite a long time, it could be back in my head, you see, because in those years I was reading him almost daily.

MW This question of the true and false father is also there in *All the King's Men* isn't it?

RPW I've been told, and I think it's true, that the true and the false father are in practically every story I've written. Now what that means, I do not know!

MW What is so interesting is that the alignment of the true *father* and the truth of the *situation* is very close.

RPW That's right. If I were asked (I haven't ever said this before, or even thought it, I guess) to relate that fact to what we were talking about before I should say, probably, this attempt to put the two halves of the world together, the halves being the fact and idea, or these various splits of this kind, the Emersonian and the Hawthornian, all these things we were talking about in Brown— the perfect father will do that, but the perfect father is only in heaven, of course. This story is about an attempt at finding the true model—

MW You mean the point where fact and idea coincide, the perfect fusion?

RPW Well, it's not in our world I guess. But we constantly want to have it in our world, and we only find it by finding a new father, I guess, beyond us, beyond this world.

MW Does this make our case hopeless do you think?

RPW No. It just makes it interesting, gives us something to talk about! But this question of *finding* the father, this perfect father, is, in one way or another, in the various stories.

MW I'd like to ask you a little about the process of redefinition that's gone on in your work. Part of the 1957 interview with Ralph Ellison [15] puzzled me a little and I wonder if you could say something more about it. He asked you about the progression from the essay on the Negro in *I'll Take My Stand* to the stance of, say, *Band of Angels* and then, of course, to *Segregation* and *Who Speaks for the Negro?* Now, in your reply there, I think you suggest that you were writing the essay at the same time that you were writing your first serious piece of fiction. I felt that possibly you rather glossed over the question of what was happening to your own *beliefs* by talking about a new interest in a different *form*: not the form of the socio-political essay or analysis, but rather the form of fiction. Did you, fairly soon after that essay in *I'll Take My Stand*, begin to rethink the whole question of the position of the Negro?

RPW I didn't begin to 'rethink' anything systematically. It was by accident. Put it this way: I wrote the essay on the Negro for *I'll Take My Stand* at the same time as I was writing a novelette—'Prime Leaf'—which was also about the South. The connection, let's say, is this: thousands of miles away in England, doing these two things—both are ways of looking back at your origins, your homeland, and all of that. They both had great emotional charges, as it were, more than I realised at the time, I'm sure. On the essay —this is part of that fatalism that was deeply engrained in the Southern mind. Nobody—except Negroes—saw anything except some system of what the sociologists then called super- and subordination based on and modified by all sorts of legal guarantees of 'separate but equal'. This is what the Supreme Court saw. This is the way the world was. At the same time, many people were uncomfortable with it, many whites. Of course you can be damn certain a lot of *Negroes* were uncomfortable! But a lot of whites too, It's a question of trying to rationalise the inevitable, what seemed to be the inevitable structure of the world. Now, at the same time, in writing fiction for the first time, in this foreign country, about the world of my boyhood, the *feelings* then came into it, not in the essayistic frame, not in terms of a social apology, but in terms of, simply, *response.*

MW I don't quite follow.

RPW Not *interpretative*—the *essay* was a social apology, an analysis and an apology, but *fiction* involves, simply, your reseeing in your imagination a world, and brings the problem of your immediate response, your immediate *feeling* about what you are seeing, without justification, without intellectualisation.

MW Just what's to be seen there?

RPW Just what's there, and having to face it as *there*. Its *thereness* is all. Now immediately after this, within six months, I was back in the South, and the Depression was coming on. I was living in the country a great deal—not in town—and you'd see more acutely than ever, first from having been away from it for so long, second from having to think about it during the years of absence, and then seeing this starvation-poverty that was coming on for whites and blacks and also certain aspects of the brutality of the system in its psychological way, which I'd been too young when I'd lived there before, or too stupid, to be aware of. So there was this long drift for several years of looking at the world again and seeing two things, one the immediate kinds of degradation involved. personal, psychological and spiritual degradation, plus the poverty. At the same time the effect on the Southern white society became more and more obvious—the great cost, both money cost and spiritual cost. Also I made acquaintances who were aware of this. It was being *talked* about more. At the same time certain friends of mine, like Davidson, became more *frozen* in their opposition to change, and the issue became drawn for me. So I had to see it, bit by bit.

Five years later I couldn't possibly have written that essay because I had lived into the world now in a different perspective and a different age. Also, one other thing I'll say. The Depression did a great deal to destroy the sense of historical fatalism, because you *had* to have action or die. There was a crisis there which *demanded* action. You could not accept history as finished, which is part of the Southern disease, and you had to reorder society, and this meant you had to reorder all sorts of relationships. The fact that you thought things *could* be reordered opened the whole question, psychologically. At the same time your acquaintance with the old, the Civil War generation, like my Grandfather— their attitude towards race had been very different from attitudes towards race in the 1900's in the South.

MW More paternalist?

RPW Well, they were more deeply aware of certain splits. My Grandfather was against slavery—at least he said that he had thought it was a bad system—but held some slaves.

MW Why would he hold them?

RPW Just like a socialist who is a banker now, you see, or hired by a business. It was the only structure of actual living. If you're going to farm you have to have labour. That was the only labour available.

MW So right in there, there was a split between fact and idea—in the Southern inheritance.

RPW Right there. In the whole question of the Southern story this split is deep, from Thomas Jefferson right on down—to take it at the grand level—to Robert E. Lee who was an emancipationist; and Grant held the last slaves legally held in the United States, I think. There are no *morals* in this, it's just part of the comedy of our history; but segregationism was a very late development in the South, it only became legal quite late, and the old people had been *against* segregation because they didn't have that kind of racial antipathy. They might be the boss but they had no racial antipathy. It was a question of the structure.

MW The two books that seem to me to have been most adversely criticised are *Wilderness* and *Band of Angels*, leaving aside *Flood*, which I think has been generally misunderstood. It seems to me that there's a very considerable clue to the way your imagination quite naturally operates in the discussion of 'Pure and Impure Poetry' in that early essay: this notion that an ideal or a purity has always to withstand the blast of irony. Perhaps what is lacking in *Wilderness* and *Band of Angels* is this Mercutio in the underbrush. There's something, somehow, too *straight*, too 'pure' about them. I would like to suggest that one of the strengths of *Flood*, and something that has apparently been missed by the critics, is that in this novel the conversion of Lettice Poindexter is something we *can* accept precisely because it's earned, because throughout the whole novel Mercutio has been sniping from the underbrush. We accept this as more than sentimentality because of the book's continual scrutiny of every ideal posture that comes up. This kind of running scepticism is lacking in *Wilderness* and it's lacking in the melodrama of *Band of Angels*; but I think that Mercutio returns to the underbrush of your fiction with real power in *Flood*. Now does this make any sense at all?

RPW I hope it does.

MW Does this notion seem to you to say anything about what happens?

RPW Well, I think it does. The problem of *Wilderness* involves a technical matter too. It started out to be a novelette, and began to exfoliate in terms not of the central character, but in terms of the objective world, so that the development of the central character did not keep pace with the development of the experience he went through, objectively considered. I became enraptured, as it were, with the world outside of him, the people outside of him, and he never developed to go along with this development of the story. You have the strange effect of a central *hollowness* with a rich context, with the central character as an observer that is a *mere* observer. He's involved *intellectually*, but *only* intellectually. The story is never fleshed out in enough depth so that the world of context is related to his experience in the right way. And this is partly scale: it started out to be a novelette, say twenty-five thousand words, and it winds up as a novel; but the character does not develop to fit the context.

MW Would you agree that this quality of irony—what I've said about ideal notions or ideal stances continually being undercut and evaluated by, say, the voice of a Jack Burden or by the counterpoint of an Ashby Wyndham narrative—is characteristic of the novels that are really strong?

RPW It's characteristic of many of my novels anyway, and it is not true of this book.

MW Do you think it's true of *Band of Angels*?

RPW Well, I think you're right about that. One thing there: the narrator is wrong. There's not enough richness and depth in the experience of the narrator—at least, it isn't brought out—and the same is true of the other book.

MW Would you say that in your writing life there have been phases in which prose or the imagination associated with prose has been dominant and other phases when poetry has been dominant? It seems to me, looking down the list, that after *Band of Angels* there is a poetic phase and then again after *Flood* a very strong poetic phase. Is this so: is it phased like that?

RPW It worked out this way as far as I can tell: poetry was my *central* interest for many years, up until the middle nineteen-forties. I read it all the time and worked at it all the time, and fiction was definitely a secondary interest. Of course, when you are in the middle of a novel it *can't* be secondary, it becomes your life for a year or so. But behind this, the novels I was writing, came the notion that somehow they might be poems: the first conception of them. *All the King's Men* started as a verse play, you see, and the other novels had very much the same background of feeling— came out of a sense that they might *be* poems if one wrote long poems like *that*. So the composition of novels didn't feel like a break between prose and poetry. Of course there are obviously *great* differences, but they are tied to the poetic interest or commit-ment, or whatever you should call it, in a very definite way.

Now something happened about '45. I got so I could not finish a short poem. I wrote, started many over that period of years. I never finished one—I lost the capacity for finishing a short poem. I'd write five lines, ten lines, twenty lines—it would die on me. I lost my sense of it. I was working in those years, for five or six years, on a long poem, *Brother to Dragons*, and that was absorbing, I suppose, all the juice. But anyway the short poems did not work out. Then, some little time after I had finished *Brother to Dragons* I felt a whole new sense of poetry. I felt freer than I had felt before. The narrative sense began to enter the short-poem— as a germ, that is. So in the summer of '54, when Eleanor and I and a then-baby daughter were living in the ruined fortress in Italy, there was suddenly just this new sense of *release*—so the short poems began to come in that year.

MW Of course a lot of the poems are about that place—

RPW —about that place, because the place and the events all tie together in this sense of a new way into poetry. Look, I could start it from the immediate thing freely, or the immediate thing might be something I was thinking about that happened twenty-

five years before. This has been a whole different kind of feeling
for writing poems.

MW You once made a rather Jamesian statement about getting the
germ of a story in a flash. Would you be prepared to say anything
about the germ of the new novel, *Meet Me in the Green Glen*?

RPW I don't know how I'd put it. The germ—I know exactly what
it was: it was on a hunting trip with my brother, in Tennessee,
some years ago. We went up a stream bed in an old army jeep.
It was a wilderness, but had once been a prosperous valley. We
saw the ruins of a nice house in there, and this totally abandoned
valley, now a game reserve, a park, began to grow in my mind—
this sense of a lost world in that valley. Then some other stories
that I knew began to flow in and populate it with other echoes
of episodes I had known.

MW Episodes in real life?

RPW Some, yes: and in just that way, you see, it came as the feel
of a place.

MW Place is very important to you, isn't it?

RPW I think so, that's why I'm so tied to that world there—*one*
reason. Let me say one thing on the question of start. Almost all,
I guess *all* of the novels I've written and many of the poems get
started years before they are written, many years before. In fact, the
Audubon book was started twenty years ago, and all the novels—
Flood went back twenty odd years. Usually there's a long period
of thinking the story over, staying with the story or staying with
the poem. These things flow along and the actual finishing may
come quite late after the idea, or after even the starting of the
writing. It's a very slow process that way.

MW When you look at the current American novel—Bellow, Malamud, Barth, Pynchon—do you feel very much that these writers
are of a different generation? Do you feel that they're talking
about a different world, concerned with different things, interested in different techniques? Do you feel apart from them?

RPW Well, one *has* to feel apart—I'm older—apart from them in that sense. But I feel very close in my *interests*: I feel very close imaginatively to Saul Bellow's work. He's a wonderful writer, a powerful imagination. And of course in one sense he's writing about a strange, Jewish world which I know only by report and through friends like Saul Bellow or through the work of people like him. But I think there's a strange kind of possibility of *rapport*: Jewish writing in America has a minority psychology to it, so does Southern writing. As my wife once said, 'You're just like Jews, you Southerners', and I think there's some truth in that. This is reflected, I think, in the literature. There's a certain *inside-ness* of the *outsider*, and intensities of inside effects sometimes look queer to those who are not inside. Malamud I admire greatly, and Styron. I think Styron's last book, *Nat Turner*,[16] is very powerful and deeply felt.

M W This caused a lot of argument about the authenticity of Negro feeling that Styron had been able to imagine. There was a lot of criticism, wasn't there, by Negro intellectuals?[17]

RPW Oh yes there was. This is politics. Put in its simplest form, as one black graduate student said to me when he asked me how I liked the book and I told him, 'Well, it wasn't fair; he took our boy and ran with him'. Simple as that. This is not the whole question—part of it is this, crudely stated. It's part of a historical moment, of a political moment. At the same time, deeper than that, there is the fact that the sexual treatment makes the white woman the dream girl of Nat, who refuses the black women, you see, who are available to him. Now this was offensive and you can see why. At the same time I think there are some grounds for accept-ing this as valid. Also—I don't want to go into an elaborate discussion of the book but this is part of this historical moment— one little item which was attacked by one of the black militants was taken by Styron out of the autobiography of Frederick Douglass—a very cunning little device of taking something out of a legitimate autobiography of a slave and a hero of the blacks and embedding this as part of Nat's story and *this* being singled out for attack then by blacks. By the way, my sympathies are with Black Power—as I would interpret it. The psychological need I'm deeply sympathetic with, and I think Black Power in terms of its long range meaning, is essential. I was in no sense sneering at that, except that the manifestations of it in some particular cases, I think, are somewhat short-sighted. Sometimes viciously short-sighted. I would say also, I think I know quite enough about Southern chauvinism to understand black chauvinism.

MW How do you view the contemporary scene in criticism? I'd like very much to know how you respond to McLuhan.

RPW I haven't read him enough, but I respond negatively. I think that this is not going to stick. He is a terribly clever writer—I've read at him some—but I'm not going to have any long-bearded theories about this. I just don't think it covers the case.

MW Do you think there's anything on the critical scene that *does* cover the case?

RPW There's *never* anything on the critical scene that covers the case. I think good criticism usually is almost inevitably *ad hoc* in some deep sense; it's trying to make sense of some *particular* thing before it, in terms of values that are much broader than that.

MW Well, that's a good Coleridgian position to take. Are there any particularly vivid contemporary ideas or technical notions that you feel attracted to?

RPW Well, there are certain things you can't avoid as being important whether you like them or not. What's happening to modern America, maybe the modern world, is something that is appalling and inspiring, I suppose, at the same time. My guess is that nothing has happened like this since the rise of Christianity—a fundamental change. Human sensibility, human instinct for value, is changing. Now to *what*, nobody knows yet. It's the world of the Roman Empire again. Things are falling apart, and we don't know quite how to define this. You can make some guesses—but at the same time that you make the big guesses I think you have to quote two authorities: one is Jefferson, that liberty is gained by inches, so you have to nag along inch by inch. I was talking to David Riesman a few weeks ago, and he was saying that apocalyptic solutions and apocalyptic analyses and diagnoses don't interest him really, because it's the little things, day by day, picking up the garbage in this village, that makes life *work*, and the values will finally take their shape from these thousands of little efforts, of little decencies, little organisations that give the *ground* for social continuity.

MW It's interesting that so many of the recent novels especially from America have been, in a sense, apocalyptic. One thinks particularly of books like *Catch-22*, which is a kind of comic apocalypse, of Thomas Pynchon's books, or of John Barth's *Sot-Weed Factor*.

RPW Yes, quite a wonderful book, I think.

MW They're all comic apocalypses, contemplating a total revelation, spoofed at the same time as it's presented.

RPW Yes, that's right.

MW The apocalyptic mode is something that has certainly occupied very intelligent writers recently.

RPW And politically too. For instance, Tom Kahn, the student power man—S.D.S.—some years ago, writing about the black movement said there are many young blacks who would rather fail apocalyptically than win, and be stuck with the responsibility of running society. The great tragic moment—to fail with a great bang—is more satisfying than winning and then having to hack along to put the world together.

MW So they would opt for the fire rather than the daily grey.

RPW That's right. But this is very human and it's very young. We all have this impulse in our youth and we keep it in our age. There are two aspects of this that have crossed my mind: one is, a sense of time is fundamentally so different now to what it was even thirty-five or forty years ago. What Alfred North Whitehead said in a book now forty-five years ago or whatever it was: the time sense before the Industrial Revolution and afterward—there was a crucial difference. A man had no sense of *change* before the Industrial Revolution: he might have a sense of vicissitude, disasters, plagues, wars, deaths, but the *world* did not change. It was the same world. Then the world began to change, and the change accelerated up to the time he wrote. But what's happened *since* is incredible: the process now is so fast that disorganisation sets in. You see this even among very young people. The shock, then, of accelerating change is a fundamental shock, it seems to me; it's something that is really disorienting. It's *too* much. Plus

R

the fact that now society does not *show* the child the nature of life. The picture is no longer this: on the one hand a babe in arms, on the other hand a grey-beard, and in between people who are more or less in the prime of life. Now we have no time sense we can recognise in terms of human experience. Nobody talks to the older people, the older don't talk to the young, even the mother and daughter, the daughter of five and the mother of twenty-five or thirty, they don't have the relation that was once there because the mother no longer teaches the child the same way, or the father the son. And this sense of a lack of continuity from one phase of life to another is part of the *destructiveness* (for the moment) of this change in time sense. And the other crucial thing is the hereditary attitude towards nature which is tied to this. More and more there's no relation between physical nature and man, and man's life, and this does something to us.

MW You mean less and less garden and more and more machine?

RPW That's right. Man's rôle in nature, as being part of nature, is no longer felt and this is tied to the sudden passion now in America to save something, save a patch of green, save a few acres of forest. The 'hippies', in their blundering and uninstructed way, represent a protest at being uprooted from nature. Theirs is a last effort to restore not the patch of green for picnickers, but something to the soul. This effort is important; don't forget that there are many people who actually *hate* the idea of the green place, the hill, the woods, the stream; they hate it with a passion, loathe it because they are afraid of it, are afraid of it because they don't understand their relation to it. They hate it the same way they hate a library.

And we don't know the end of this story; but something is happening deep in the gut or the soul of modern man that we just don't know the meaning of now. The social structure is such, this impotence is so great, that you feel what's the use, why vote, why do this, why do that. The minimal activity though, is important. Bertrand Russell, years ago, was saying the only hope is to find the small organisation that will allow man to feel important, significant within it. This is the only hope. It's the inches business again.

MW Two more small points. Saul Bellow, a year or two ago, re-pined that the writer today has sunk, he said, from the curer of souls, which was his proper business in the nineteenth century, to the level of the etiquette page, advice to the lovelorn, something of that sort.[18] Would you agree with that?

RPW The writer now gives a hand-book of fornication—the number of positions is what the novel has, in most recent times, taken as its subject.

MW Yes, well, that, I suppose, is a form of etiquette! Do you think that the writer *might* reasonably regard himself as a curer of souls in the twentieth century?

RPW I think he had better not take himself too seriously in that rôle. The soul he ought to cure is his own, put it that way. Literature springs from the attempt to inspect one's own soul rather than from the attempt to cure the souls of others, although it happens that good literature may cure souls; but not because it set out to do that.

MW Round about when you were thirteen, I understand, you read Buckle's *History of Civilisation*.

RPW Oh, somewhere around then. Later, I expect. In those days there were not many books to read.

MW But this was on every educated shelf, wasn't it?

RPW That's right.

MW And after believing for a while in Buckle's great geographical key to everything—

RPW Everybody wants a big solution to everything. For a long time I would stop people in the street and explain to them what made the world change!

MW Well, you became disenchanted with this one-answer system. Now I wonder whether you found any describable substitute for the one-answer system?

RPW No. I didn't. Marx didn't serve. Me, anyway.

MW Has anything else worked?

RPW Neither did the church.

MW Any other contestants?

RPW No.

MW Do you anticipate finding any describable substitute?

RPW No. Hack along. Inches, again.

Appendix—Notes

¹ According to Louise Cowan the Fugitives 'were a quite tangible body of sixteen poets who, having no particular programme, met from 1915 to 1928 for the purpose of reading and discussing their own work.' See Louise Cowan, *The Fugitive Group, A Literary History*, p. xvi. The sixteen were John Crowe Ransom, Donald Davidson, Allen Tate, Robert Penn Warren, Merrill Moore, Laura Riding (Gottschalk), Jesse Wills, Alec B. Stevenson, Walter Clyde Curry, Stanley Johnson, Sidney Mttron Hirsch, James Frank, William Yandell Elliott, William Frierson, Ridley Wills and Alfred Starr. Laura Riding, 'in her connection with the magazine . . . functioned only as a contributor, not as a real member' (Cowan, p. 184). Andrew Lytle was a Fugitive *de facto* though not by formal election. Warren joined the group in 1923.

² The first issue of *The Fugitive* was published in Nashville, Tennessee in April, 1922, the last in December, 1925.

³ Dr Edwin Mims, Chairman of Vanderbilt University English Department, 1912–1942.

⁴ The prize Warren refers to was donated to the magazine in its second year by the Associated Retailers of Nashville. Only one of the three judges gave first place to Hart Crane's poem, 'Stark Major', the other two placing it twelfth. The one-hundred-dollar prize was divided equally between Rose Henderson and Joseph Auslander. See *The Fugitive*, **2** (Dec, 1923), 162 and Cowan, pp. 138–39.

⁵ MacDonnell, Archibald Gordon, *Napoleon and His Marshals* (London: Macmillan, 1934).

⁶ Professor of History at Vanderbilt University, 1920–1949.

⁷ With some revision this version was later produced, thanks to the intervention of Eric Bentley, at the University of Minnesota, and at some twenty-five other little theaters in the country. The later prose

version was first produced by Erwin Piscator, at the President Theater in New York, in 1948, with many later productions, including Frankfurt and Moscow (Note by Mr Warren).

[8] *The Faerie Queene*, Book V.

[9] American writer on political and social conditions, especially those of Latin America.

[10] *Brother to Dragons*, p. 29.

[11] Shortly before he dies, Willie Stark says to Jack Burden, 'It might have been all different, Jack' (AKM, p. 425).

[12] Wilson, Edmund, *Patriotic Gore, Studies in the Literature of the American Civil War* (London: Deutsch, 1962).

[13] Sartre, Jean-Paul, 'Le Bruit et la Fureur', in *Situations I* (Paris: Gallimard, 1947), pp. 70–81. Originally published in *La Nouvelle Revue Française*, **52** (June, 1939), 1057–1061, and **53** (July, 1939), 147–51. English translation published in *William Faulkner, Three Decades of Criticism*, ed. Frederick J. Hoffman and Olga W. Vickery (East Lansing: Michigan State University Press, 1960) pp. 225–29.

[14] The Seventh Circle of the *Inferno*.

[15] Cowley, Malcolm, *Writers at Work*, pp. 165–86.

[16] Styron, William, *The Confessions of Nat Turner* (New York: Random House, 1967).

[17] See, for example, *An Exchange on Nat Turner, New York Review of Books*, **7** Nov., 1968, pp. 31–36.

[18] In an interview with Henry Brandon, 'Writer versus Readers', *Sunday Times*, 18 Sept., 1966, p. 24.

Bibliography of Works Cited

(1) Works by Robert Penn Warren in order of publication.

BOOKS

John Brown: The Making of a Martyr. New York: Payson and Clark, 1929.

Thirty-Six Poems. New York: The Alcestis Press, 1935.

Night Rider. Boston: Houghton Mifflin Co., 1939; re-issue, New York: Random House, 1948.

Eleven Poems on the Same Theme. Norfolk, Conn: New Directions, 1942.

At Heaven's Gate. New York: Harcourt, Brace and Co., 1943; re-issue, New York: Random House, 1959.

Selected Poems: 1923–1943. New York: Harcourt, Brace and Co., 1944.

All the King's Men. New York: Harcourt, Brace and Co., 1946; re-issue, New York: Modern Library, 1953.

The Circus in the Attic, and Other Stories. New York: Harcourt, Brace and Co., 1947.

World Enough and Time, A Romantic Novel. New York: Random House, 1950.

Brother to Dragons, A Tale in Verse and Voices. New York: Random House, 1953.

Band of Angels. New York: Random House, 1955.

Segregation: The Inner Conflict in the South. New York: Random House, 1956; re-issue, London: Eyre and Spottiswoode, 1957.

Promises: Poems, 1954–1956. New York: Random House, 1957.

Selected Essays. New York: Random House, 1958; re-issue, New York: Alfred A. Knopf and Random House, Vintage Books, 1966.

The Cave. New York: Random House, 1959.

All the King's Men: A Play. New York: Random House, 1960.

You, Emperors, and Others: Poems, 1957–1960. New York: Random House, 1960.

The Legacy of the Civil War: Meditations on the Centennial. New York: Random House, 1961; re-issue, New York: Alfred A. Knopf and Random House, Vintage Books, 1964.

Wilderness: A Tale of the Civil War. New York: Random House, 1961.

Flood, A Romance of Our Time. New York: Random House, 1964.

Who Speaks for the Negro? New York: Random House, 1965.

Selected Poems, New and Old, 1923–1966. New York: Random House, 1966.

Incarnations: Poems, 1966–1968. New York: Random House, 1968.

Audubon: A Vision. New York: Random House, 1969.

Homage to Theodore Dreiser on the Centennial of His Birth. New York: Random House, 1971.

Meet Me in the Green Glen. New York: Random House, 1971.

Or Else—Poems/Poems 1968–1974. New York: Random House, 1974.

All the King's Men. London: Secker and Warburg, 1974.

Democracy and Poetry. Cambridge, Mass. and London: Harvard University Press, 1975.

Selected Poems: 1923–1975. New York: Random House, 1976.

A Place to Come To. New York: Random House, 1977.

POEMS NOT PUBLISHED IN THE ABOVE BOOKS

'The Golden Hills of Hell'. *Driftwood Flames*. Nashville: The Poetry Guild, 1923. P. 41.

'Crusade'. *The Fugitive*, **2** (1923), 90–91.

'After Teacups'. *The Fugitive*, **2** (1923), 106.

'Midnight'. *The Fugitive*, **2** (1923), 142.

'Three Poems'. *The Fugitive*, **3** (1924), 54–55.

'Death Mask of a Young Man'. *The Fugitive*, **3** (1924), 69.

'Portraits of Three Ladies'. *Double Dealer*, **6** (1924), 192.

'Alf Burt, Tenant Farmer'. *The Fugitive*, **3** (1924), 154.

'Easter Morning: Crosby Junction'. *The Fugitive*, **4** (1925), 33.

'Heat Lightning'. *Times Literary Supplement*, 5 May 1978, p. 491.

ARTICLES

'The Blind Poet: Sidney Lanier'. *American Review*, **2** (1933), 27–45.

'T. S. Stribling: a Paragraph in the History of Critical Realism'. *American Review*, **2** (1934), 463–86.

'John Crowe Ransom: A Study in Irony'. *Virginia Quarterly Review*, **11** (1935), 93–112.

'Literature as a Symptom'. *Who Owns America? A New Declaration of Independence*. Ed. Herbert Agar and Allen Tate. Boston and New York: Houghton Mifflin Company, 1936. Pp. 264–79.

'Some Don'ts for Literary Regionalists'. *American Review*, **8** (1936), 142–50.

'The Reading of Modern Poetry'. (With Cleanth Brooks) *American Review*, **8** (1937), 435–49.

'The Present State of Poetry: III. In the United States'. *Kenyon Review*, **1** (1939), 384–98.

'Notes'. *Modern Poetry, American and British*. Ed. Kimon Friar and John Malcolm Brinnin. New York: Appleton-Century-Crofts, 1951, Pp. 541–43.

'A note to *All the King's Men*'. *Sewanee Review*, **61** (1953), 476–80.

" 'Blackberry Winter,' A Recollection". *Understanding Fiction*. Ed. Cleanth Brooks and Robert Penn Warren. 2nd ed. New York: Appleton-Century Crofts, 1959. Pp. 638–43.

'Introduction: Faulkner: Past and Present'. *Faulkner, A Collection of Critical Essays*. Ed. Robert Penn Warren. Englewood Cliffs, N.J.: Prentice-Hall. 1966. Pp. 1–22.

'Hawthorne Revisited: Some Remarks on Hellfiredness'. *Sewanee Review*, **81** (1973), 75–111.

(2) Other works cited, listed alphabetically

Aiken, Conrad. *A Reviewer's ABC*. London: W. H. Allen, 1961.

Anon. 'Fables for Our Time'. *Times Literary Supplement*, 27 Nov. 1959, p. 692.

——. 'Old Kentucky Style'. *Times Literary Supplement*, 21 April 1972, p. 439.

——. Review of *Flood*. *Times Literary Supplement*, 5 Nov. 1964, p. 993.

——. " 'Thirty-Six Poems' by Robert Penn Warren". *Nation*, 25 March 1936, p. 391.

Auden, W. H., *The Dyer's Hand*. London: Faber and Faber, 1963.

——. *Collected Longer Poems*. London: Faber and Faber, 1968.

Audubon, John James. *The Birds of America; from Original Drawings by John James Audubon*. London: The Author, 1827–1838.

——. *Ornithological Biography, or An Account of the Habits of the Birds of the United States of America, Accompanied by Descriptions of the Objects Represented in 'The Birds of America', and Inter-*

spersed *with Delineations of American Scenery and Manners.*
Edinburgh: Adam and Charles Black, 1831–1839.

Barrett, William. 'Readers' Choice'. *Atlantic Monthly,* **213** (June, 1964), 134.

Beatty, Richmond C. 'The Poetry and Novels of Robert Penn Warren'. *Vanderbilt Studies in the Humanities.* Ed. R. C. Beatty, J. P. Hyatt, and Monroe K. Spears. Nashville: Vanderbilt University Press, 1951. **I,** 142–60.

Bellow, Saul. *Herzog.* London: Weidenfeld and Nicolson, 1965.

—— and Henry Brandon. 'Writer versus Reader'. *Sunday Times,* 18 Sept. 1966, p. 24.

Bentley, Eric. 'The Meaning of Robert Penn Warren's Novels'. *Kenyon Review,* **10** (1948), 407–24.

Bergonzi, Bernard. 'Nature Mostly American'. *Southern Review,* **6** (1970), 205–15.

——. 'Tales From the South'. *The Observer,* 1 May 1977, p. 24.

Bohner, Charles H. *Robert Penn Warren.* New York: Twayne Publishers, 1964.

Bradbury, John M. *The Fugitives: A Critical Account.* Chapel Hill: University of North Carolina Press, 1958.

Brooks, Cleanth. *The Hidden God: Studies in Hemingway, Faulkner, Yeats, Eliot, and Warren.* New Haven and London: Yale University Press, 1963.

——. *Modern Poetry and the Tradition.* Chapel Hill: University of North Carolina Press, 1939.

——. 'A Plea to the Protestant Churches'. *Who Owns America? A New Declaration of Independence.* Ed. Herbert Agar and Allen Tate. Boston and New York: Houghton Mifflin Company, 1936. Pp. 323–33.

——. *A Shaping Joy: Studies in the Writer's Craft.* London: Methuen, 1971.

——. *The Well-Wrought Urn: Studies in the Structure of Poetry.* New York: Harcourt Brace, 1947.

——. *William Faulkner: the Yoknapatawpha Country.* New Haven and London: Yale University Press, 1963.

——, Lewis, R. W. B. and Warren, Robert Penn eds. *American Literature: The Makers and the Making.* New York: St Martin's Press, 1973. **I,** 1061–70.

Carter, Everett. "The 'Little Myth' of Robert Penn Warren." *Modern Fiction Studies,* **6** (1960), 3–12.

Cary, Joyce. *To Be A Pilgrim.* London: Michael Joseph, 1942.

Casper, Leonard. *Robert Penn Warren: The Dark and Bloody Ground.* Seattle: University of Washington Press, 1960.

s

Clark, Eleanor. *Eyes, Etc., A Memoir*. London: Collins, 1978.

Coleman, John. 'Property Values'. *Spectator*, 4 Dec. 1959, p. 836.

Coles, Robert. *Farewell to the South*. Boston: Atlantic-Little-Brown, 1972.

Conrad, Joseph. *Lord Jim*. London: Dent, 1946.

Cowan, Louise. *The Fugitive Group, A Literary History*. Baton Rouge: Louisiana State University Press, 1959.

Cowley, Malcolm. 'Luke Lea's Empire'. *New Republic*, 23 Aug. 1943, p. 258.

———, ed. *Writers at Work: The Paris Review Interviews*. London: Secker and Warburg, 1958. The interview with Robert Penn Warren is pp. 165–186.

Curtiss, Mina. 'Tragedy of a Liberal'. *Nation*, 29 April 1939, pp. 507–08.

Davidson, Donald, Unpublished Letters and Papers. Nashville, Tennessee: Joint University Libraries. Bequeathed May, 1967, Open to the public from April, 1968. Examined by the writer in June and July, 1968.

Dickey, James. 'In the Presence of Anthologies'. *Sewanee Review*, **66** (1958), 307–09.

Donoghue, Denis. 'Life Sentence'. *New York Review of Books*. 2 Dec. 1971, p. 28.

Eisinger, Chester E. *Fiction of the Forties*. Chicago: University of Chicago Press, 1963.

Farelly, John. Review of *The Circus in the Attic, New Republic*, 26 Jan. 1948, p. 32.

Faulkner, William. *Intruder in the Dust*. Harmondsworth: Penguin Books, 1960.

———. *The Mansion*. New York: Random House, 1959.

Fiedler, Leslie A. *Love and Death in the American Novel*. 2nd ed. London: Jonathan Cape, 1967.

———. *No! in Thunder: Essays on Myth and Literature*. London: Eyre and Spottiswoode, 1963.

———. 'On Two Frontiers'. *Partisan Review*, **17** (1950), 739–43.

———. 'Romance in the Operatic Manner'. *New Republic*, **133** (Sept. 1955) pp. 28–30.

Fitts, Dudley. 'Exercise in Metrical High Jinks'. *New York Times Book Review*, 23 Oct. 1960, p. 32.

Forster, E. M. *Aspects of the Novel*. London: Edward Arnold, 1949.

Gill, Brendan. 'One Bourbon on the Rocks, One Gin and Tonic'. *New Yorker*, 24 June 1950, pp. 89–90.

Gransden, K. W. Review of *The Cave*. *Encounter*, **14** (1960), 78.

Gray, Richard. 'The American Novelist and American History: A

Revaluation of *All the King's Men'. Journal of American Studies*, **6** (1972), 297–307.

Guttenberg, Barnett. *Web of Being: The Novels of Robert Penn Warren*. Nashville: Vanderbilt University Press, 1975.

Hardy, John Edward. 'Robert Penn Warren's *Flood'. Virginia Quarterly Review*, **40** (1964), 485–89.

——. Review of *You, Emperors and Others. Poetry*, **99** (1961), 58–62.

Hoffman, Frederick J. and Vickery, Olga W. eds. *William Faulkner, Three Decades of Criticism*. East Lansing: Michigan State University, 1960.

Holman, C. Hugh. *The Roots of Southern Writing*. Athens, Ga: University of Georgia Press, 1972.

Huff, Mary Nance. *Robert Penn Warren: A Bibliography*. New York: David Lewis, 1968.

Huxley, Julian. *TVA: Adventure in Planning*. London: The Scientific Book Club, 1945.

Hyman, Stanley Edgar. 'Coming Out of the Wilderness'. *New Leader*, **44** (1961), 24–25.

Irving, Washington. 'The Legend of Sleepy Hollow'. *The Penguin Book of American Short Stories*. Ed. James Cochrane. Harmondsworth: Penguin Books, 1969. Pp. 11–41.

Isherwood, Christopher. 'Tragic Liberal'. *New Republic*, **31,** May 1939, p. 108.

Jarrell, Randall. 'On the Underside of the Stone'. *New York Times Book Review*, 23 Aug. 1953, p. 6.

Justus, James H. 'On the Politics of the Self-Created: *At Heaven's Gate'. Sewanee Review*, **82** (1974), 284–99.

——. 'The Concept of Gesture in the Novels of Robert Penn Warren'. Unpublished Ph.D. dissertation, University of Washington, 1961. Abstracted in *Dissertation Abstracts*, **22** (1962), 3201.

Kallsen, Loren J., ed. *The Kentucky Tragedy, A Problem in Romantic Attitudes*. Indianapolis: Bobbs-Merrill Co., 1963.

Lask, Thomas. 'On the Frontier'. *New York Times*, 13 Dec., 1969 p. 37.

Linenthal, Mark, Jr. 'Robert Penn Warren and the Southern Agrarians'. Unpublished Ph.D. dissertation, Stanford University, 1957. Abstracted in *Dissertation Abstracts*, **17** (1957), 2611–12.

Longley, John Lewis, Jr., ed. *Robert Penn Warren: A Collection of Critical Essays*. New York: New York University Press, 1965.

Lytle, Andrew. Unpublished Papers. Nashville, Tennessee: State Library and Archives. Examined by the writer in July, 1968.

McDowell, Frederick P. W. 'Robert Penn Warren's Criticism'. *Accent*, **15** (1955), 173–96.

MacDonnell, Archibald Gordon. *Napoleon and His Marshals*. London: MacMillan, 1934.

MacNeice, Louis. *Modern Poetry, A Personal Essay*. London: OUP, 1938.

Malamud, Bernard. *The Fixer*. Harmondsworth: Penguin Books, 1967.

Martin, Terence. '*Band of Angels:* The Definition of Self-Definition'. *Folio*, **21** (1956), 31–37.

Marx, Leo. *The Machine in the Garden: Technology and the Pastoral Ideal in America*. New York: OUP, Galaxy Books, 1967.

Matthiessen, F. O. *American Renaissance: Art and Expression in the Age of Emerson and Whitman*. New York: OUP, 1941.

Meriwether, James B. and Millgate, Michael, eds. *Lion in the Garden: Interviews with William Faulkner, 1926–1962*. New York: Random House, 1968.

Merrill, Boynton, Jr. *Jefferson's Nephews: A Frontier Tragedy*. Princeton: Princeton University Press, 1977.

Miller, J. Hillis. *Poets of Reality: Six Twentieth Century Writers*. Cambridge, Mass: Harvard University Press, 1965.

Mizener, Arthur. 'The Uncorrupted Consciousness'. *Sewanee Review*, **72,** (1964), 690–98.

O'Connor, Flannery. *Everything That Rises Must Converge*. New York: New American Library, 1967.

O'Connor, William Vann. Review of *The Circus in the Attic. Western Review*, **12** (1948), 251–53.

Orwell, George. *The Collected Essays, Journalism, and Letters of George Orwell*. Ed. Sonia Orwell and Ian Angus. Harmondsworth: Penguin Books, (1970) **1,** 454–504.

Owsley, Frank. Unpublished Papers. Nashville, Tennessee: State Library and Archives. Examined by the writer in July, 1968.

Poenicke, Klaus. *Robert Penn Warren: Kunstwerk Und Kritische Theorie*. Heidelberg: Carl Winter, Universitätsverlag, 1959.

Prescott, Orville. Review of *The Circus in the Attic. Yale Review*, **37** (1948), 575–76.

Purdy, Rob Roy, ed. *Fugitives' Reunion: Conversations at Vanderbilt, May 3–5, 1956*. Nashville: Vanderbilt University Press, 1959.

Quinn, Sister M. Bernetta, O. S. F. 'Robert Penn Warren's Promised Land'. *Southern Review*, **8** (1972), 329–58.

Ransom, John Crowe. *God Without Thunder: An Unorthodox Defense of Orthodoxy*. New York: Harcourt Brace, 1930.

———. "The Inklings of 'Original Sin'," *Saturday Review of Literature*, 20 May, 1944, pp. 10–11.

———. *The New Criticism*. Norfolk, Conn: *New Directions*, 1941.

———. 'Poetry: I. The Formal Analysis'. *Kenyon Review*, 9 (1947), 436–56.

———. 'Poetry: II. The Final Cause'. *Kenyon Review*, 9 (1947), 640–58.

———. 'Thoughts on the Poetic Discontent'. *The Fugitive*, 4 (1925), 63–64.

———. *The World's Body*. New York: Charles Scribner's Sons, 1938.

Revel, Jean-François. *Sur Proust: Remarques sur A La Recherche Du Temps Perdu*. Paris: Rene Julliard, 1960.

Richler, Mordecai. 'The Big Southern Novel Show'. *Spectator*, 30 Oct. 1964, p. 981.

Root, Judy. 'Lea Property Auction Worth $5,184'. *The Nashville Banner*, 21 Dec. 1967, p. 12.

Rubin, Louis D. Jr. 'All the King's Meanings'. *Georgia Review*, 8 (1954), 422–34.

———, and Robert D. Jacobs, eds. *Southern Renascence: The Literature of the Modern South*. Baltimore: Johns Hopkins Press, 1953.

Samuels, Charles Thomas. 'In the Wilderness'. *Critique: Studies in Modern Fiction*, 5 (1962), 46–57.

Schwartz, Delmore. 'The Dragon of Guilt'. *New Republic*, 14 Sept. 1953, pp. 17–18.

Shepherd, Allen. "Warren's *Audubon:* 'Issues in Purer Form' and 'The Ground Rules of Fact'." *Mississippi Quarterly*, 24, (1971), 47–56.

———. 'A Critical Study of the Fiction of Robert Penn Warren'. Unpublished Ph.D. dissertation, University of Pennsylvania, 1965. Abstracted in *Dissertation Abstracts*, 26 (1966), 7325–26.

Sheppard, R. Z. 'Sacred and Profane Grit'. *Time*, 14 March 1977, p. 58.

Sochatoff, Fred A., *et al*. *All the King's Men: A Symposium*. Pittsburgh: Carnegie Press, 1957.

Solotaroff, Theodore, *et al*. 'Symposium: Violence in Literature'. *The American Scholar*, 37 (1968), 482–96.

Sontag, Susan. *Against Interpretation*. New York: Farrar, Straus and Giroux, 1966.

Southard, W. P. 'The Religious Poetry of Robert Penn Warren'. *Kenyon Review*, 7 (1945), 653–76.

Spears, Monroe K. 'The Latest Poetry of Robert Penn Warren'. *Sewanee Review*, 78 (1970), 348–57.

Stevens, Wallace. *Opus Posthumous.* New York: Alfred A. Knopf, 1957.

——. *The Collected Poems of Wallace Stevens.* New York: Alfred A. Knopf, 1954.

——. *The Necessary Angel: Essays on Reality and the Imagination.* New York: Random House, Vintage Books, 1965.

Stewart, John L. *The Burden of Time: The Fugitives and Agrarians.* Princeton, N.J.: Princeton University Press, 1965.

Stitt, Peter. 'An Interview with Robert Penn Warren'. *Sewanee Review*, **85** (1977), 467–77.

——. 'Robert Penn Warren, The Poet'. *Southern Review*, **12** (1976), 261–76.

Strandberg, Victor H. *A Colder Fire: The Poetry of Robert Penn Warren.* Lexington, Ky: University of Kentucky Press, 1965.

——. 'The Incarnations of Robert Penn Warren'. *Shenandoah*, **20** (1969), 94–98.

Styron, William. *The Confessions of Nat Turner.* New York: Random House, 1967.

Symons, Julian. 'In the Southern Style'. *Times Literary Supplement*, 29 April 1977, p. 506.

Tate, Allen. '*The Fugitive*, 1922–1925: A Personal Recollection Twenty Years After'. *Princeton University Library Chronicle*, **3** (1942), 75–84.

——. *Reactionary Essays on Poetry and Ideas.* New York: Charles Scribner's Sons, 1936.

——. *Reason in Madness, Critical Essays.* New York: G. P. Putnam's Sons, 1941.

Theroux, Paul. 'A Lifetime of Writing'. *The Times*, 2 May 1977, p. 11.

Trollope, Anthony, 'The Genius of Nathaniel Hawthorne'. *North American Review*, **129** (1879), 203–22.

Twelve Southerners. *I'll Take My Stand: The South and the Agrarian Tradition.* New York: Harper Brothers, 1930; rpt. New York: Harper Torchbooks, 1962.

Wells, Anna Mary, Harding Vincent and Thelwell Mike, 'An Exchange on Nat Turner'. *New York Review of Books*, 7 Nov. 1968, pp. 31–36.

West, Paul. *Robert Penn Warren.* Minneapolis: University of Minnesota Press, 1964.

Williams, T. Harry. *Huey Long.* New York: Alfred A. Knopf, 1969.

Wilson, Edmund. *Patriotic Gore: Studies in the Literature of the American Civil War.* London: Andre Deutsch, 1962.

Winnington, Richard. 'Films of the Month: *All the King's Men*'. *Sight and Sound*, June, 1950, pp. 163–64 and 168.

Wilson, Angus. 'The Fires of Violence'. *Encounter*, **4** (1955), 75–78.

Woodward, C. Vann. *The Burden of Southern History*. Baton Rouge: Louisiana State University Press, 1960; rpt. New York: Random House, Vintage Books undated.

Zabel, M. D. 'Problems of Knowledge'. *Poetry*, **48** (1936), 37–41.

Zinn, Howard. *The Southern Mystique*. New York: Alfred A. Knopf, 1964.

Index

Titles of Warren's poems, collections and sequences of poems, stories and essays are given in Roman type; titles of books in italic. The main entries for items which are frequently mentioned are also in italic.